SADAHARU OH

SADAHARU OH

A ZEN WAY OF BASEBALL

SADAHARU OH and DAVID FALKNER

Times
BOOKS

All photographs courtesy of *Baseball Magazine Sha.*

Published by TIMES BOOKS,
The New York Times Book Co., Inc.
130 Fifth Avenue, New York, N.Y. 10011

Published simultaneously in Canada by
Fitzhenry & Whiteside, Ltd., Toronto

Library of Congress Cataloging in Publication Data

Oh, Sadaharu, 1940–
  Sadaharu Oh: a Zen way of baseball.

  1. Oh, Sadaharu, 1940–   . 2. Baseball players—
Japan—Biography. 3. Zen Buddhism. I. Falkner,
David. II. Title. III. Title: Zen way of baseball.
GV865.O13A375 1984   796.357′092′4 [B]   83-45922
ISBN 0-8129-1109-1

Designed by Marjorie Anderson

Manufactured in the United States of America

84 85 86 87 88 5 4 3 2 1

This book is dedicated to:

Hiroshi Arakawa, Kyoko Oh

—S.O.

Jenny, Ellen, Ivan, and Maggie

—D.F.

Acknowledgments

The following people extended time, talent, and wisdom to the making of this book: Mary Beth Dickman, Makiko Funato, Marty Kuehnert, Tom Mori, Daniel Siff, Peter Skolnick, Roger Straus III, Keiji Suzuki, Daigo Tamura, and Ichiro Tanuma. Particular thanks to Yoshikazu Demura of Japan's *Baseball Magazine,* whose help from start to finish was invaluable.

D.F.

SADAHARU OH

Prologue

Outside, the warm autumn sun shone on the grass. The grass had yellowed during the summer and was dying now. White clouds floated in the clear sky above. The light of the sun, so particular now, carried a hint of winter. The sounds of the crowd filling the stands came to me like the low rumbling of an island surf. The game would be starting soon. Everything was as usual, except. . .

> *The sound of the crowd.*
> *The clear colors of the sky.*
> *The warmth of the sun.*
> *The light of winter coming.*

My last game, my very last game. Twenty-two years leading to this moment—a whole lifetime. I realized that I was standing alone in this locker room. I had not meant to linger behind, but I had—and now I was by myself in an empty room that seemed more like a warehouse: row on row of lockers, empty trunks of equipment, signs of life everywhere but no one to be seen. I felt enclosed in this space, as though in a dream just before waking, unable to stir myself past those final restraints of sleep. Why was I standing here? I wanted to follow my teammates, but I didn't. I became

3

conscious of how foolish I felt just standing there alone. I moved to a bench and sat down. I was thinking about my uniform number.

My uniform number was One—all the years I was in high school and all the years I was a major league ballplayer. Number One. People made something of that. BIG ONE the press blurbs read. Big One! What is a "big one"? I don't put that down. I enjoyed it too much. But I know who I am—or who I have been. I am ordinary. No larger, no smaller than life-size. But my number matters to me. In my mind's eye, I see my number on my uniform jersey in the only way that it has ever been important—showing toward the pitcher as I assume my batting stance. When I was at my best, I turned my back almost ninety degrees toward the pitcher. I felt like a rough Japanese sea. My number suddenly rose toward the pitcher like a dark wave just before I struck.

I blinked. I looked down and saw that I had been gripping my cap so tightly in both hands that I was in danger of tearing it. I wiped my face. I had been crying. So strange. Why was I behaving like this? Get up, go out there, join your teammates! But I was not ready.

I am a professional ballplayer, I told myself. A professional. The word has meaning for me as few others in my vocabulary do. There is a standard of performance you must maintain. It is the best you are able to give and then more—and to maintain that at a level of consistency. No excuses for the demands of your ego or the extremes of your emotions. It is an inner thing. I held myself to that standard for twenty-two years. It is my proudest achievement.

I saw my face in a locker-room mirror used for shadow batting. A kind of mirror I had stood before for perhaps thousands of hours in my pro career. My face looked odd to me, eyes a little swollen, the expression open and easy, almost as if I were a child again rather than a man of forty.

"Get yourself together, Number One!"

"Easy, give the man time. He has it coming."

4

My voices. For me, the tough one, the hard one nearly always wins out:

"It is November 16, 1980. You are in Fujisakidai Stadium in Kumamoto, Kyushu. The opponents are the Hanshin Tigers. Your teammates and the fans are waiting. . . ."

The other:

"This is your very last game, last time you will swing the bat. This game is for you, just you. There is something in it for you. Take your time. Be kind to yourself. . . ."

I have been a pro baseball player for so long. More than half my time on earth. I barely had the time of my boyhood just to myself. I hit 868 home runs. More than Babe Ruth or Hank Aaron, more than any man on either side of the Pacific. I was a home-run champion for fifteen years, thirteen of them in a row. I hit thirty or more home runs for nineteen consecutive seasons. I led the league in RBIs thirteen times, in batting five times. I won the Triple Crown back to back in 1973 and 1974 and was the league's MVP nine times. I walked more than 2,500 times, leading the league in walks for eighteen straight seasons. In 1972, Japanese professional baseball introduced fielding awards—the Diamond Glove—equivalent of the Golden Glove awards in America. I won a Diamond Glove thereafter for nine consecutive seasons till I retired.

But I am not Babe Ruth or Hank Aaron. I cannot compare myself with them any more than they might have compared themselves with me. I am the Japanese Oh Sadaharu. And I should probably qualify that, too. I am only half-Japanese! I take my records seriously, of course. Athletes are very fond of saying that they look forward to having successors come along to break their records. There is always the figure of the former record holder trotting out on the field to embrace the new record holder. It is part of the show. But if it happens to me, I'll be sad. I'll be photographed smiling and shaking hands and embracing like all the other old-timers, but I'll be very sad. I want my records to stand. And yet, while I am proud of my records,

I am prouder still of this matter of duration. It represents something different, harder to explain. . . .

There are two figures who have been a constant inspiration for me throughout my career. Lou Gehrig and Miyamoto Musashi. Gehrig was a home-run hitter, but his greatest achievement was as "the Iron Man," playing 2,130 consecutive games. That is not just an athletic record (which it is and will be most likely forever), it is more an event of the spirit. It is impossible to play through fourteen straight seasons simply as a body showing up. You must be filled with something in your soul that enables you to withstand bruises and injuries and pressures of boredom and fatigue. The stretch of so many years and so many games leaves you with that one game, that one day where you simply sit down. But Gehrig never did. There was something in him—not necessarily physical strength—that enabled him to endure. The Japanese word for spirit-power is *ki*. It is both spiritual and physical. They are not to be separated. Thus the *quality* of Lou Gehrig's play during that incredible stretch was as much determined by his spirit as by the "iron" in his body. He was a man whose great talents were enhanced by spirit-discipline. He wanted to retire later than he did. His physical body betrayed him. His spirit never did. On Independence Day, 1939, knowing that he was dying, he told fans in Yankee Stadium not only about how lucky he was but also that he was truly happy. It was his Independence Day.

Musashi, the legendary Japanese samurai, beat his archrival Kojiro with more than strength and technique—it was also spirit-discipline. Musashi began as a young, headstrong boy and learned through years of daily practice that he was the possessor of something far more important than his sword. Kojiro was probably the better technician, but Musashi, in the end, beat him. And then gave up fighting.

The sound of a wave is an ordinary happening
in this world . . .

But who can sound the wave a hundred feet below?

The mirror across the way did not show me what was in my own body now. Beyond the doorway was the warm sun of Kyushu, a crowd of people, my teammates, another baseball game. I was not retiring just because my body would no longer permit me to play; nor was I, like Musashi, retiring to seek out solitude in the mountains. I was leaving because in this, my final year, I had also discovered that I no longer had the desire to play. My heart was no longer on fire. I could no longer play up to my own standards.

Records come and go. So does celebrity. Because my profession took place in the public eye, people have attached more importance to my comings and goings than they might have otherwise. I have been asked all kinds of questions in my career—questions about war and peace, art, politics, religion—and I've always had this odd feeling of being both flattered and embarrassed. The opinions of someone who has spent his life chasing a little white ball around a field really ought not be offered as oracles from the Buddha. I was a home-run hitter (as I later became an assistant manager). But I found in the world of baseball something I might never have found if I had done something else. It was surprising and unexpected. Baseball was for me, too, a form of spirit-discipline, a way to make myself a better person—although I surely never sought discipline for such a reason. It became my Way, as the tea ceremony or flower arranging or the making of poems were the Ways of others.

"Mr. Oh, it is time!"

"Yes. I'll be there."

The crowd in Kyushu, like the weather, was warm and encouraging. A good day in a good atmosphere to end it.

"Batting fourth, Number One, Oh. Number One, Oh!"

Last time as cleanup hitter, last time to swing the special Ishii bat, last time to try for one more, just one more. . . .

Yes, of course I wanted to go out that way. In the last game of the official season I had gone hitless. I wished God had let it be otherwise. But there had been only this gift of an extension of the regular season, so peculiar to Japanese baseball. In America the season ends with the World Series. Here, after the Japan Series, some of our teams regularly make trips to remote areas of the country that normally don't see live major league baseball during the season. It is done as a tribute to the fans, and the games, though considered exhibitions, are well attended and hard fought.

Our opponent that afternoon was our traditional rival, the Hanshin Tigers. It was the bottom of the fifth inning. The newspapers, the day following, said it was exactly 1:56 in the afternoon. The Tigers' pitcher—Norikazu Miyata— was young and inexperienced, and he threw me a ball I saw well. I hit it into the bleachers in right-center field. I circled the bases for the last time. (By coincidence, my first hit as a major leaguer had also been a home run.) Yes, this was the way I wanted to end it. But, then, a curious thing happened. As I crossed second base, heading toward third, I saw the players on the Hanshin bench leave the dugout and come toward the third baseline. By the time I reached the bag, they were lined up from third base to home plate. Some of the players in the field had also joined them. Even though they stood formally, at attention, there were expressions of genuine affection on their faces. I was very moved. I slowed my trot so I could shake hands with each of them in thanks. As I approached each player, he took off his cap, bowed to me, and shook my hand. At home plate, the manager of the Tigers presented me with a large bouquet of yellow autumn flowers. The crowd cheered. I waved to them, and bowed to the stands and the other players, then I went out to the mound to encourage the Tiger pitcher and to wish him well in the future.

My opponents lifted my spirits and, in doing so, reminded me of something that I had spent twenty-two years learning. That opponents and I were really one. My strength and skills were only one half of the equation. The other half was theirs. And standing there that day in Kyushu as my past became the future in a single moment, the years dropped away and I was a young boy again, coming out of high school to this strange, exciting world of professional baseball. How full of hope and strength and eagerness I was! I saw in the faces of the young players near me on the field the same look of expectation. In their eyes was the same will to combat, the same dream of creating records; and to me, because I was a celebrated old-timer now, they were kind enough to pay respect for a job well done.

But my job is not done, it is only beginning—and where the future will take me I do not know. I learned as a boy, because fate put me in the way of a master teacher, that practical training in skills, if done in a certain way, was also a method of spirit-discipline. And in combat, I learned to give up combat. I learned in fact, there were no enemies. An opponent was someone whose strength joined to yours created a certain result. Let someone call you enemy and attack you, and in that moment they lost the contest. It was hard to learn this—perhaps I am only just beginning to follow its lead—but my baseball career was a long, long initiation into a single secret: that at the heart of all things is love. We are, each of us, one with the universe that surrounds us—in harmony with it, not in conspiracy against it. To live by being in harmony with what surrounds you is to be reminded that every end is followed by a new beginning—and that the humblest of life's offerings is as treasured as the greatest in the eyes of the Creator.

Chapter One

I believe Fortune, like a breath of wind on my cheek, has always hovered close to me in this life. I was born of a Chinese father and Japanese mother at a time when China and Japan were at war; I was born a twin, but my twin sister died at fifteen months. I was born left-handed but spent years believing I was right-handed until one day I was to discover the meaning as well as the fact of being left-handed. I mention this only to set my sights straight on the road ahead. There are bridges to cross, places to travel I never imagined I would see. I am not a religious man, but I have been accompanied every step of the way by powers that are not mine alone. And so it was left to me always to make the most of the life I had. For myself and for what I am merely custodian to. I am a simple man and would gladly have lived out my life in obscurity, working hard and doing my duty. But I am also a twin. And if Fortune has taught me anything it is that I have two lives in me, two that I must live for, two that I must honor, two that I must allow to live with and against each other. Fortune places good opportunity before everyone. In making the most of this, I have had the strength of two rather than one. My story begins and ends with that.

I was born on May 10, 1940, although my birth certificate reads May 20. The reason for the discrepancy was that I was a fraternal twin, the punier of the two, and, according to the old medicine, very likely to die as a consequence. My parents, convinced that I had only days to live, changed the official date of my birth so they would not have to go through the rigmarole of filling out a separate death certificate later on. As I clung to life, my mother did what she could to preserve me. She went to a well-known hospital in Asakusa and consulted a doctor who was steeped in the old mysteries of these odd births. My mother was told to carry me outside naked twice a day, at ten in the morning and two in the afternoon, so that by exposing me to the elements I would therefore become strengthened. This my mother dutifully did, to the amazement and amid the whisperings of our neighbors. For years afterward, people regarded her as slightly crazy. But I survived and eventually grew fat and happy. My mother says she wondered about me at that time because I had very large eyes, which, when I was feeding at her breast, I apparently fixed on her in a way she said was strange. I, of course, did not know what was going on around me then, but I must have sensed something in my body. I did not learn to walk until I was two. When my sister died from measles (or lack of available medical care, really), I simply went on trustingly at my mother's breast. However, my body, almost immediately afterward, began to grow strong. Later, my mother said to me, "Hiroko took all your weak points with her. You should be grateful to your late sister." There were tears in her eyes when she said this. Though I was only six or seven at the time, I understood from then that my life—and my strength—were never meant to be my exclusive property.

We lived in Sumida-ku, one of the oldest parts of Tokyo. It was a merchant area right at the center of Edo when it flourished under the Tokugawas. It was a poor but very respectable neighborhood in my childhood. People were close—physically and spiritually. Houses were packed in one upon the other. The sense on the streets all the years I lived there was somehow of a very large family all crowded into the same area. My parents ran a small Chinese noodle restaurant that served people in our area and in Asakusa, the neighboring community, just over the bridge on the other side of the Arakawa River. Neighbors, along with my older brother and two sisters, often looked after me when my parents were working. The houses in the neighborhood were always open. It was nothing to wander from one house to the next, to go inside when no one was home, sit down on a chilly afternoon, put your legs under the draping of a *kotatsu*, warm your feet, and take an orange from a bowl and eat. There were always people from the neighborhood in each other's houses.

The first years of any child's life are protected—somewhat—by shrouds of forgetfulness. One lives through these years as in a dream, remembering certain details, forgetting others, always invisibly learning. I remember that when I was very young my parents tied me to a pole with a sash when they were downstairs working. They were afraid I might wander off and fall down the staircase when no one was watching. My mother told me this story, too: one day, she came up to the second floor to see how I was doing. She was surprised to see me throwing a toy with my left hand. She rushed downstairs and told my father, "Sada is left-handed. It's awful. I saw him throwing a toy with his left hand." Because left-handedness was considered a curse in those days, I was trained to use a pen and chopsticks with my right hand. But, as fortune would have it, left-handedness was too deep in me ever to be completely eradicated. Toy throwing, it turns out, was only the beginning of my career as a southpaw!

These first years of my life were also years of war. Because I lived in the heart of Tokyo and because my father was Chinese, the war, I am told, was doubly hard. My father went away one year. I don't remember it. He was arrested by the police, suspected of being a Chinese agent. In reality, his crime, I think, was that he was Chinese. Because we lived in an area where many people worked late into the night and because my father always made it a point to be helpful to others, he kept his restaurant open past the time of curfew. The authorities apparently saw something sinister in this. So my father was taken away. But it wasn't until I was nineteen, when I signed my first pro baseball contract, that I learned exactly what had happened. My father spoke to the press then. I read in the papers that the police had held him in prison for many months. And tortured him, leaving a scar across his neck that I always believed had been the result of some old accident.

We were bombed. I have some memory of that. I used to go outside in the evening and look up at the night sky crisscrossed with searchlights looking for the B-17s and B-29s, whatever they were, floating by. They seemed beautiful. I looked forward to seeing them. But one day in March 1945, Tokyo was fire-bombed. The entire city was destroyed, and whatever was left standing was finished off by another raid two days later. Our neighborhood was among the hardest hit on that first day. I remember the fire-bombing—but as though it happened on another planet at another time. The sky was red. I had never seen such a color before nor have I since. And it was night. Or so I thought. Actually, it was morning, but the smoke, my mother later told me, was so thick it turned day into night. But, for the most part, I was asleep on my mother's back through it all. When the bombing began, my mother put me in a sling on her back and fled with the rest of the family to the banks of the Arakawa River. We sought shelter in a junk that was moored there. But that was no more secure than any place else. We hid under the floor of a nearby shrine with other people from the neighborhood. But the shrine soon caught fire. Still carrying me on her back, my mother joined a bucket brigade going to and from the river bringing back water, vainly hoping to douse the flames.

As our house and neighborhood were utterly destroyed, we moved to Yokohama for six months. But we reestablished ourselves and our restaurant shortly after the war, and that is when my memories begin to solidify. The time was a happy one for me. Block after block was flat with just a building or two poking up through rubble. People were everywhere, going about their business, making do with what they could in the midst of disaster, seeming to share the fruits of plenty. Children played in the streets, in areas cleared of rubble—something like fields but not fields. There was considerably less traffic then. I had lots of friends. We played in twos and threes in groups and teams. We played as long as there was light and time to play. We played a game with spinning tops called *begoma* and a card game called *menko*, very Japanese, in which you placed cards on the ground, then tried to flip them over—in order to capture them—by hitting them just so with another card. And then there was wrestling. We drew circles in the street and had sumo wrestling contests. Because I was big and thick, I won often. I was also a bit of a bully and big shot. I used to make a point of saving up my allowance and walking over to Ryogoku, where the national sumo stadium was located, and paying my way in to see the matches. Actually, there was an entrance for kids, and it was easy to get in. I not only saw top-notch sumo wrestling, but I managed to meet a couple of the champions. I made a real show of a passing acquaintance with Yoshibayama, one of the great champions of the time. I tried to be very impressive with my friends.

This tendency to be a big shot eventually brought me to grief. Sometime around the second or third grade, I had a terrible run-in with my father. It happened this way: every day, after school, my friends and I walked home together. We used to go past this *yakitori* shop from which the most delicious smells would emanate. One day, one of my friends said, "I wanna eat, I wanna eat."

"Wait here," I said. My friends looked at me questioningly. "Wait here," I repeated with a tone of bragging and certainty that simply stopped my friends in their tracks.

I ran home and stole some money from my parents' restaurant and bought some *yakitori* for them all. I repeated this several more times. It was easy. My parents did not keep their money in the cash register but in a basket hung from the ceiling on an elastic string, which, because I was so tall, was simple to reach.

One day my father caught me just as I was reaching for the basket. He must have been waiting for me, knowing that money had been missing. He said nothing, but it was obvious that he was furious. I made a stupid excuse—that I was only trying to be helpful to others—thinking to soften him with his own philosophy, but it only seemed to make him madder. He beat me—with his fists. I have never stolen since. I like to think, also, that my career as a big shot ended on that day, too. I still carry vividly in my mind the image of my father's fists raining down on me. I will to the day I die. It was the only time my father ever beat me. The memory is dear to me.

Then, of course, there was school. In those days there were no gleaming buildings teeming with expensive equipment. The first school I attended two years after the war was in an old four-story building that had survived the bombing. The upper two stories housed the homeless. The school, grades one through six, crowded into the two stories below. Then, as now, we went to school six days a week (half days on Saturdays) from 8:30 in the morning until 4:00 in the afternoon. We worked hard. Though competition for grades and advancement was not as keen as now, we had heavy responsibilities. Classes were fifty minutes each with ten-minute breaks. We had lunch consisting, nearly always, of bread and soup. We studied Japanese (oh, so difficult for students barely able to write their names!), math, social studies, natural science. At the bidding of my parents, I worked diligently and faithfully. My best subject was math and, in particular, the abacus. By the third year of elementary school, I had reached second-level proficiency (just below top grade). After school I attended abacus class. Computers have long since replaced the abacus, and while I am embarrassed by my ignorance of computers (my daughters shame me with their questions!), the abacus has served me well through my adult life. I will confess it now—and leave it at that—but there was never a time in my twenty-two-year career in baseball when, in the seconds following a hit, the bone disks didn't click across my brain, exactly calculating the change in my batting average. By the time I reached first base, I always knew what I was hitting!

The time of my childhood was also the time of the Occupation, a special time for all Japanese and a peculiarly important one for me. For all of us, America was everywhere—American movies, American dress, American values, American music seemed to sweep in upon us like a strange wind from the sea, ominous and attractive at the same time. At the behest of our school authorities, who wanted students to be exposed to English early, we went off in orderly groups to see American movies. We dutifully trooped through bombed-out streets, past old alleys whose shops and doorposts still reflected Japan of the fifteenth century, to the local movie house to see such films as *She Wore a Yellow Ribbon*, *Stagecoach*, *Roman Holiday*, and, of course, all the films of Deanna Durbin!

At home, my parents—as immune as any people in Japan to the siren songs of the West—installed their own music-maker in the living room of our house—a small organ. The hope was that it would provide not only musical inspiration for the children but evenings of traditional family singing as well. There *was* musical inspiration of sorts. I learned to play almost any keyboard instrument from that little organ, and that has stayed with me, a pleasure and a consolation to this day, although I play mainly by ear and my skills are hardly worth mentioning. The most immediate result of the Oh family organ, however, was that "The Tennessee Waltz" became a kind of theme song in the house—threatening to drive everyone crazy. It was odd music to hear coming from overhead in a Chinese noodle shop.

Another American engine of change shortly followed— TV. In those days, few families had TVs, but because we ran a restaurant, my parents decided that it would be good for business if we got one. So a cumbersome and very formidable looking box was installed in the restaurant downstairs. On the nights when there were wrestling matches, the tables in the restaurant were cleared away and rows of chairs installed so people from our neighborhood could crowd in and watch the thrilling exploits of the Sharp Brothers, Ricky Dozan (master of *our* karate chop), and other great pro wrestlers.

But the Occupation was even more special for me because my family—owing to my father's birth—was Chinese, not Japanese. Because of this, we were considered friendly rather than occupied subjects by the authorities. So, as a matter of course, we were regularly given rations that were denied to Japanese families. Sweets, chocolates, cookies, wafers—real prizes in those days—were turned over to my parents, who hid them in the house, mindful of the conspiracies of my sisters and me to get our hands on them.

What I experienced then was only the child's play in it all. I did not understand the meaning of being Chinese. There were other examples. Once my family and I went to visit Hokkaido. We took a shuttle ferry from Alomori on the Honshu side to get there. The ferry was a large, one-cabin boat. The Occupation authorities divided the cabin with a rope into two separate areas—one for Japanese nationals, the other for unoccupied subjects. On this particular occasion, the Japanese side was packed, the other side, save for the members of the Oh family, was empty. I remember my father suddenly saying in his broken Japanese to the people beyond the rope, "Please, there's a lot of room over here, come and join us." No one moved. No one said a word. People simply stared at us. But it wasn't until years later that I began to understand why.

In the middle of all this was baseball. Baseball was everywhere in those years following the war. You could no more avoid baseball as a boy in Japan than a Canadian child could avoid skates. Even though we had no real fields to play on, though our equipment was handmade and very crude—balls fashioned from wound string and strips of cloth, bats made from tree limbs and discarded sticks— baseball seemed to grow from the very rubble itself, like some mysterious blossom of renewal. There were pickup teams from the neighborhoods, sandlot teams, school teams, and the reemergence of the pro teams. Baseball had always been popular in Japan (an American missionary, so the story goes, introduced the game here in 1873; pro baseball began in Japan in 1936, although it was suspended during the war). But now, in the ruins of the Occupation, streets and alleyways became meeting places for sudden games of catch, eruptions of ground ball, and pop-fly drills. I was a very typical Japanese boy. From the earliest time, I simply loved baseball. The country was baseball crazy, and so was I!

I came to play baseball for the first time this way: my brother, Tetsushiro, ten years older than I, was already an established baseball lover in the neighborhood. He played— and starred—on one of our Sumida sandlot teams. He also had the misfortune—fortune for me!—of being my chief baby-sitter. This meant that when he had baseball practice he had to find a way to divide his time. My brother, being as smart as Solomon, figured out an answer. One day he picked me up and put me on the rear fender of his bicycle and drove off through the streets.

"My brother," he announced to me, "this is called the strategy of killing two birds with one stone. You are going to see some baseball. Your only obligation is to keep your mouth shut about it."

And off we went to his practice field. I was under strict instructions that day to sit quietly and watch—to do absolutely nothing that might draw attention to the fact that my brother, Tetsushiro, aside from being a baseball star, was also an ordinary nursemaid! Above all, Tetsujo said, my parents were not to know about this. So I watched. I decided then and there that I liked the game of baseball. I enjoyed watching the ball come flying. Over and over I listened to the sounds of the ball striking the bat, whispering along the ground, smacking into a glove. The sound of the ball against the bat when it was hit well was one kind of sound. The sound of a badly hit ball was another. It was all very pleasing. Then one day I decided that it would be fun to hit like the others. My brother, though, allowed an increase of activities for me only to the point of picking up balls and equipment after practice. I enjoyed this, too, but still, I wanted to hit.

My brother must have started feeling sorry for me, or perhaps he grew scared that I might tell on him. At any rate, one afternoon, toward the end of practice, as it was growing dark, he called to me:

"Hey! Don't just sit there. Come on over! It's your turn!"

My turn! I was there, almost before the words had left his mouth. My turn! But what was I to do? Everyone was getting ready to go home. I didn't have much time for practice. I understood only what I had observed in others. I picked up a bat. My heart was pounding. What do you do with a bat? I copied what all the batters on my brother's team did. I stepped to the right side of the plate, assuming that batting right-handed was one of the rules of the game. There were a few players left in the field. My brother tossed a pitch toward me. I swung and got a clean hit. The sound of the ball, the click of pressure in the bat, the blur of the ball in the air are sensations that are still with me as though they happened yesterday.

It was just one hit that lured me into the world of baseball!

Over thirty years have elapsed since that day, a lifetime filled with more baseball than I would ever have imagined. And yet I go back to that day—and to my brother, Tetsushiro. He was the one who first introduced me to the game, first taught me about it, first led me to its charms. It was he who took me to Korakuen Stadium to see the Giants play for the first time. The Giants! The team of my childhood dreams, the team of my twenty-two-year professional career! He would point out the skills of this or that player, the strategy of the game as it unfolded, the fabulous history that lay behind the action I was watching. It was from Tetsushiro that I first learned about Eiji Sawamura, the beloved young pitcher who was killed in the war, who as an amateur, in 1934, lost a heartbreaking 1–0 game to a team of American all-stars headed by Babe Ruth, Lou Gehrig, and Jimmy Foxx, and who in that game struck out Gehrig, Ruth, Foxx, and Charley Gehringer in succession. It was because of Tetsujo that I first saw with my own eyes Masaichi Kaneda, who would win 400 games and strike out an amazing 4,490 batters, including a batter named Sadaharu Oh in his very first appearance as a professional ballplayer! At Korakuen I saw the unbelievable batting feats of the Hanshin Tiger star Tomio Fujimura, Japan's first authentic home-run hitter; and also the wizardry of the Giants' Tetsuharu Kawakami, our "God of batting," who was later to become my friend and manager.

It was also at Korakuen that I learned the meaning of an autograph. Like most boys, I eagerly waited around the Giants' dugout in the hopes of getting this or that player to sign my autograph board. Almost always, the players would walk past me as though I didn't exist. My brother would tease me because I always wound up feeling so hurt that I wanted to cry. But one day a young Giants' star named Wally Yonamine looked directly at me, smiled, and stopped. He took my board, asked my name—which I could barely get from my lips—and signed his autograph. I have that autograph today. When I became a player it was always remarked how readily I gave autographs—which is true—but I did so for the best of reasons: because of the joy Wally Yonamine brought into my life one afternoon in my boyhood.

More than anything, though, baseball was a neighborhood game. Every day when school let out, we would run home, drop our bags of books, and run out to play. Because I was bigger and stronger than most children my age—and because my brother was a catcher and an indulgent brother— I became a pitcher on the very first team I played for: a right-handed batter and a left-handed pitcher. I could throw the ball hard for someone my age, hard enough as a sixth grader to lure my friends into believing our boys' team might take on a team of older players and do well. We looked around until we came up with a prize challenge.

There was a soft-drink bottling factory near the school I went to, and, in typical Japanese fashion, this factory fielded its own baseball team. Because the field and the factory were in such close proximity to our lives, we saw the bottlers play many times. They played other factory teams, other sandlot teams, improvising games as they went. A good number of the players, though many years older, were no bigger than I was. Our players talked it over. The bottlers, though older, were surely not supermen. They weren't professionals, there were no sportswriters following them around telling the rest of the world how good they were. Above all, these bottlers had access to one of the more treasured luxuries of our youth: soft drinks. Our team decided to challenge them, in the hopes that, somehow, whatever transpired, a few free sodas might be the result. The leader of our group of boys, true to the custom of Japanese neighborhoods, was the oldest, a junior high schooler. He was not an especially imposing spokesman, but that, perhaps, created exactly the desired effect. The bottlers were amused by our leader's challenge and, demanding no recompense if the contest went their way (which was inevitable), they accepted. Little did they know what a case of soda would mean to a group of thirsty boys on a muggy Tokyo afternoon in early summer!

We had a team meeting, and it was determined that our best chance depended on my pitching a strong game. It was my obligation to do this. I welcomed the challenge. I found very quickly that the fastball which was so effective against my peers was also effective against these older players. It was probably surprise more than anything else. I pitched quickly, trying to give these older players little time to think about what they were up against. What was supposed to be an hour's amusement offered as an indulgence to neighborhood children turned into a real, if somewhat improbable, baseball game. My pitching held them at bay, and a combination of a few meager hits and some slipshod fielding by the bottlers actually was enough to carry the day for us. We claimed our trophy of drinks as though we had just won a world championship—to the amazement not only of the bottlers and ourselves but also of the small group of spectators who had gathered to watch and, then, to cheer us on.

Word of our triumph spread quickly through the neighborhood. Succeeding games with the bottlers, who could not very gracefully avoid playing us, drew larger crowds. To be sure we lost our share of games. But we won, again and then again, filling our summer and our bellies with more soda than we ever imagined we could consume— more, I'm sure, than was healthy for us to drink.

The logical next step for me was junior high school baseball, but this—fortunately as it turns out—was barred to me. The baseball club at Honjo Junior High School in Sumida was overenrolled, so I enjoyed other school sports. I was the leading high jumper and shot-putter on the school track team, the captain of the Ping-Pong team, a mainstay on the wrestling team. I was left to play neighborhood baseball—but in Japan during the early fifties this was serious business. Every ward had not only many different teams but different leagues as well. These leagues and teams had sizable followings within the wards, and though there was not much interward play, rivalries between the wards could become very intense. In our area, for example, because playing space was so limited, we would travel across the bridge to Asakusa looking for room on one of the fields there. This sometimes led to challenge games that would wind up drawing crowds of partisans from both wards. People from Sumida were naturally resentful of people from Asakusa because there was always a little more affluence, a little more put-on sophistication over there; people from Asakusa in turn regarded us as somewhat inferior, more rooted in the old ways, more oafish in manner.

Because of my success in the games against the bottlers, I soon found myself in demand within the ward leagues. I played for my own team in a boys' league, but I also played for teams composed of high school players and even a team of adults. At each level, I did very well. And the stakes for winning went up, too! A winning effort among high school or adult players most often meant a good warm meal of rice and pork cutlets, while losing meant cold noodles.

My brother was an important part of this phase of my life, too. A couple of years earlier, when I was in the fourth grade, he had entered Keio University as a medical student. It was my father's deepest wish that his two sons would become, respectively, a doctor and an electrical engineer. Instead of bedtime stories, he told us this over and over again:

The village in China where he grew up had neither electricity nor a doctor and there was terrible suffering as a result. It was his dream that—one day—his children would in their own careers give back to life some of what he had seen taken away.

Tetsujo's acceptance at Keio was therefore a great joy. And surely it was Tetsujo's intention to honor the commitment he was about to make. Only my brother's passion for baseball had not diminished one iota. At Keio he organized a doctor's team and became a star on it. Not only that, in late February and March he and his colleagues would hold a regular spring camp, actually living together in an old abandoned shrine so they could ensure their work together as a team. On some weekends and spring vacations I lived with my brother and his friends at the shrine—and I went to their practices, willing to pick up balls and equipment for the few opportunities of swinging a bat and playing catch that were afforded me.

As my playing improved—and as I got physically bigger—I found myself more and more included in the workouts of the doctors' team. By my second year in junior high school I was a full-fledged member of the team, pitching and winning many games for them, doing some heavy hitting as well. Though my brother was shortly to leave baseball for good, his approach to the game taught me some very basic lessons about effort and discipline that remain with me to this day.

My brother's career ended suddenly. One day, in a league game in our ward, he slid into second base and broke his ankle. Examination time at the university was not far off, and he suddenly found himself in the hospital, having to prepare without what he normally would be getting from class and the library. My father was beside himself. He forbade both my brother and me to ever play baseball again. His own dreams were lying broken on that hospital bed. Tetsujo accepted this verdict honorably—and also because he had no choice. I, too, accepted, but unfortunately was healthy enough to have a choice. Unknown to my father, I continued to play. It was the only time in my life that I consciously disobeyed him. I kept my equipment hidden in the house and stealthily went on with my own baseball career.

The only problem was that it was hard to keep a secret like that. My own best efforts, it turned out, meant nothing. Because my reputation in the ward games had grown, many people invariably stopped by my parents' restaurant and complimented them on my play. "Oh," they would say to my father, "Sada is such a wonderful player. You should have seen him today. He did such and such and such and such." My father would grin and nod, seemingly pleased, inwardly seething. I never knew how close I was to having my own baseball career ended before it began. But just at that moment, Fortune once more interceded. It happened this way:

One of the teams I was playing for, the Umayon Cape Hearts, had crossed the bridge for a game in Asakusa. Word had gone through both neighborhoods for days that this game was going to take place, and there was a very large crowd gathered to watch it in Asakusa's Sumida Park. I was the pitcher, and the game was very close going into the late innings. I came to bat in the eighth inning with a chance to win the game for us. The large crowd of followers from Sumida began cheering and chanting. Just at this moment, it turns out, my father was in the area delivering food orders to local customers. Hearing a lot of commotion, he came over to find out what was going on. One of the fans explained to him.

"It's that kid, Oh! That damned kid, Oh!"

"What about him?"

"A hit and those miserable so-and-so's from Sumida go ahead! Come on, Asakusa, take care of that miserable kid!"

My father said that despite the feeling of having been betrayed, he suddenly found himself cheering for me. I got the hit that won the game, and my father began jumping up and down with the bags of food in his arms! He did not tell me this story till years later, but neither did he ever confront me with my having disobeyed him. My baseball career was saved.

Fortune moves in and out of people's lives like a living

25

spirit. Because all of us are susceptible, sometimes we wind up seeing things; other times we scarcely know that our lives have been touched. For a young boy, distinguishing between the real and the imagined is especially trying. Right at this time in my life there was a professional psychic living in my neighborhood. He was a small, spare man who wore a gown and had a terrible habit of looking sideways when he spoke directly to you. Perhaps he had a glass eye. At any rate, he was brought to me one day by an older friend. We were introduced.

"Oh, Sadaharu," he said to me, very ominously, "I am able to see the future."

"Y- . . . yes?" I stammered, very impressed.

"There are two things you must do immediately."

"Yes?"

"First, you must keep the image of a dragon with you at all times for as long as you live. A dragon is your protection. Do you understand that?"

"I do," I assured him.

"Second, and this is most important, you must change your name for one year."

"Change my name?"

"Yes. Most important. And it must be for a whole year."

"And why must I do that?" I asked, almost whispering.

"You must," he said. "Your life will be in jeopardy otherwise."

Believe me, I did. For one whole year my name—to the consternation of friends and relatives alike—was Hisoshi Oh. And to this day, wherever I am, there is an image or a statue of a dragon to protect me.

I am a modern Tokyoite. Like most modern people, I am attracted to and skeptical of the invisible world at the same time. It is all too easy to look to the stars in this uncertain world. But I do know from over forty years of life that Fortune, however mysterious its origins, is as real as the ground you walk on, its effects as palpable as a touch.

I hope dragons protect me. I won't take the chance of finding out that they don't. But when I was fourteen, Fortune did enter my life again. Of this I am as certain as I can be of anything in this world. I even remember the date. November 30, 1954.

It was toward dusk. We were playing a practice game in Sumida Park in Asakusa. There was a good chill in the air. Winter was coming. You could feel it, but it didn't matter. I was pitching for our side, we were winning 5–0. Then, suddenly, there was a commotion on the field. One of the players recognized a man walking a dog nearby. The man was Hiroshi Arakawa, an outfielder for the Mainichi Orions, one of Japan's major league teams. We tried to continue with the game, but it was almost impossible. We watched the man following the dog—the dog pulling forward on the end of a taut leash—as they came closer and closer to our field. When he reached the area where we were playing, Arakawa-san stood behind the backstop at home plate and watched the action. All of us—players on both sides—became so keyed up! I felt my body fill with fighting spirit. I pitched as powerfully as I could. At bat, I swung from the heels, trying to send the ball clear across the river. Between innings, as I was about to leave the bench for the mound, my life changed. Arakawa-san left the backstop area and threaded his way between the players, who seemed to step aside before him in awe. He was making his way toward me! I felt myself freeze in place. I couldn't believe what was about to happen. He wanted to speak to me! He nodded to me and smiled, very gently. I very stiffly bowed to him.

"How come you pitch left-handed and bat right-handed?"

Sounds gurgled in my throat, but I had no words. I so badly wanted to make the best impression. I nodded my head, wanting to show that I accepted what he said—whatever he said.

"You know, you're probably wasting your talent that way. You look left-handed. Why don't you try to bat left-handed next time you come up?"

"Y-... yes, yes I will, of course, I will," I finally blurted out, so ashamed of myself that I raced back out to the field at top speed. I expected Arakawa-san then to leave the area, to go on with his evening's stroll. But, no, he took a seat on a bleacher bench behind the plate!

It seemed like a year before my next turn at bat, and all the while I felt Arakawa-san's eyes on me. The game, the cold, the time of day, everything seemed to drop away. There was only this need to live within the cocoon of Arakawa-san's words. Finally, it was my turn to bat again. For the first time in my life I stepped to the plate to bat from the left side. I swung the bat back and forth. It felt easy, natural, as though I had done it always. I seemed now to come to my senses. I could feel everyone on the field watching me, as though in envy because a major league ballplayer had spoken only to me. I felt like a star! I knew I would hit! Nothing was going to stop me. If a building had fallen from the sky, I'm not sure I would have paid any attention to it, even if it had fallen on my head. I waited for the pitch I wanted. My bat met the ball squarely. For a moment, I watched the blur of the ball as it streaked out over the infield. Then I put my head down and ran. I looked up again at second base. I had lined a clean double to the fence in right-center field. I looked toward the bleacher bench behind the plate. Arakawa-san was still there. He gave me a big nod of approval. My body filled with goose-flesh.

When the inning was over, he came up to me again.

"See that," he said, "that was a really nice hit."

"Thank you! Thank you!"

"No reason to thank me. How old are you?"

I responded crisply, "I'm in the second year."

"Ah, good," he said, "then you'll be thinking of university next year. You might think of Waseda University.

I went there. It has an excellent baseball program, and you will have a chance to develop your talents to the fullest."

I stood rigidly at attention.

"I am in the second year of *junior* high school," I said.

"Oh, I see. I thought . . . well, never mind what I thought. Perhaps you'll go to Waseda High School, then."

"Yes. Yes."

"You're a very good player, you know."

He smiled. We shook hands, and I bowed to him deeply. Then, with his dog, he turned and walked away. It seemed like only a few feet between where we were standing and the darkness surrounding the field. I tried to call to him. But I couldn't. Just like that, he was lost in the shadows as surely as if he had evaporated.

Chapter Two

Strange are the ways of the Goddess. The last idea in my mind was to pursue a career in baseball. My father's dreams were very clear and forceful. My brother was already on his way to becoming a doctor. I was going to become an electrical engineer. My father had an opinion of baseball players as well. "It is a foolish profession for a man to enter," he said. "It depends almost entirely on having a stout and healthy body. And a man can have that for only a short while. Even the very best players will be finished while they are still young." I couldn't have agreed with him more. A man's purpose, my father has insisted to this day, is to be of genuine service to others. In my last year at Honjo Junior High School I took the entrance examinations to Sumidagawa Public High School, fully intending to honor my father's goals for me.

It was not easy to get into Sumidagawa. The high school entrance system in Japan, though somewhat more easygoing in my day than now, is different from that in America. Much depends on what sort of high school a student winds up going to. If you go to one kind of high school, your future will be more or less tracked toward business or the professions; another kind of high school will mean an entirely different sort of future. The system is difficult, exacting, and sometimes cruel. I knew this then, as every schoolboy did, and I worked very hard to guarantee my future. My parents later had a laugh at all this, because my brother, who turned out to be a doctor, was really a lazy student while I, who turned into a baseball player, was actually a diligent one. The night before exams of any sort, I never slept—though I have always had the gift of being able to sleep like a horse through almost anything. The nights before the high school entrance exams were terrible. Wired to my books, I studied and studied and studied.

I thought I did well on the exams; still I knew it would be close. And close it was. I missed Sumidagawa by one point! Besides my father's obvious disappointment, I felt crushed. What was I to do now? I did get into Waseda Commercial High School, but I never thought that I would go there. I really wonder after all if there isn't something like Fortune, something beyond understanding or description that enters into our ordinary lives. One more point on that exam and I would have had a very different life. There is really no question of that. At the time, however, all I or my family could see was the stern and cheerless face of misfortune. There was no immediate answer to it either. At first, I was undecided that I would even go on to Waseda.

There was at this time a man living in our ward who ran a sporting-goods shop. He was a neighborhood sports fan and got around quite a bit. He followed ward baseball closely and was a regular on both sides of the river. He had a high regard for me and a neighborhood catcher named Obata. When he heard that both of us had gotten into Waseda Jitsugyo (Commercial), he asked permission of our families to be allowed to escort us—the catcher and I—to Nerima Ward, clear on the other side of town, so that we might see the grounds.

I believe my father may have first thought that this was to be a visit to the school proper, but of course it turned out to be a visit to the grounds where Waseda played baseball. Nevertheless, we went. And, nevertheless, for me, this was a real adventure. Aside from the times when I moved with my family to Yokohama or went with them as a child on brief vacations, I had never traveled so far away from home. This trip across Tokyo by rail might as well have been a trip to distant lands. It took over an hour to get there. I leaned out of the window of this packed railway car. We went through areas where there were no buildings, only low-hanging trees that touched the train as we passed. Dust swirled around us, the sound of the train slowly pounding in my ears—it was the other side of the world we were heading to!

When we finally got off the train, my eyes were wide as saucers. The area of the city was totally unfamiliar, and as I walked I heard a weird chant that seemed to grow louder as we moved along the street. I looked at Obata, who seemed as nervous as I. We exchanged smiles. Our chaperone, however, walked confidently on, a step ahead of us.

The chanting, it turned out, was coming from the practice field we were being taken to. There were many players in dirty uniforms on the field (in my dreams big-time baseball players always wore white uniforms!), and gathered at the backstop, standing in very precise rows, were 150 to 200 boys, freshman hopefuls for the baseball team it turned out, chanting loudly, rhythmically, energetically.

Over the next two weeks I learned rather forcefully about tribal ritual. Waseda Jitsugyo—or Sojitsu as everyone called it—was indeed a baseball factory. In fact, it seemed everyone who went there wanted to join the baseball team. Only, quite obviously, there were not enough places on the team to go around. In April, when the school year starts in Japan, the 150 to 200 freshman candidates who came to try out were normally forbidden to take part in any actual play on the field. Instead, they were herded into this mass cheering section along the backstop, under orders to chant slogans of encouragement as loudly as they could. If an individual boy's chanting was not up to standard, he would be slapped by an older classman. I developed a good, loud voice from that experience. I made sure I was never slapped. Practice was hard, and encouragement was necessary to keep everyone's spirits up. The role of chanter, it was thus explained, was an integral part of the baseball program. The incoming freshman was invited to feel as much a part of the team as anyone else by performing this necessary task. And when he got tired, he was allowed to sit. In the periods of sitting, which alternated with the periods of standing, boys sat cross-legged, not allowed to stand again until their feet were numb.

There was a practical reason behind all this of course. With such a regimen imposed on this crowd of new boys, not many of them stayed for very long. The ranks of those who wanted to give their all for Waseda baseball were gradually thinned until only the hardiest souls remained. This was Showa 31—1956—such a long time ago. I think back to that time, which seemed so frightening and severe then, with a kind of fondness. Yes, it was painful to be subjected to such harshness. But those who left the baseball program did so not because they were told they were not good enough but because they themselves chose not to put up with it. The ones who remained, curiously, demonstrated just that degree of tenacity and fighting spirit needed on a winning baseball team. I chanted loudly that first day— and for the two weeks following. I was then invited to come out of the line and, surprisingly, join the practice. But I am rushing things. There was, first, the matter of my father.

When my father learned that my trip to Sojitsu was for the purpose of introducing me to the baseball program, he was outraged. He made up his mind on the spot that I was not going to be allowed to go to Waseda. There was just no way that his son was going to be seduced into the world of baseball. Never mind its spartan trappings, serious people who had the capacity to be helpful to others did not devote themselves to such a way of life. My father's anger— except for that one time in my boyhood—was nearly always expressed as stubbornness. And what I was confronted with now was an almost immobile determination to keep me from going to Sojitsu. A crisis was at hand. I wanted to go to Waseda now—and yet I would never have disobeyed my father. I could not persuade him that he was wrong—I did not even believe that he was. At any rate, I had no power of my own—none that I knew of—to make him change his mind.

My brother and my uncle, after many hours, finally talked him into it. It was touch and go for a while, but the turning point was that my father allowed himself to look into my heart. Though I could express it only with confusion and uncertainty, I wanted to play baseball. Everyone—my father included—knew that. We were at a crossroads. I think if my brother or my uncle had tried to be tricky, my father's defenses would have stood.

"If he goes into Waseda, it could mean that he will end up pursuing a career in the world of baseball," my father said. "Do you understand that?"

"Shifuku-san, this is true," my uncle said.

"It's a *strange* profession," my father said, after what seemed like an interminable silence.

"Dear father," my brother, Tetsushiro, quietly answered, "let there be one strange profession in this family."

I don't remember the precise moment when my father softened and finally relented—more than thirty years separates me from that time. But relent my father did, and, very reluctantly, offered his permission to have me enter a new and—for him—frivolous world.

There is a popular story in the Japanese press that I wore threadbare clothes and had on *geta* (wooden sandals) that first day at Sojitsu. It is a colorful story designed, I imagine, to illustrate my family's poverty. Fortunately, it is fanciful. Though my parents worked hard and had not much to show for it, they prided themselves on what they were able to give their children. I don't know what I wore on my feet that first day, but I do know that I had leather shoes and sneakers when I was growing up. Going to school, I regularly wore sneakers. I liked sneakers. The story comes back to me now, because I knew what cost there was for my father in having me go to a baseball school. It had little to do with what kind of shoes I had on my feet. That was never the point.

By all rights I should have been a chanter for a year before I was allowed to practice with the baseball team. I said I was surprised to be pulled from the line and asked to join the team on the field. And so I was. I was even more surprised to learn that Mr. Miyai, the manager, and Mr. Daigo and Mr. Tokutake, the captain and co-captain of the team, had heard of me. From whom? From Arakawa-san, it turns out! Arakawa-san, graduate of Sojitsu and Waseda University, was a faithful alumnus and unappointed scout for the baseball teams of both schools.

Another "coincidence." The great star in Sojitsu baseball history to that point was a player named Kishichi Enomoto, a powerful left-handed batter whose home runs traveled legendary distances. There was a dirt bank that served as the fence in right field, beyond which was a street. Very few players had the power even to reach this bank, let alone clear it. Enomoto, it was said, regularly put the ball onto the street beyond. He did it easily. I made a slogan for myself in those early days: "Catch up to Enomoto and go ahead." It kept me concentrating and striving, though I could not reach the street no matter how hard I tried. Most curious, however, was that Enomoto, when he went on to play pro ball with the Mainichi Orions, became not only "rookie of the year" and a top batter but also Arakawa-san's first pupil. Many years later, Arakawa-san told me this story:

Enomoto would come home after games and work with the sword. He would swing at trees. All the trees in his garden were eventually cut. One day he came to Arakawa-san and said, "I can't use this anymore, the blade is too blunt." Arakawa-san replied, "A blade is never dull, only a man," and proceeded to demonstrate for him that even the bluntest sword could cut through objects hard as a helmet.

But I am jumping ahead again.

Arakawa-san, at this point, was a man who had appeared and disappeared one evening in Sumida Park.

Though I was honored to be asked to take part in practice, life on the team was very hard. I traveled almost an hour to the training ground every day after school. With other teammates and chanters, we would drop our bags in a pile near a bakery that was next to the bus stop at the grounds. There would be over a hundred bags piled up as we rushed off for the field. With other first-year players, I not only underwent hard training, I was also expected to perform grounds-keeping and other chores, often staying afterward, working under starlight to smooth the infield for the next day's practice.

As a first-year boy I dressed in a room with thin wooden walls and an earthen floor. My locker consisted of a nail in a post against a wall. In the cold of early spring and late fall, my body would tremble in the dark when I dressed or when I stayed to pick up after the seniors, who dressed in an equally flimsy room, different from ours only in having board floors. Even though I quickly made the starting team, batting in fifth position as the number-two pitcher on the squad, I was never exempted from these chores. No freshman ever was. Freshman year on the baseball team was for learning that the individual always subordinated himself to the team. The game as we knew it was incomprehensible otherwise.

There was a special way that freshmen were obligated to deal with the mistakes and errors they inevitably committed. The slogan was "The error of one is the error of all." It was wrong and destructive to permit a new teammate to believe that an obvious error—in conduct or in performance—was his alone. Instead, when such infractions occurred, we freshmen formed two lines face to face and were required to hit each other. By doing this, each one of us could feel that it was necessary to be both sorry and responsible. There was no slacking off either. The upperclassmen who watched would make you hit again if they felt the blow you delivered was too light. I always hit hard because I did not want to be made to strike a second time. I hit hard and in turn was hit hard myself. This happened more times than I can remember. When I was an upperclassman, I presided over this ritual as those before me had, willingly and unreservedly. It is not easy to acquire a sense of shared responsibility. People by nature look out for themselves first and for others second. But it is higher consciousness to learn to care for others, to acquire a sense of genuine responsibility for the actions—good or ill—of the team or group to which you belong. On a baseball team, there is simply no avoiding this demand. The lesson is painfully learned—but it is learned. One more word. The person in this sense who suffers the most is the one who made the mistake in the first place. The shame is all the more for the pain he winds up inflicting on others. And that is precisely the point. What you do on a team has consequences for everyone else—not just for yourself. A player caught like this inevitably resolves never to make a mistake like that again. He is forced to confront his own sincerity. And this kind of feeling, in turn, has consequences, too. Ties are created between players that are deep and lasting.

What I remember most from that time is the sense of togetherness we shared. I can recall day's end, when practice was done and we trooped together back to our bags of books. The smells from the bakery assaulted our sharpened senses. And in the early dark of the evening we bought hot loaves of bread and milk and wolfed them down. The name of the bakery was Minerva. We had bruises on our faces and on our bodies, warmth and nourishment in our bellies. I have eaten in many fancy restaurants since then. But no food anywhere has been quite so exquisite as the milk and bread of Minerva!

Aside from our approach to the game, high school baseball in Japan is quite different than it is in America. The games in Japan are very well attended and receive quite a bit of media attention. Twice a year there is a national high school tournament held at Koshien Stadium in Osaka. The games are played before crowds of 60,000 and a nationwide television audience. For the two weeks or so that the tournament continues, the entire nation gets caught in its grip. It is an amazing spectacle, which, probably more than anything else, demonstrates just how baseball-crazy Japan is. Even among pros, it is nothing to be caught up in Koshien. Players on the Giants regularly sat before clubhouse television sets saying, "Look, there's my team," or "One more win and we're in"—as though their high school allegiances were as fresh as ever.

The two Koshien tournaments are actually a little different. In the spring tournament, teams are selected by a committee. The larger summer tournament involves winning your way there—through preliminary tournaments held in each prefecture. These preliminaries are also intensely followed. That first year I went to Sojitsu, our team reached the finals of a preliminary tournament, the Kanto High School Tournament for Tokyo. The team we played that day was Nichidai-Sanko, our archrival. The Sanko-Sojitsu rivalry was as fierce as any in Japanese sports, and a contest matching our teams in the finals of the Kanto tournament drew thousands of excited spectators from all over the city. Though I was the number two pitcher on our team, the luck of the schedule made it my turn to pitch that day!

I felt good and strong, full of fighting spirit in the early innings. I was pitching a shutout through four innings. In the bottom of the fourth, we pushed across a run to take the slenderest 1–0 lead. Now the game was different, tighter, more tension-filled. In the fifth, Sanko's lead-off batter tripled. The opposing bench, the stands, were suddenly in a frenzy. Runner on third, no one out, Sanko's cleanup hitter coming to the plate.

"Come on, Namiki! Let's go, Sanko!"

"NA-MI-KI! NA-MI-KI!"

Concentrate, concentrate, I told myself. I summoned all the power I had in my body. See the catcher's mitt! Put the ball there! Don't think about anything else! I struck Namiki out and followed by striking out the next batter, too. The threat had subsided. The last batter rolled out to second, and the lead was preserved. And as if that were the catalyst, I got stronger through the rest of the game. Meanwhile, we upped our lead to 4–0, so that in the ninth inning I found myself pitching with more confidence than ever. With the final out, I got so excited that I threw my glove high into the air, jumping and yelling in celebration! We were the best in Tokyo! Koshien was within reach! What a memorable day it was!

Only now, thirty-two years later, it was memorable for a very different reason. My brother saw that game. He had come to cheer me and our team on, and he had enjoyed our victory quite a bit. But he had a bone to pick with me. Afterward, when we were by ourselves, he lashed out at me.

"What you did today was a disgrace!"

I could scarcely believe what I was hearing.

"What did I do?"

"What did you do? Are you a first-year man?"

"First-year man? Yes, yes," I stammered, still uncomprehending.

"Where do you get off carrying on like that?"

"Like what?"

"Throwing your glove in the air, rubbing salt in their wounds. Wasn't it enough you beat them? Did you have to humiliate them as well? Have you no respect for the feelings of your opponents?"

I didn't know what to say.

"Shame on you!"

My brother's words cut into me like a whip. I believe these were the hardest words I ever heard. At least I can't think of any others that hurt quite so much. I neither cried nor lowered my head—just took in what my brother said, sitting across the way from me. His words were more difficult to bear than any defeat. From that day forward, save for one notable exception—for both me and my brother—I never again showed my feelings in public. Oh, yes, I raised my arms from time to time when I hit an important home run, but I did so only because photographers asked me beforehand to try to show some gesture of gladness that they could record. But I lived having his words as a discipline. And I believe to this day that one should not show one's emotions so easily. In ways that I did not fully appreciate then, my brother passed on a gift that enabled me to survive in the world of professional baseball.

The following day, six days before my sixteenth birthday, my name was in the Tokyo papers for the first time. My family and relatives, people in the neighborhood were proud of me—yet unaware of what else had happened the previous day.

Sojitsu played hard all through that spring and early summer as we pointed toward the Prefecture Tournament, scheduled for mid-July. We established our dominance over Nichidai-Sanko and over other likely rivals as well. Everything seemed to be moving our way, and yet, for me, there was a cloud on the horizon to which I had barely paid attention before.

In early July, we played a practice game against a team called Hosei Niko. I was pitching. Going into the seventh inning, we led 3–0. Suddenly (I have no idea why to this day) I couldn't get the ball over the plate. I had had these unexplained lapses of control before, but they had never been quite so sustained. Our manager, Mr. Miyai, made no move to replace me. When the inning ended, I had walked in five runs. In the eighth inning, I was even worse, walking batter after batter, moving them along with wild pitches. We were routed. Nothing I tried worked. It was as though some power bent on undoing me simply had taken over my body and would not let go. I could not explain myself to my teammates or, worse, to Mr. Miyai. Mr. Miyai ordered me to sit.

"Assume the *seiza* position," he said. This is a meditative pose, basic to all martial arts, where you kneel and then sit back fully on your heels. I obeyed.

"You are to contemplate on why this has happened to you so that you may avoid it in the future."

"Yes," I said. But my head was filled only with turmoil and confusion that I could not begin to resolve. I had no idea what was wrong. I could only hope that I would be spared this humiliation in the upcoming quest for Koshien. That was everything!

On July 17 the National High School Tournaments to qualify for Koshien opened: 1,739 teams all across Japan took part, including 124 in the Tokyo area. As though my prayers were answered, I pitched a no-hit, no-run game in our second outing in the tourney as we swept toward the final against Meiji High School. We beat Meiji, too, on an unusually cold and cloudy day. I hit a home run in the fifth inning of that game (off a pitcher named Genichi Murata, who coincidentally surrendered my first professional home run three years later). We were leading at the time 2–1, and this could not have been a better omen as far as I was concerned. My spirits as we went off to Koshien were fully restored.

Crowds of schoolmates and well-wishers waved goodbye to us at Tokyo station as we boarded the train in our traditional school uniforms, carrying the banner of Waseda for the seventeenth time since 1914 to distant Osaka. The train headed across low farmland as we all pressed excited faces to the windows waiting to get a good look at Mount Fuji, which grew larger and larger as we went. It was August, and everything was brown and green; only the top of Fuji was hidden, its wonderful mysteries and secret powers coming ever closer, hiding high up, away from the punishing heat of our Japanese summer. What lay on the other side of this world? We would know soon enough now!

August 12, Showa 31—the opening of the thirty-eighth National High School Tournament at Koshien Stadium in Osaka. Sixty thousand people were in the stands for the day's opening ceremonies and for the games that followed. We were scheduled that first day, the third of four games. We played Shingu High School. I batted fifth and played left field. In the bottom of the first with two out, we had two runners on base. I made my first appearance at bat in the games. I grounded to the pitcher, killing our chance to score. In two succeeding at-bats I walked, but that hardly mattered. Shingu eked across a run early in the game and made it stand up. We entered the last of the ninth inning trailing 1–0. We got our first two men on, however, and suddenly the complexion of the game was dramatically different. We had a chance, a real one. I was sent up with orders to sacrifice, and I did better than that. I bunted perfectly, loading the bases. We then won the game with two successive squeeze bunts. A 1–0 loss had, at the very last, been turned into a 2–1 victory. We had begun our Koshien quest in the most auspicious way we could, with a hard-fought, perfect team victory. And I had managed to contribute after all.

In our second game, against Gifu Commercial High School, I was the starting pitcher. This, it turns out, was the real test for me, because what had gone on before was at some distance from what I really had to face. And that was standing alone on the mound in front of 60,000 people. Nothing had prepared me for that moment.

I was excited, more so than I have ever been on a baseball field. My adrenaline was almost like a tidal wave roaring through my body. I imagine I had more strength than I possibly knew what to do with. There was only one problem. Standing on the mound, peering in to get the sign for the first pitch, I was unable to see! The catcher, the umpire, and the batter were all part of a single blur. No matter how hard I tried to focus, my vision was fixed and frozen. I was horrified. My breath felt like the rasping of a file moving in and out of my lungs. My head was swimming. I tried, simply, to remember what the pitching motion was and hope for the best. Though I could propel the ball plateward, I had no idea at all where it was going. I couldn't begin to pitch effectively. I was out of the game before I knew it, our team on the way to a terrible drubbing, as Mr. Miyai was forced to use our number-one pitcher, Mr. Ohi, who had barely begun to recover from his winning efforts the day before. Our dream was over. Just like that. We returned to Tokyo, no one's spirit hurting more than mine. I felt that I had personally been responsible for my team's undoing.

I have my manager, Mr. Miyai, to thank for leading me slowly back to a semblance of self-confidence. In that period following our defeat at Koshien, I frankly hated myself and cursed this force in my body, whatever it was, that could so completely betray me. Mr. Miyai saw this and was quite anxious, though he had really run out of ideas about what he could do to cure me. Instead, he brought a consultant to our training ground one day. Mr. Kubota, a former So-jitsu star, after much observation and consultation, made an analysis. My head, he said, was too large. Thus, when my arms swung up and behind in the pitching motion, my big head got in the way, disturbing the rhythm of my delivery. The cure, he and Mr. Miyai agreed, was to keep my arms at waist level until I was ready to release the ball. I thus became the first pitcher in Japan—at any level—to use the no-wind-up delivery.

The Japanese press later reported that this episode occurred on October 9, 1956—one day after Don Larsen pitched his perfect game against the Dodgers in the World Series. I honestly don't remember the date, but I rather doubt that it was the one given by the press. For one thing, this neat progression from West to East is undermined by the international date line. October 8—the date of Larsen's perfect game in New York—was simultaneously October 9 in Tokyo. I somehow have the feeling that I began work on this no-wind-up delivery earlier than that. I know that I worked on it for some time during the fall, eventually using it in our games, discovering that, in fact, I was able to pitch with control using it.

I mention this only because Don Larsen *did* serve as an inspiration for me—but not in the way it was reported. The real story is far more curious. On New Year's Day that winter, Mr. Kubota said that he wanted me to watch a film of Larsen's perfect game. I went to a house in Toshima Ward to see it. There was nothing special about the house. It was small, unpretentious, typical of many in that area of Tokyo. But it belonged to Arakawa-san!

I could scarcely believe it when I saw this shadowy figure of my boyhood dreams standing there in the doorway to greet us. What did this mean? Did he remember who I was? Was this only the wildest coincidence, or had Arakawa-san all the while remembered me and been keeping tabs on me at Waseda? I bowed to him and shook his hand.

"We meet again," he said with a smile.

No coincidence at all!

But I could not bring myself to speak or to ask questions. I was there because it was determined that I should see this film, and that was all I permitted myself. The film, obviously, confirmed the correctness of what I had been working on. I saw what was possible at the highest level of professional play using this style of delivery, and it immediately compelled my attention. I watched Larsen's motion very carefully, making notes as I went. I studied the position of hand and glove at the waist, the way in which the turn of his body helped hide the ball till the last moment before the whip of the arm, how the stride forward left him balanced and in perfect fielding position. All the while I tried to see this in a kind of reverse mirror, checking each of these points against the movements I made as a left-hander. Yes, of course, it could be done. More than that, just because it eliminated so much excess motion, it might be the ideal counterfoil to the destructive effects of my nervous system. I was full of hope for the new year and the new season, which was shortly to begin.

I felt tremendous gratitude to Mr. Miyai and Mr. Kubota for helping me. But toward Arakawa-san I felt something I could not begin to explain. It was as though, in re-entering my life at this point, he had all along been a kind of invisible helping spirit, watching me from afar, interceding just at those moments when I needed help the most. I wanted to say some of this to him, but it was all too confusing.

I bowed deeply to him when I said good-bye. I wondered if he saw what was in my heart. I did not want to embarrass him, and yet I wanted to convey some sense of this powerful upsurge of thankfulness. He smiled and nodded, and the glint in his eye, whether a glimmer of recognition or the simplest light of good feeling, was enough to send my spirits soaring.

At any rate, it was my impression then that this meeting was a kind of circle closing on a magical story. I knew I would be all right now. But I still had no idea at all that the story had not yet even begun.

Chapter Three

In the spring of Showa 32 (1957) we were invited to take part in Koshien once again. Because this was the spring meet, there were fewer teams competing, and hence our chances—along with teams from nineteen other schools—were improved. But there was a drawback, too. A serious one. Spring Koshien occurs shortly after the end of one school year and the beginning of the next. As a result, practice time is limited. In the weeks before the end of the school year, baseball is put aside for examinations. And so it was for us. I, being a conscientious student, worked hard to do as well as I could on my exams. In my own mind, the future, as my father still insisted, lay in the classroom and not on the playing field. And though I knew Koshien was coming, I put it out of my mind for many weeks.

When we did resume practice in April, all of us were rusty and ill equipped, really, for the rigors of a physical campaign. Training was thus accelerated. We tried to do in a matter of days what we normally would have taken weeks to accomplish. Bumps and bruises, aching and strained muscles were common. For me, a pitcher, the problem was that the skin on my fingers had become too soft. My fingers throbbed and burned after several minutes of hard throwing. This was as it should have been. We simply had to get ourselves in shape for Koshien.

One day, however, we had an unusually hard practice. We arrived at our training ground early, and we stayed until we could not distinguish other players on the field. During this session I pitched longer than I probably should have. I injured two fingers on my pitching hand.

At first I paid little attention to the injury. It seemed nothing more than the formation of blisters on my fingers— a problem common enough and relatively easy to deal with. There was pain, of course, but I disregarded it. It would only be temporary. My fingers would soon toughen up again. At the end of the day, however, I noticed that these blisters were a good deal deeper than I had thought and, more ominously, were filled with blood. The blistering and bleeding carried so deep beneath the superficial layer of the skin that there was no way I could lance them or effectively treat them other than by complete rest—which I could not allow myself at that point. The danger was infection and a more serious injury, but I simply had to go ahead. I had no choice. To pitch in Koshien! I could not miss that. In all other respects I was ready. In our practice and in our preliminary games, my no-wind-up delivery was more and more effective. I was a year older, had already had Koshien experience—never mind the result—I was not going to miss now! My task was simple and twofold. One, to go out and pitch as best I could and, second, to hide my injury from my teammates so that they would not suffer any loss of confidence going into the tournament. I was the number one pitcher on the team now, and my responsibilities were clear.

In our first game, against Neyagawa High School, I reinjured myself in the third inning. I could feel the raw burning on my fingers. But I was prepared for this. I would not let myself be beaten by pain. Mr. Tamura, our catcher, however, called time. I was upset with myself. Surely I hadn't revealed anything. Or had I? Why was he coming to the mound?

"Please," he said, "look." He handed me back the ball.

"Look," he said. I took the ball from him. There was a streak of blood on it.

"Is anything wrong?"

"Nothing," I said.

"You're okay?"

"I'm fine."

He trotted back to his position. I walked around the mound, carefully rubbed the bloodstain from the ball, then casually reached down for some dirt to help speed the drying of the blister that had burst. In all other respects, I was strong and full of good fighting spirit. We handled Neyagawa easily. I gave up only two hits in the course of the game, and struck out ten, and my control was fine. Even more important, I did no further damage to my fingers. Save for the pain, I was ready for the next day's game.

At 8 A.M. the following morning we played Yanai Commercial High School, and this time I pitched into the eighth inning before I injured myself again. This time Mr. Tamura knew exactly what was wrong.

"Please say nothing," I told him.

He looked at me.

"Please."

He nodded and went back to his position. The pain was quite severe now, but I was lucky because the game was nearly over, and once again, I could still throw well enough to preserve victory. We beat Yanai, and along the way I recorded eleven more strikeouts and, even better, walked no one. But in order to win the championship, we still would have to get through two more games on two successive days. I now doubted that I would really be able to finish the job for our team. My fingers hurt terribly, so much so that I was unable to sleep or to clear my mind. What was I to do? There really was no one else to pitch for us, and as long as I was physically able to throw the ball, my mechanics were now sound enough to at least take a chance. Above all, I wanted to make sure that I did not give away the extent of my injury either to my teammates or to our opponents. The way in which teammates and opponents alike perceived me was crucial.

We beat Kochi-Sho the next day, and I pitched another complete game—although I am not sure how. I was never in so much pain in my life. I rubbed more dirt into my torn blisters than I care to remember. But only my friend and battery-mate Mr. Tamura knew what was going on. I kept my injury hidden as best I could.

Everyone on our team was excited. The newspapers, the fans in Osaka were buzzing about our prospects, what with my strong pitching aided so much by this new no-wind-up delivery that gave me both the necessary control and stamina. All that stood in the way of our bringing home a Koshien pennant was victory in the final game against Kochi-Sho the following day.

During our stay at the tournament our team lived in an old-style boardinghouse called Sansui-Kan, just across the way from the Nishonomiya railway station. I lay on the tatami-mat floor of my room the night before that final game, my fingers aflame with pain, my mind aching as well. The truth of the matter was that my fingers simply would not work. I reached for a baseball in my equipment bag and could not feel the ball for the pain that throbbed upward from the base to the tips of the fingers. I had gone as far in this tournament as I could go. Meanwhile, my teammates were in high spirits, happy and joking, full of determination for the next day's action. It was dark, and I could hear all my friends carrying on beyond the *shoji* of my room. How in the world was I to break to them the knowledge that was already a dagger in my heart? Just at that moment, however, my thoughts were interrupted.

"Mr. Oh, a guest for you," a woman of the inn said, gently sliding open my door. I raised myself up, distracted from anguish. What was this? I tied on a *yukata* and went downstairs, baffled. Standing there in the dingy foyer, wearing worn clothes and carrying an old-style bundle of baggage, was my father. I was flabbergasted. What in the world was he doing here? He was supposed to be in Tokyo, 350 miles away!

"Papa! Papa! You here? What is the meaning of this?"

"Shh," he said, taking me by the elbow, "where is your room?" I led him back in that direction. Still at my elbow, suspicious of being overheard, he whispered:

"Your fingers are injured, are they not?"

"What! You know!"

"Never mind now."

We got to the room, and I slid the door closed behind us. In a low voice, I asked him the meaning of this. How in the world did he know what was going on with me?

"I've been watching the games on television," he said simply. "I could tell from the way you held your fingers something was wrong."

I don't know if I was more surprised by my father's almost offhanded acknowledgment that he had taken time out to watch me play or by his having discerned what he did and come such a long way to be with me just at the moment when I needed support the most.

"Are you in pain?" he asked.

For the first time I was able to tell someone. "Yes," I said, "very much. I can't grip the ball anymore." When he took my hand to examine it, it trembled from the pain. He lowered my hand and then turned to the bundle he had brought with him.

"Borrow a bowl and a grater for me, would you?"

"A bowl and a grater?"

"Yes, if you please."

He had taken out a bottle of Chinese wine and a block of what looked like brown cork and laid them carefully out on a cloth—all of which he had removed from the opened *furoshiki*. I went to the kitchen area of the inn and returned with the bowl and grater, thoroughly mystified by what my father was up to. He thanked me and took the bowl, laying it alongside the bottle of wine. He held the grater in his hands.

"I could tell you had dangerous blisters on your fingers," he said as he began to grate the corklike substance into the bowl. "You moved your fingers in a peculiar, unnatural way, as though you were trying to hide something. I came immediately."

"What is it you're doing?" I finally asked my father.

"We would treat this this way when I was in China many years ago," he explained. The corklike substance was actually ginseng root, and, mixed with this particular wine, it was an ancient remedy. When the ginseng was fully grated and mixed with the wine, he soaked my fingers in it. After a short while, he removed my hand.

"You'll be okay now," he said. "Don't tell anyone about this. Tomorrow, pitch with all your strength." With that, he placed his things back together and wrapped the *furoshiki* into a bundle once more.

What was most amazing was that the pain actually had lessened. I could feel it go as I was soaking my hand, and now as I looked at my fingers, the raw red gashes seemed shriveled and duller. I could feel the normal sensation of my nerve ends in my fingertips once more. I wanted to weep for joy, but more than that I wanted my father to stay and spend the night with me. I thought that if my father stayed and talked with me through the night my anxieties about the upcoming game along with my pain would be stilled. But he had come only to give me a treatment. Having packed up, he was ready to leave.

"Please," I said, "won't you stay just the night? It's late. You can go in the morning."

"No," he said, "Mother needs me. She'll be too busy by herself. No worry now. Pitch as much as you can, okay?"

I nodded without a word. My father stood holding his *furoshiki*-wrapped bundle.

"Good-bye," he said.

To this day I remember his incredibly massive back retreating through the small door of my room. I will remember the image of his back till the day I die.

"Father! Father!" I called. Not a word. He was gone.

The next day, Sojitsu played Kochi-Sho in the championship game. For the fourth straight day, I was the starting pitcher (it was customary in those days, even at the pro level, for one pitcher who was unusually effective to pitch on many successive days). The first inning came and went, and, though I could feel pain when I threw the ball, my fingers seemed all right. In the bottom of the first, with a runner at first, I hit a double over the left fielder's head, and we had a run on the board. In the second, we scored again, and meanwhile, I pitched free enough of pain. For a time I thought my arm might even give out before my fingers, but in any case my father's words to pitch with all my strength were as much a balm to me as the actual medicine he had applied to my hand. We built our lead to 4–0 by the eighth inning, but by then I had reinjured myself—and this time badly enough so that not only my teammates but the opposition as well knew what was going on. Every ball I threw in the eighth inning became smeared with blood. The sense of feeling in my fingertips once again gave way to raw, pulsing pain. The Kochi-Sho batters waited, making me throw as many pitches as possible. My control began to desert me along with much of the velocity I had started the game with. At inning's end, our lead had been cut to 4–2.

In retrospect, I logically should have been removed from the game at that point, but there was no thought of it—either in my mind or in our manager's. The spirit a player shows in a game is valued—especially in high school—as highly as his talent. In fact, sometimes more so. In any event, we had come this far with me as pitcher, so we would go just one more inning with me as well. If my spirit was strong, it would make up for whatever my fingers or my arm no longer possessed. Somehow, I got the first two outs in the inning. Call it spirit, call it sheer luck, or whatever—all feeling save unbearable pain had left my torn, bloody fingers. I wished I was numb from head to toe, but all I could do was try to pitch. I walked the next batter on four pitches, none of them near the mark! What was I to do, what could I possibly do in such a situation? If I had myself removed from the game, it would give Kochi-Sho a tremendous burst of confidence at precisely the wrong moment; if I let them know that I had lost belief in my own ability to continue, they would get the same lift; if I went ahead pitching, I risked losing the game. There was only one thing for me to try. I took my position, affecting, as much as possible, a sense of casual confidence. I gazed lazily from the stretch position at the runner at first. Then I stared long and hard at our catcher, who put down his sign. No matter what, this was my last moment on the mound in this game. The ball in my hand felt like the teeth of an animal trap tearing my flesh. I kicked my leg just as the base runner began widening his lead—he was leaning the wrong way—and my move, all the way, was to first base, not home plate. I could see the sudden look of panic on the runner's face as he tried to reverse himself and duck back toward the base. My pick-off throw was right on target, low and slightly toward the right-field side of the bag. In a single motion, our first baseman speared the ball and tagged out the runner. It was over! We were champions of Koshien!

The press in our country makes much of the "spirit of high school baseball." And it is true—as far as it goes. High school players back then—and now—give themselves to the game in ways that are both admirable and foolish. But determination has little to do with reaching the highest level of skills. The papers the next day and for some days following made much of the fact that I pitched with such an injury. It demonstrated this superb "spirit of high school baseball." But if the game had been lost—as well it might— the stories would have been different. In any case, I felt very lucky and very grateful to my father in reaching this moment.

For me, the spirit of high school baseball is somewhat

more personal, because it is about the teammates with whom this and other dear moments were shared. At the closing ceremony, it was customary for the captain and co-captain of the winning team to receive the champion's banner and cup to take home. My teammates decided that I should carry home the cup that year even though the honor rightfully belonged to others. It was a wonderful gesture, and returning home, riding through city streets in an open car with people cheering us, was certainly the biggest thrill of my early baseball life, but the spirit of high school baseball was more than winning or losing as far as I was concerned. As my teammates supported me in victory, so they were there for me in very different circumstances a short while later. The "spirit" of Waseda baseball, as I knew it, had finally to do with friendship. It is with me to this day.

A short while after winning Koshien, our team was selected to be the Tokyo representative of still another national tournament—this one called Kokutai, or the National Amateur Athletic Competition. Our team was to travel to Shizuoka Prefecture early in the fall to take part in these annual games—which, I learned at that time, were for Japanese nationals only. I learned this in the most abrupt and surprising way. A teacher at school called me into his office to inform me that I would not be allowed to take part in Kokutai because I was Chinese. I was stunned—as were my teammates, who had to be talked out of refusing outright to go to Shizuoka. What with the protest of my teammates and the immediate support and sympathy I received from my manager, teachers, and the Tokyo press, it seems hard to believe that such a rule would stand. But stand it did. There were no exceptions. Ever. It was there just for the reasons stated. Kokutai was for Japanese only.

To say I was hurt and confused means almost nothing. I was more hurt than I have ever been in my life. My confusion was even deeper. How could this happen to *me, who was a Japanese*! My father was Chinese, and I was his son, that was true, but I had grown up as a Japanese, treated fully as such by neighborhood friends and schoolmates alike. It never entered my mind that I was "different." I had never felt "different." But now, suddenly, images came back to me . . . the Occupation, the privileges we received from the authorities, the hidden treats. . . . What had I thought? The Japanese people packed in on the other side of the rope refused to come over to the side where *my father* was. It was also the side where *I* was! Realization tumbled in upon me. As though a giant wave of anger tossed me to and fro, then threw me up on a strand, I came to an understanding:

"Hey! They're damn right, I'm *not* Japanese!" Of course. How could it be otherwise? And what in the world could I do about it? Could I change my fingerprints, my face, my father? There was only one error in all of this, and it had nothing to do with rules. It had to do with my own thinking, which had led me to deceive myself into believing I was someone other than who I was. What to do about it, then? I vowed then and there to make sure that at least I would keep my feelings to myself.

I think of all the people this hurt, my father was most affected. Though he never showed anger or lashed out or seemed bitter, his pain was all too obvious. I believe that he had come to see in the progress of his sons the lifting of a lifelong burden. And particularly in this national baseball meet, my inclusion would have meant for him that measure of acceptance that had been always denied. It would have represented a day he had been waiting for since 1921; it would have meant freedom for his sons that he had never known for himself. But he was an old hand at this, far more practiced than I—or anyone I have ever known—in the arts of endurance. He had heard that my teammates were going to refuse to go to Kokutai as a gesture of support for me. He said:

"The National Athletic Competition is a festival for Japanese. You should not trouble other people because you cannot attend. The fact that you are a player of the Sojitsu team does not change, although you cannot take part in the festival. You must always learn to repay hatred with virtue."

My brother, too, accepted this as inevitable and seemed simply resigned to it. My sisters, though, made no attempt to hide their feelings. They were furious. "Why, why, why?" they said. "It makes no sense. It's stupid. Everyone worked so hard together, went to Koshien together . . . you're the star pitcher on the team. Why, why, why!"

My mother, who quietly went about the business of going to the district government to see if the rules couldn't be changed, later said that she felt very sorry for me in all this because I didn't show any emotion, seemed almost to make light of it.

"Yes, yes," I told my sisters, "a rule is a rule. Don't worry, I'll be at Koshien next year. This tournament doesn't matter like Koshien, you'll see me next year at Koshien."

That was the slogan I adopted—for myself and for everyone else—out of my father's endurance and my own confusion. With friends and family alike, I took a light, almost joking air. At school—and especially with my teammates—I carried this through to the point where I made sure they knew that of course I would work out with the team as usual, that I would travel with them to Shizuoka, and that, yes, of course I would stay and watch the games. I did want my team to play in Kokutai, to accept an honor that was legitimately theirs. And because I knew in my heart how bad they all felt for me, my father's words gave the strength of sincerity to what I had not yet honestly worked out for myself.

I said before that the "spirit of high school baseball" came to me in the form of friendships that went beyond victory and defeat. On the opening day of Kokutai, there was a traditional parade of teams in their uniforms into the stadium—Kusanagi Stadium in Shizuoka. Before this event, we had a team meeting. One of our players said, "We are representatives of Tokyo—so are you. You put on your uniform and march with us." My teammates cried out in acceptance. Mr. Miyai, though this may have been a transgression against the rules, showed support by keeping silent. I was deeply moved by this. I marched with my friends into Kusanagi Stadium, wearing my Sojitsu uniform. And afterward, I stayed, sitting right behind home plate, leaning my face against the wire net, watching the action on the field.

All this was a long time ago. I had never thought about discrimination till then, and the meaning of it for me—if there is any—is that it caused me more pain than anything else in my forty-three years of life. To this day I cannot go into Kusanagi Stadium as a professional without recalling that time. Because I received such loving support from so many sources then and because my father's example and his words made such an impact, I believe that I received far more reward than penalty in this situation. My life might have turned out differently. I have been asked many times now why I haven't become a Japanese national—even though my public position would certainly have allowed me to. The answer I always give is that it would be useless because everyone knows I'm Chinese anyway. Does that make sense? Let those who need answers to that which is essentially unanswerable find it in the feeling of being so deeply hurt and in the effort it takes to repay hatred with virtue. As for my teammates—boys who took upon themselves more responsibility than their years demanded—I say this: if I could be reborn in one of the seven lives we have, I would like to be a high school baseball player again, so that I might enjoy the comradeship and mutual dreams that are the lot of ordinary students.

In the spring of 1958, my final year of high school, our team returned to Koshien. It was a brief visit, because we lost in our second outing—I pitched well enough to win our first game against Gosho Commercial High School but was hit very hard by Seisei High in the game following. Still, I carved out a moment for myself in this tournament.

I hit home runs in both games, the first time a player had ever done that in successive games in the spring meet. And even though we lost, most everyone said we would be back for the more important summer tournament after we won the Tokyoto—the Tokyo qualifying tournament—to get there. We believed this, too. At least we were determined to work so hard that our path to Koshien would be assured. For me, after Kokutai, this effort took on almost religious fervor.

On August 3 of that year, we reached the finals of Tokyoto. Before 35,000 people at Jingu Stadium in Tokyo (home of the professional Yakult Swallows), we took on Meiji High School for the right to go to Koshien, which was to open five days later. Because of the closeness of Koshien, there was an extra aura of excitement surrounding this game. All of the particulars of travel and hotel arrangements—for both teams—had not yet been worked out; the plans of thousands of people, quite literally, were up in the air, part of the electricity charging the atmosphere that day. In fact, the day itself was typical for Tokyo at that time of year—very hot and humid, a day begging for a thunderstorm, which our teams were supposed to supply.

In the games leading up to this final, our pitching had been done mainly by my friend Mr. Kawaharada. On this day, though, because I was strong and well rested, I was the choice to face Meiji. I was as ready as I could be.

Through four innings, neither side scored. But in the top of the fifth, Sojitsu scored the all-important first run of the game (lack of team power in Japan, at all levels, makes the scoring of this first run psychologically more important than it is in America). In the bottom of the sixth, however, Meiji tied the game on a squeeze bunt. And so we remained deadlocked at one as the game moved into the eighth, ninth, and then extra innings. The level of tension on the field seemed to rise with each batter. The grandstands behind each dugout were oceans of confusion and cheering—I'm not sure if the game or the heat of the day or the tremendous and unresolved logistical problems of getting to Osaka were affecting people most, but whatever it was, the sense of frenzy everywhere was undeniable.

In the top of the twelfth inning, our thunderstorm arrived—Sojitsu exploded for four runs; I managed a double in this rally—and we took a 5–1 lead. Behind our dugout, general frenzy gave way to hurried preparations for the on-field ceremonies that would shortly be coming up. One of our teachers, to the cheers of the crowd, made his way out of the grandstand to telephone for train tickets and hotel reservations. The moment we were waiting for was at hand.

I got the first out easily in the bottom of the twelfth. A pinch hitter whose batting style I was not too familiar with followed and hit a hard bouncer to third. Too hot to handle. It went for a hit. Still, there was no great problem. The ninth hitter in the order was coming up, and he proceeded to hit a routine grounder to second—only Mr. Iyase, our second baseman, bobbled the ball, and all hands were safe. Meiji's lead-off man then dumped a short single over the infield and suddenly the bases were loaded. Time out! Conferences on the mound, in the infield, cheering and screams from the Meiji side of the field, silence from ours.

"Nothing to worry about. Four runs ahead!"

"Cheer up! Don't be discouraged!"

I was still strong—and excited—and full of spirit. But when I turned to face the number-two man in Meiji's order, a hard-hitting fellow named Nomura, my best intentions and all my strength were undermined by something I could neither see nor touch nor begin to bring under control. I could not get the ball over the plate. All the work I had done on the no-wind-up delivery, all the worries and nerves I thought I had put behind me boiled up once again. I walked Nomura on four straight pitches, none of them close to the plate—it was as if I had given him an intentional walk with the bases loaded—and then Mr. Miyai came out of our dugout and removed me from the mound. I was sent to right field, and Mr. Kawaharada, who had pitched his heart—and his arm—out to get us to this final game was brought in. We were still ahead by three runs, and though the bases remained loaded, we needed to get only two last outs. On a one-one pitch, Nishihiro of Meiji hit a high drive toward me in right field. I turned and went back and back, looking for the ball over my shoulder. It sailed over my head and to the wall. When I finally ran it down and got it back to the infield, Nishihiro was standing on third, the bases had been cleared, Meiji had tied the score! The noise was so deafening in the stadium we could communicate only by hand signals. And now the hand signal was for me to return to the mound. This I did, on the run, determined not to let my teammates down. I took the ball and tried as hard as I could to concentrate on the task at hand. I knew what to do. Above all, this batter, Miyazawa, and the one who followed him would see strikes from me—and not ones they could count on hitting either. Miyazawa, their cleanup hitter, had done nothing against me all day. I observed him choking up on his bat as he stepped in to hit. Cutting down his swing, looking for my fastball was he? All right, let's see what he does with a screwball. I waited for my sign, got it, kicked, and threw. Miyazawa hit a clean single into left-center field. The game was over!

In a lifetime of playing baseball, that was the toughest defeat I ever experienced. It was unbelievable. Amid the craziness that followed, most of us on the Sojitsu team were simply numb. Games were not lost like that. Cheap dramas would not resort to endings so improbable. But improbable had turned to certain right in front of our eyes and in full sight of 35,000 witnesses. In my heart, I believed I was responsible. It was as though I had brought a curse on my friends and teammates and on all our fans. I felt as damned as a leper, a living corpse. I could not begin to apologize for what I had done. The next day, August 4, I went down to Tokyo station by myself and got lost in the crowd that came to say good-bye to the victorious Meiji team. I stayed on the train platform, long after the train had pulled out and the fans had gone, staring at the stretch of empty track that should have been the strip of road bearing our Sojitsu team to Osaka.

Defeat, like victory, is a passing thing. It is with you only as long as you insist on keeping it. It turns out that I was a good deal luckier than my teammates on Sojitsu that day, because this defeat was really the beginning of another phase of my baseball life. For most of my friends, though, in fact for most boys who play high school baseball, victory and defeat, at least in terms of baseball, are futureless. That is precisely why the spirit of high school baseball, so widely praised in our country, is deficient. What kind of advantage is there in staking everything on one game, only to have it all disappear with one bounce of a ball or one crack of a bat? No matter how hard the practice or ardent the dream, everything is gone in a day of defeat, or becomes a memory the day after victory. A futureless game that depends as much on luck as on skill is too heavy a price to pay. It is sad and it is hurtful. There are many talented players in high school, some who go on to college, most who disappear from the baseball world, finally, in the wider world of jobs and family concerns. The few players who go on to the professional ranks learn something very different about the game of their youth. They learn that it does not take one game or one season or two to gain real skills. It takes years and years. But in the climate of heroic and spiritual effort fostered by high school baseball, it all rides on a single game won or lost, on dreams and tears too easily filled and too painfully given. It is really not right to place this all on young boys who should be allowed to grow more freely. There are people in my country who argue that the kind of spiritual power found in this setting is important for later life, that it teaches one to survive defeat and to become a better person. I'm not so sure.

In fact, in the high school baseball world, spiritual power

as much as baseball is presented in a distorted way. To turn spiritual power toward the fulfillment of a one-day dream is to make illusion out of spirit. The skills necessary for any craft, practiced day in and day out over many years, are what separate the professional from the amateur. The acquiring of skill is also a spiritual as well as a technical undertaking and is a far more natural setting for fostering growth of "spiritual power." The professional world enabled me, after many, many years, to understand that what I did every day mattered far more than the glory or the grief of a moment. To lose in the professional world means you have a chance the next day, to win means that you must come back and do it again before you congratulate yourself too much. And in any case you are left with yourself each morning.

My high school baseball career ended, as many do, with a single, shattering defeat. In this period of time, ripening slowly, certain changes had already taken place in my and my family's life. The possibility of my becoming a professional ballplayer rather than going on to college had moved from the stage of unwelcome speculation to acceptance. For our big-league teams had been visiting my family. There were ten calling cards—including one, I learned much later, from a man named Arakawa of the Daimai Orions—sitting on the mantelpiece at home. Discussions, plans, proposals had been in the air. The big thing was that my father had given me his blessing. I think he conveyed this to me that night he visited me at Koshien. I am not sure, because we never talked about it directly. But at any rate, in the aftermath of this final high school defeat, it was simply understood that beyond the ruins of the moment lay the horizons of professional baseball.

Chapter Four

In those days there was no draft system. Thank God. If there had been such a system, I never would have fulfilled my dreams. I can look back on it now and feel this sense of tremendous blessing—one which includes the sense that I am somehow a person from another age—but I feel anger for what was ultimately surrendered.

The draft system, this peculiar lottery of talent that is supposed to give all teams an equal opportunity to stock their rosters, is one of the most unfortunate changes to affect modern professional baseball in Japan.

It is argued that the draft cuts down the costs of management in pursuing young players, that a kind of order is created in an otherwise chaotic situation, that the sickliness of many teams is prevented by cutting out the advantages of robustness in one strong team (*i.e.*, the Giants). Well, all of that sounds reasonable, and perhaps it is—but it also is destructive of something very essential in baseball—a dream of fans and players alike.

Imagine a young amateur player, as I once was, looking forward to playing professionally. In the heart of that young person, if he has passionately followed baseball from his boyhood, is loyalty and longing. His mind is crowded with so many memories of wonderful players and games, triumphs and failures, the years of his growing up with "his" team. What does it mean when that youngster, if he is good enough to be a professional, has no say whatsoever in which team he plays for? What does it mean when the fans of a team see their management unable to choose players whose loyalties have led them to the team in the first place? The answer in both instances is a tremendous loss in the charm of baseball itself. The charm of the sport is so much more than the outcome of games. And yet the draft system reduces everything to that. Players become mere technicians, engineers of results, with loyalties created out of business arrangements rather than naturally, from the heart.

I can almost hear the objections now. That's fine if you belong to the Tokyo Giants, but what about all the other teams? Most boys in Japan grow up rooting for the Giants; everyone wants to play for them. You can't have nine hundred players on one team and one on the other. And let's not forget money. The strongest team has the strongest bankroll, and don't you think that a boy's loyalties for, say, the team from Hiroshima might be changed when he is confronted with a far bigger offer from the Giants?

First things first. What's so wrong about a professional league where interest is built up around everyone else trying to beat the one big team? This kind of competition is genuine and very healthy. The joy of beating Goliath is unsurpassable, and such victories as these become lasting in memory. In our culture, the leading samurai warrior held his position only as long as he could hold off the inevitable challenges that came his way. When he lost, not only was his life at stake but his deepest self-respect as well. And for the new champion there was a sense of accomplishment and transformation that was not about money. The charm of baseball involves a world in which the outcome of games is only one of many parts.

I longed to play for the Giants. The fact that I did wind

up playing for them allowed me to achieve what I did in baseball. I am completely convinced that if I had played elsewhere, as the current draft system might have dictated, I would never have set the records I did. It meant everything to play for a team I truly loved. I strove with all my might to answer to my dreams—which fortunately were not reduced to the single dimensions of money and personal accomplishment. I played hard and better as a result of being with the Giants. The Giants, with their wonderful talent and tradition, gave me every bit as much as I ever could give them.

I initially believed that I would not play for the Giants. Of the many teams that had expressed interest in me, the Giants seemingly was not one of them. I say "seemingly" because in fact they were—though I was unaware of it. The Giants were, in fact, the first team that expressed interest in me—a full year before I graduated from high school. At the time, my family was still thinking that I would go on to college. My father told this to the representative of the Giants at the time, and there the matter lay. When it became clear that I was going to go into professional baseball, no one in my family informed the Giants of that decision. As far as the Giants knew, my family's decision to have me go to college still stood. Sometime later, in the chaos of other teams pursuing me, it became clear to the Giants what had happened, and their representative reappeared on the scene. Before that, however, I had almost made up my mind to join another team.

A representative of the Hanshin Tigers, Mr. Sagawa, had taken great pains to explain to me and my family what advantages there would be for me if I played in Osaka. The team was particularly suited to me because it was made up in large part of high school graduates, some of them familiar rivals of mine. Teams like the Giants, on the other hand, were composed mainly of college graduates. Competition would be easier, I would feel more comfortable with a team like the Tigers. When I thought that the Giants were not going to make an offer, I was inclined toward accepting Mr. Sagawa's offer. So were my parents, who knew that Mr. Sagawa was a decent and courteous man. The Tigers' offer was very handsome, not as large as some other teams, but certainly good enough. The issue, anyway, was not money. That became absolutely clear when the Giants, at the eleventh hour, entered the picture to make their offer.

Initially, I did not know what to do. Instead of feeling elated, I felt awful. Not only did I feel obligated in some way to the Tigers, but Mr. Sagawa had been so thoughtful in his representations that I wondered if it wouldn't be stupid on my part to reject them.

Sometime later—no more than a day or two—my brother, Tetsushiro, came to see me. He shook me from the protective cocoon of lethargy and misery that I had spun for myself.

"Look," he said, "our parents are anxious about Sagawa-san, this is true. But there is a decision to make here, and, you see, it must be yours. What do you want to do?"

"I should go to the Tigers."

"Why?"

"Oh, well . . ." I searched for answers. The Tigers, as I had been told, had many top high school players like my old rival Teruo Namiki from Nichidai-Sanko and others. . . .

"Yes?"

"And it will be easier to break in. . . . "

"Yes?"

"And the Giants . . . " The problem was that whenever I thought about the Giants, I was a star-struck boy again. I could no more get rid of that than breathing. The Giants may have been university players, but they were *gorgeous*. Mr. Kawakami with his brilliant, flashing red bat, Mr. Chiba and Wally Yonamine and Mr. Bessho and, above all, the great new star, Nagashima. . . .

"What *about* the Giants?" my brother insisted.

"It's my dream to play for the Giants!" I blurted out.

"Then choose the Giants!" he said.

And so I did.

My brother and I informed our parents of our decision. My parents, far from being critical, supported me tenderly.

"Sada," my father instructed me, "since you have chosen your own way, you must now do this as fully as you can. Give yourself to it wholeheartedly. No halfway effort." And then he added:

"If, in spite of all your effort, it does not work out as you hope, you may leave the team and come home. It will be difficult. But you leave the team and come home. You can take over my job."

"Yes," I said, bowing deeply to my father.

What followed was a formal meeting in which the family made its decision. While it seems now to be a postscript to what had already taken place, it certainly had the feeling of something else then. To begin with, the meeting was in Yokohama, where many of our relatives lived. Getting to and from Yokohama was not all that easy, what with the considerable amount of press activity around our house. Scouts and officials from other teams—including the Chunichi Dragons, who had most recently fattened their offer to an incredible 20 million yen—were close by as well. Getting to Yokohama, therefore, required some doing. Before dawn, the day of the meeting, my mother left the house alone and boarded a train for Yokohama. An hour later, my father boarded another train. I got to Yokohama by first going with Mr. Miyai to Ueno station, ostensibly to say good-bye to our new Sojitsu team, which was traveling that day to a road game. But Mr. Miyai stayed behind, and amid the crowds in the station, we slipped away and went on to Yokohama together. Tetsujo, making his own arrangements, arrived in Yokohama in midafternoon.

Our family meeting broke up before evening and Tetsujo immediately telephoned the Giants' office with our decision. By the time we returned home that night, a team official was en route to our house with cameramen and reporters. Although the formal announcement would not come until October 4, almost a month away, it was all set. I was to sign a contract for 13 million yen (about $60,000), more money than I could possibly want—and, yet, far below what other teams were offering. It hardly mattered. Futureless baseball was not the baseball of my dreams. As a boy of eighteen, who had known only the narrow, demanding world of a Tokyo high school, what more could I have hoped for?

The matter was not entirely settled. When the press announced my decision to join the Giants, my family and I were concerned that Mr. Sagawa would rightfully feel that his claim to my services had been usurped. For a few days the press was concentrating its attention almost exclusively on the question of whether the Giants would use me as a hitter or as a pitcher. Then one day Mr. Sagawa was discovered visiting the commissioner's office. He finally commented on the situation. "What I hope for," he said, "is that Sadaharu's talents will be used to the fullest. He's going to be a hitter, so if the Giants use him as a pitcher, they will waste lots of money. Please tell the Giants to use him as a hitter." And that was all. To this day I think of Mr. Sagawa with friendship and gratitude.

The formal signing was a circus of sorts. There were so many reporters and photographers—and members of the Oh family—covering the event that they had to move it to a large banquet hall in downtown Tokyo. Amid the whir of cameras and the pop of flashbulbs and all the noise and heat, what I remember most clearly is a photograph of a very young person in a stiff high school uniform, looking skinny and out of place in his close-cropped military-style haircut. Did I feel like a big shot at that moment? I look at that picture now almost with the forbearance of a father remembering one of his children's special moments. A uniform shirt was handed to me—I would have the same number I had had in high school—Number One. Good-natured jokes were made about it. "He's the number one high school player in Japan!" "Number one for number one!" Someone using my Chinese nickname said, "Wan and wan, very good combination!" All the while, I grinned from ear to ear, my heart pounded, my head was in the clouds. But in the back of my mind I knew even then there was a difference between all this fuss and what lay ahead.

At first I had only ceremonial matters to deal with—press interviews, photographers, signing autographs, nothing that was so startlingly different from the world I was about to leave. I wanted more than anything to get right to work. I went to the Giants' Tamagawa campground on the outskirts of Tokyo in the early part of October to work out with our farm team, which was housed there. But I was ahead of myself. Spring training was still months away. There's simply no way to hurry time, to create challenges that have not yet been defined.

One part of waiting was observing. The Giants, a little later that fall, were in the Japan Series. This is our equivalent of the American World Series, and that year—1958—the Giants, winners of Japan's Central League pennant, were up against the Nishitetsu Lions, champions of the Pacific League. I went to the first two games of the series at Korakuen Stadium. Though I was a spectator, I no longer felt like one of 50,000 as I had those many times I had visited Korakuen in the past. I was now a part of *this* team, these Giants. And Giants they were! My teammates were my boyhood idols. I was one of them now—but I was still a boy. Amid the organized chanting, the sound of drums, and the waving of the long colorful streamers and banners, characteristic of fan involvement with our game, I was the most excited person in the place. However, Time was busy fashioning its own story at this point.

The Giants won both games I attended and traveled on to Fukuoka, hoping to take the series without having to return to Tokyo. They took a long step toward this objective by winning game three, thereby standing on the brink of a clean sweep. Fortune or, more likely, crafty management then intervened. The Lions' best chance for any kind of recovery in the series lay with their great right-handed pitcher, Kazuhisa Inao. But Inao had already been overused and would surely not have been at his best if he had had to go to the mound in game four, as scheduled. The Lions' management, after an overnight rainfall, called off the game at ten o'clock that morning—though the sun was bright in the heavens and fans were lined up at the gates of the stadium!

With a day's extra rest, Inao returned to the mound— as a relief pitcher—in an early inning and battled the Giants the rest of the way. In the last of the ninth, though, the Giants led by a run with two out and no one on base (my recent high school experiences should have been fore-warning for what was to come). A ground ball just over the bag at third—which Giant fans to this day swear was foul—went for a double. A long and fruitless argument followed, but the third-base umpire's call stood. The following batter singled to center, tying the game. And then, in the tenth inning, Inao himself hit a two-run "sayonara" home run to win the game for the Lions, 6–4.

With that win, Inao came back the very next day and pitched a complete-game 4–3 victory. With another day off for travel, and a legitimate rain-out, Inao returned fully armed for game six. He shut out the Giants and, the fol-lowing day, led the Lions to the series title with a complete-game 6–1 victory, marking the only time in the history of the Japan Series that a team down by three games came back to take the championship.

Apart from Inao's outstanding personal accomplishment (even at the major league level, it was then traditional to use the same pitcher, game after game), this defeat really marked the end of an era. By the following spring, when I began my first season of active play, changes were already under way. Mr. Kawakami retired, and Wally Yonamine was shortly to be shipped to another team. The Giants team of the next decade was to be built around two new players—

one of them, myself. The meaning of that amazing defeat for the Giants in the fall of '58, the real story Time was working there, was in this change of guard.

Obviously, I knew none of that. There was only the whirl and thrill of these unprecedented days of my youth. Shortly before the end of the regular season, I met my new teammates for the first time. How could anything more important than that be going on? I was taken to Tokyo Station one day to meet the Giants' players as they set off by train for Hiroshima. I remember literally trembling as I was escorted along the platform to the train. As I approached, the players thrust their heads from the windows of the train to greet me. Everyone shook hands with me—and what I remember now is how big their hands were and how stout they looked framed in those windows—middle-aged men good-naturedly welcoming a boy.

Among those players was Nagashima-san. No player in recent memory had so captured the imagination of the fans. There was no one like him. And yet, the strongest memory I have of that day was of his being set apart. The window in which I saw Nagashima-san's face for the first time seemed to be shining! His face and body were actually engulfed in light, and when he, too, thrust out his hand to shake mine, I could think only, this is Nagashima-san, the one with such great batting skills, the one all of us are talking about. It was like looking into the face of the sun. It was too much. He gripped my hand and I gripped his. He offered words of encouragement to me. What they were, I don't remember. I'm not sure I even heard them. I was filled with the feeling of a fan shaking hands with a star he has longed to see!

I said that Time was working its own story in this period, making a new Giants team. I could perceive this only as a youngster looking forward to the adventure of his life. Baseball in America is a game that is born in spring and dies in autumn. In Japan it is bound to winter as the heart is to the body. Our season ends in late November, pre-camp begins shortly thereafter. Spring training begins in early February. When the cherry blossoms bloom in Japan, our players are already fully hardened for combat. I looked forward to this discipline as a passion. I could not wait for it to begin. I could not wait to throw myself at it full force. And yet, when I boarded a train for Miyazaki in those first days of February 1959, I was aware, even more, of leaving home for the first time in my life.

When Nagashima-san had arrived in spring camp for the first time the year before, there had been literally thousands of fans and media people there to greet him when he got off the train. This was befitting a great college star, one of the brightest ever to come out of the illustrious Big Six League of Tokyo. And Nagashima-san, as though born fully matured from the head of a god, had been ready for it from the start. When I arrived in Miyazaki, there were fewer than twenty reporters and team officials there to meet me. That was fine, I said. I was there to work hard, to do as well as possible, to answer to my team's needs and to try to fulfill whatever goals they set for me—either as a pitcher or as a hitter.

I am well aware that I have a reputation now as a very hard worker. The press has done much over the years to build this image of me as some kind of fanatic devotee of heroic labor, as though I were some sort of wonderful exception to the rule in Japan. There are two misconceptions in this—and I should set them straight before I move one step further. Many, if not all, players work just as hard as I do. Hard work is a professional's obligation. He has no business taking credit for it any more than a musician should take credit for practicing scales. Another point: I am not a "natural" hard worker. I have two in me, one is weaker, the other stronger. The weaker one always looks for a way out, wants fun and good times—and usually finds them; the other is therefore forced to work overtime to catch up. Praise or blame half of me for being a hard worker. Because I am so conscious of not wanting to work, or of being exposed without means of holding my head up, I push myself to do better. In Miyazaki I worked simply to prove—to myself and everyone else—that I belonged there, that I could be both a good teammate and a good fellow. And that first spring I worked hard, if only to quiet the mad beating of my heart.

We were invariably out of bed shortly after sunup and at it through the day and into the night, till just before bedtime at ten o'clock. We had drills to toughen our bodies—running distances and sprints with ropes tied to our waists, dragging heavy tires behind us; as a team we did calisthenics and warm-ups as well as field drills and obstacle-course exercises; we took our meals together morning, noon, and night. We went to the far end of Miyazaki by the sea, and by the Shrine of Aoshima, ran around and around the palm-tossed island that is said to be the very place where the God of the Sea rose up out of the waters to create the nation of Japan. We prayed at the shrine for safety and good results in the coming season.

We drilled to the clock, honing our baseball skills. From ll to 12 we practiced special fielding plays, cutoffs, relays, ground-ball positions; 12 to 12:30, lunch together of, say, noodles, miso soup, and rice balls; 12:30, batting practice—ten minutes each player; 1:45, batting practice with defense in the field in order to simulate game conditions; 3:15, sliding practice; 3:35, special practice for young players—thousand-ground-ball drill; *tokushu* for catchers and infielders; 4:15, *tokuda*, special batting practice. Then meetings and running and dinner and night practice. Oh, yes, all of it. Every day.

But try as I might, I could not get over the feeling of being a boy among men. No matter how hard I tried, one part of me stared wide-eyed at these fantasy figures who passed back and forth, wearing uniforms of the same team I now belonged to.

In those first days in Miyazaki, there were two hotels for the players. One was for the players most likely to join our farm team, the other was for the regulars. I was housed in the hotel for the regulars. And my first roommate, of all people, was Nagashima-san himself!

To this day I cannot figure out why Mr. Mizuhara, our manager, arranged this—except that I know his motives proceeded from utmost kindness toward me. Perhaps he wanted me to get a taste of professional life as quickly as possible, to learn from the best example around. Maybe he wanted me to understand something about the differences between public and private life. I don't know. However, what happened was that I found myself on tenterhooks to please this new older brother, to be the perfect roommate and friend. I obliged photographers often by allowing them to take pictures of my serving tea to Nagashima-san—to prove their contention that among new Giant players I was a most earnest and serious young fellow. What I wanted more than anything was to have good, easy times with Nagashima-san. After ten days, though, I was suddenly transferred to another room—a common dormitory room for young players.

Actually, I felt a lot easier there, because I was with people who were most like myself. But I was anxious about why I had been transferred. I went over and over in my mind what I might have done to displease Nagashima-san, and I could not figure it out. Sometime later I learned the reason was that Nagashima-san's sleep was disturbed by my big snoring. Yes, of course. This was true. I felt relieved when I heard this. It's odd to feel anything like pride over so strange a thing as snoring, but I have always counted myself lucky to be such a heavy sleeper—even if the consequences sometimes produced these unwelcome results.

In fact, big sleeping is very much a part of understanding the early relationship I had with Nagashima-san. It has been written that Nagashima-san is a man of such stature that his head was in the clouds, that mere mortals would have a hard time being in his company. This is, of course, completely untrue. He was when I first met him—and always—very natural in manner, outgoing and friendly—and very, very dedicated to his craft. He was a genius at what he did, a man who comes along once in a century—and from the start the sense I had of him was always colored by this. He and I were never really friends, though. We have never drunk together or had a social evening together in the more than twenty years we have known each other. In these first days, however, I did not perceive distance as such between us—only that there was authority and presence on the one hand and my fatheaded clumsiness—and snoring—on the other.

Once, in these early days, we took a road trip to Hiroshima. While trips to Hiroshima today are made by air, then we went by sleeping car. When our train pulled into the station at Hiroshima that morning, I was still sound asleep. I woke up, thinking I was in a dream with someone shouting over and over, "Wake up! Wake up!" In fact, when my eyes cleared, I found Nagashima-san standing over me, his face set with sternness and frustration.

"Huh?"

"I'll get your baggage! Hurry up, put on your clothes! Hurry, there's no time!" He shouted at me again and handed me my shirt, necktie, and jacket one by one. I put on each article of clothing as it was handed to me, and then, still half-asleep, I ran out into the aisle, telling myself, my God, I've got to get off before the train pulls out of the station. Nagashima-san, taken by surprise, ran after me, carrying my shoes and socks.

"Hey! Hey! What's the matter with you? Wait!"

There was another time, too. We went to Vero Beach early in 1961 to train with the Dodgers. We stopped overnight in Los Angeles on the way, intending to catch a plane early the next morning for Florida. When the time came for us to assemble in the lobby for the trip to the airport, I was not there. Yes, I was once again 20,000 leagues under, swimming near the ocean floor. And it was Nagashima-san, knowing exactly the cause of absence, who rushed off to my room.

I don't know how long he pounded on my door in a vain effort to wake me. I never heard him—and my door was locked. The first glimmering I had of his torment was when I woke to his thunderous shouting and saw him—or that is, half of him—stuck in the transom over my door, his face contorted with the effort of shouting. As in Hiroshima, we went through this bizarre ritual of my stumbling into clothes that he handed me piece by piece. And this time, too, because I was so out of it and because time was so short, Nagashima-san packed for me—also, very carefully, article by article, as though his deliberateness was a method he was adopting to keep from murdering me on the spot.

It was so long ago; Nagashima-san and I are both middle-aged men now. He is out of baseball completely, and I spend more and more time thinking about what I might do when the last of baseball is behind me. In that first spring, though, the big questions for me were how I would fit in with this team, how my teammates would take to me, and what position I would at last wind up playing.

I did try to make myself very agreeable because I was so happy to be where I was. I think I may have amused people without knowing it. Mr. Fujita, a future manager of the Giants, a quiet and very dignified man, was always willing to let others step before him into the limelight. He was a superb pitcher in his day and a leader on the Giants when I first got there. He jokes now to reporters:

"You should have seen Oh in those days. He used to say '*Hai* [yes]' to everything. Ask him the time of day, he'd say, '*Hai, hai*, it's twelve o'clock.' Ask him his name and he'd say, '*Hai, hai*, Oh Sadaharu.' He was very enjoyable to us."

My friend Mr. Hiroka, alas, has the same memory of me. Once he asked what I had done the night before. The conversation, he says, went like this:

"What did you do?"

"Yes, yes, I went to the movies."

"The movies?"

"Yes, yes."

"What did you see?"

"Yes, I saw *Damn Yankees*."

"That's an interesting movie."

"Yes, yes."

"Did you like it?"

"Yes."

The coaching staff of the Giants was meanwhile puzzling how exactly to use me. It is not true, as some have written, that I was tormented by doubt and uncertainty about whether I'd be a pitcher or a hitter. I wasn't sure, of course, but I had my ideas. I practiced with pitchers and hitters and fielders. I probably wound up practicing more than I might have otherwise, as a result. In the middle of one set of drills, someone would come over to me and say, "Go to the bullpen," and I'd run off to the bullpen. In the bullpen, someone would come and say, "Go join the outfielders for fly-ball drill," and I'd trot off to the outfield. In the outfield, someone would come and order me to take thousand-ground-ball drill as a first baseman—and off I'd go again.

I believe the coaching staff was divided for a time on what they should do with me—Mr. Makao, the pitching coach, thought I should be a pitcher. Mr. Hiroka advised that I might really be a switch hitter. Mr. Mizuhara, our manager, took his time. "No need to hurry, plenty of time till opening day," he said. When I stood down in the bullpen, though, and watched the Giant pitchers warming up, I knew in my heart that I was no pitcher. The velocity with which they threw the ball was simply astonishing to me, far beyond what I could do. If I threw a ball anywhere near eighty miles an hour, I was surely in high gear. These major leaguers could surpass that just playing around. I also knew, from my last disappointing days at Sojitsu, that I wasn't quite the pitcher everyone thought I was. And if I really needed any confirmation of that, I was simply clobbered when I finally wound up pitching in a Red-White intrasquad game that spring.

The question, really, was what position I would play if I did not pitch. I had played the outfield in high school, but the Giant outfield was strong at that time, and as I was a very slow runner, there was really no likelihood of my breaking in there. First base was a possibility, because Mr. Kawakami had just retired. But it was more or less understood that Wally Yonamine would cover that position. Two things happened to resolve all this. First, one of our top outfielders, Mr. Sakazaki, injured himself, thereby opening a spot in the outfield. Still, because I was thought to be too slow, there was no plan to use me. Wally Yonamine—whose autograph I still cherished with intense and secret joy—told the coaches that I was too good a hitter not to be in the lineup. He said that I already knew how to hit to left field, something that had taken him many years of study to achieve. His suggestion, therefore, was to use me at first base and send him to the outfield. Though I believe his own future with the Giants may have been at stake in this decision, he unequivocally urged it and stood behind it. By the end of camp, I was a first baseman and my pitching days were behind me.

I thought I might succeed as a hitter, and though I was slow, I felt comfortable at first base. Our exhibition games were soon upon us, and we began slowly wending our way back to Tokyo. I managed five home runs in these games—including one "sayonara" home run. It was enough to keep the press buzzing with questions about what I might eventually do. It was also enough to lull me into a false sense of what I was shortly to be up against. Just prior to the season, the coaching staff, as is traditional in Japanese baseball, reviewed the goals that were expected from each of the players on the team. There is no sense of contract in this, but there is a very strong cultural sense of obligation to which a player must answer. Obligation is a very powerful force in our lives—ours is a culture of shame—and the player who falls short of the goals established for him by his team runs the risk of having to answer to the sternest authority of all—his own sense of self-worth. What was expected from me was a batting average around .280, approximately fifteen or twenty home runs with about eighty RBIs. And given what I was doing in exhibition games, these seemed good targets to shoot for. What awaited me, however, was something no one—coaches, friends, family, or I—could have foreseen. At the summit of my young baseball life, I was about to enter a three-year free fall that nearly destroyed me.

Chapter Five

Our batting coach was Mr. Tetsuharu Kawakami, who, within two years, became the team's manager. Mr. Kawakami was a forceful and intense personality as well as one of the greatest batters in the history of Japanese baseball. He had been the Giants' first baseman since 1938, winning five different batting titles (including a career high of .377) and earning the nickname "The God of Batting" among an adoring public—whose numbers certainly included me. When Mr. Kawakami had anything to say about hitting, you can be sure I listened. I sought to follow his guidance with utmost determination.

During our exhibition games that spring, the press naturally asked Mr. Kawakami many questions about my batting technique. This was standard. In my country there is an almost overdone preoccupation with the smallest details of strategy and technique (which may be a chief reason why the average game in Japan takes far longer to play than its equivalent in America). This preoccupation is even more intense when it is turned on a player just breaking into the major leagues. A new player with a big high school reputation like me is gone over like an experimental machine of some sort, every turn and fitting of the model checked and double-checked again before being placed on line. If there is a flaw there, the fans will probably know about it before anyone else.

For myself, I was not too worried about this sort of scrutiny. I knew I was not a perfect hitter and that it took time to develop a really good technique. That was what being a pro was about. I had confidence in myself, and I was also able to adopt the slogan "Take It Easy" in order to give myself a chance. (Some of my teammates, in fact, good-naturedly called me "Mr. Take It Easy.")

Mr. Kawakami, for his part, saw things similarly. He stressed to the media that it takes one or two years for a rookie to learn good batting form. Along with Mr. Mizuhara, our manager, he emphasized the importance of patience in dealing with me. He also pointed out that my batting form was not really well defined—which was certainly the case. He reminded me—and the press—that I was a top talent but that my form was very soft. The problem, as he saw it, was that my leg and hip were really tight—and hence I could not move on the ball with the power and speed that were required.

As the exhibition season drew to a close, Mr. Kawakami's words weighed on me more and more. While I had managed to show power at the plate, my hitting was not consistent, and I would go through several games at a time where I made little or no contact, striking out often. "Hitting is with your hip not with your hand," Mr. Kawakami told me. "You should imagine that your eyes are in your front hip. You can see the ball with your hip. This is difficult, I know. Be patient and it will come." And patience was what Mr. Kawakami stressed to the press—and through them to the fans. Working with me, Mr. Kawakami pointed out that the absence of good hip movement had immediate bad consequences. For one thing, it made me pull my head up off the ball too soon. It also left me peculiarly vulnerable to left-handed pitching and to the breaking pitch in particular.

While all this was going on, the press seemed to grow

critical of Mr. Kawakami, demanding to know why he didn't teach me how to overcome these deficiencies. If they could be so readily identified, why couldn't they be as readily corrected?

About this time the St. Louis Cardinals paid a visit to Japan. On the team was Stan Musial, whose extreme crouch at the plate was the most observable aspect of his great hitting form. Mr. Yonamine was most impressed by this and tried to adopt the crouch himself, and very soon had me trying to follow suit. I could not do it. Instead of freeing me, crouching only seemed to make it hard for me to get my bat around. The impression I gave to the press, however, in changing stance so radically, was that I was confused at the plate. Why, they demanded to know, wasn't I being taught?

"It takes time to observe a hitter, please don't rush," Mr. Kawakami told them—as the season came closer day by day. As far as Mr. Kawakami was concerned, he had confidence in me. One day he and Wally Yonamine took me aside and presented me with the first baseman's mitts they had carried with them through their major league careers. They were to be mine, they said, letting me know in the strongest symbolic way they could that whatever batting problems I had were independent of my future with the Giants. I was the new Giants' first baseman. I was very moved and obligated to them for this gesture.

The fact of the matter was that the caliber of play I was seeing now was so different, so vastly superior to what I had been used to, that I naturally wondered how I would stand up to it. I had to feel encouraged that I had managed five home runs off major league pitching during the exhibitions, yet I also knew the regular season would provide the only real test.

I was not yet nineteen, and I was a member of the Giants. These two facts taken together impress me now with what was really going on with "Mr. Take It Easy." To belong to the Tokyo Giants is unlike membership on any other professional team anywhere. The Giants in Japan are a kind of national institution. Wherever we go as a team, whether to the remotest villages of the countryside or to the largest of our cities, crowds of people are sure to gather. If you are a Giant, simply coming in and out of a hotel is an adventure. People congregate in lobbies and air and train terminals, line streets and stadium entrances for our comings and goings. Swarms of professional and amateur photographers, tourists, teenagers, old people, and children greet us, photograph us, talk with us, get our autographs, share their secrets with us. It is almost as if we are a small nation, a powerful and benevolent kingdom responsible to an area and a population far beyond our own numbers. I was once asked, many years after that first season, by a Western reporter to explain my understanding of the Japanese term *yamato damashi*. This is a nearly untranslatable phrase. It is an ideal that connotes devotion to the community or the nation—but it is much more particular than that, involving obligation as well as feeling. I answered that I perceived *yamato damashi* principally in terms of my belonging to the Giants. I know, of course, that a baseball team is not really a nation, any more than a business company is—but, for most Japanese, loyalty and obligation have roots where you work. And now, suddenly, where I worked seemed to touch the lives of people from one end of Japan to the other. I did not feel "easy" about this. I felt so stirred and fired up it took some doing to convince myself that it was all real. Oh, yes, I wanted to live up to that! I wanted to be worthy and responsible.

I also wanted to have a good time! It was as though every day brought me into contact with what I had never experienced before: new towns and cities, countrysides, people, sights and smells, exotic new foods, and ways of living that months before I could not even have imagined. Was I confused about hitting, as the press said? No, I was merely calm in the eye of a storm—a giant storm of new life! Confusion doesn't begin to speak of it!

My brother once taught me a lesson about showing emotion that served me well then and serves me to this day. No need to make a display of feelings. I never imposed on anyone else what I was going through. Mr. Kawakami said to the press that he did not worry about me, that "my face was still good"—by which he meant that a confused or agitated person always revealed his state by the look in his eyes. "My sleeping style," it was also observed, "was terrific," and besides, my defense was improving.

One day on the train I sat down next to Mr. Kawakami and had a conversation with him about my future. This was as close as I could come to letting him know what was going on in my heart. The Giants have a dormitory for young players at Tamagawa in Tokyo, and very often the two or three youngest players on the team live there along with the members of the farm team. The Giant players stay there for two years before moving on.

"I am anxious," I said to Mr. Kawakami, "about whether I should live at home or in the dormitory." I sincerely wanted his advice on what course I should follow and was prepared to do whatever he said.

"Live in the dormitory," Mr. Kawakami said. "If you play on the Giants, you must stay in the dorm to really learn what it is to be a part of Giants' baseball." And with that—and a hip that was still blind—my major league career began.

In early April of that year we opened our new season at home against the Kokutetsu Swallows. The Swallows' pitcher that day was Masaichi Kaneda. Kaneda, quite simply, was Japan's best pitcher—ever. In his twenty-year career (which ended with the Giants) he won more than 400 games and struck out an unbelievable total of 4,490 men. It was certainly no disgrace to strike out against Kaneda— Nagashima-san had been his victim four times in his rookie debut the year before—and to this day I can only shrug at what happened. In my first three appearances against him, I struck out twice and walked. I never once made even the slightest contact with what he threw. On opening day at Korakuen Stadium, I had the peculiar feeling that the league in which I was now playing featured principally the use of an invisible baseball.

But Kaneda was not really the problem. Good pitching—big league pitching—of any sort was. Game two became game four became game six became game thirteen and April was almost gone. I found myself batting eighth in the Giants' order—when I played—and through my first twenty-six at-bats I still had not got so much as a scratch single. The odd thing was that in spite of the good pitching I still could not understand why I was doing *that* badly. I would feel all right in practice, I would work hard before the game—sometimes I even got up with the farm team at eight in the morning to work out with them before afternoon practice prior to our evening game—but nothing seemed to work.

It may be a little odd to talk about Fortune in this context, but I believe that I was protected in this period as much as in any other where good results were more obvious. Our manager, Mr. Mizuhara, by showing patience with me when he might more easily have rearranged his lineup, enabled me to remain in the big leagues. If Mr. Mizuhara had agreed with many of our team's critics that I was not yet ready for such a high caliber of play, I might have found myself on the way to our farm team—and from there, out of baseball. Mr. Mizuhara was never swayed by what others said, however. And so, Fortune smiled by allowing me a twenty-seventh time at bat in April. It was, ironically enough, in a game against the Hanshin Tigers. There was a scoreless tie, with two men out and a runner on base in the sixth inning, and the Tiger pitcher was an old high school rival of mine, Genichi Murata. Was more needed? All right, a good stiff wind blowing to right field—and a pitch that was probably a mistake. I hit it down the line, not hard but high in the air. I watched it graze the wall and fall into the first row of seats barely 300 feet away. I see myself in old films circling the bases easily, almost nonchalantly. What a laugh! I felt like I was airborne all the way, racing on the clouds! If you ever get to see an old film of me in this moment, watch carefully as I pass third base. The ear-to-ear grin on my face, just barely visible under that old-fashioned Giants' cap, shows the true measure of my nonchalance.

If Fortune smiled, however, it was not in getting the ball over the wall but in allowing me to continue playing. At the time, this seemed anything but a blessing. My batting average did not pick up with that first hit, nor did I have any startling bursts of power that would give anyone an indication that what I was going through might be only temporary. I did not hit my next home run until June, and in the interim what I did mostly—far in excess of average—was strike out. In fact, it was not long into the season when I began hearing fans register their feelings about what they were getting from me.

My name, translated from the Chinese, means "King." Yes, in the situation I was in, this lent itself too easily to ridicule. *"Oh! Oh! Sanshin Oh!"* some fans chanted one day. Soon, every time I came to bat, I would hear the chant, until thousands of people at the same time were all joining in: *"Oh! Oh! Sanshin Oh!* [King! King! Strikeout King!]." This chant was unjustly leveled at me. A friend or two over the years has maintained that I heard it only because I was not a full-blooded Japanese. I don't know. I understood what I had to do to still it, however, but I could not bring it off. The chant followed me from one stadium to the next, across Japan, wherever there were Giant fans or Giant detractors. *"Oh! Oh! Sanshin Oh!"* For three years I did not have it in me to still that sound. The waves of sound do not die away in memory.

My family was worried about me in this period, though I did my best to hide my hurt from them. Parents have an unerring way of sensing their children's feelings, so on the occasion of my first home run, my first hit in the big leagues, my mother and older sister presented me with a small statue of a figure with a sword. This was Kintaro, a figure in children's histories and anecdotes. He was dressed in a brilliant gold costume with a fierce-looking black headpiece. His arm was raised, holding the sword above his head, in a posture of triumph and determination.

"This is to cheer you up," my mother said, "so, now, be of good cheer."

My sister laughed with her. "And hit better."

We all knew the meaning of Kintaro, the child who, when he grew up, defeated many strong devils and promoted only good. I had to laugh, too. I held the statue in my hands, looked at it almost wishing I could borrow the fierce aura surrounding the figure. Would that he could have promoted good hitting!

"Yes, yes. Thank you. You see, I am cheered up already!"

And in some sense I was. I have never been one to drag my tail between my legs. And everything was too new and too special for me to feel so completely overwhelmed by poor performance. I was one of only a select few who had the chance to belong to a big-league baseball team—and if it was not my fate to continue, well, then, I would still have been luckier than most. And, surely, I was not about to give up all that easily.

I settled into life in our dormitory in Tamagawa. This was truly an amazing period for me, and I don't know how to describe it without being misunderstood. First, it should be pointed out that there really is no equivalent in American baseball to this phenomenon of dormitory life for young players. It exists for a purpose most valued in our culture—namely to nurture young people in the hard discipline of group endeavor. That a baseball team needs a sense of real togetherness is obvious, and that young people away from home for the first time need the helpful guidance of their elders is equally clear. But like everything, there is always a kind of balance between the ideal and the actual, and the tension between the two—in any culture—is how you begin to experience the particulars of a life.

From the outside, Tamagawa is not much to look at. Our campground is set in a large field bound in by a fence and bordered by a river. People from the area, children especially, continually congregate at the fences. A busy expressway is visible in the distance against a skyline of smokestacks and new construction. The practice field itself is rough and scruffy—more sandlot than big league in appearance. The dormitory I lived in—as young players have done after me right up to the present—was a wooden, barracks-like structure containing about thirteen rooms, a dining room, and a meeting hall. We players normally lived with roommates, under the tutelage of a dormitory master—who, as long as anyone can remember, has been Mr. Toshiyaki Takemiya, a man synonymous with both Giants baseball and strictness.

The usual dormitory routine begins at seven in the morning when a loudspeaker wakes you. Shortly afterward players gather in a circle and take breakfast together, a traditional Japanese breakfast of rice balls and fish or miso soup, and by eight, practice, hard practice is under way. Players from the major league team have the option of joining this practice (and sometimes the farm game that follows), but all are bound by dormitory rules, which promote the utmost in clean, ordered living and bind one and all to the demands of a 10 P.M. curfew. The problems of the day, of the team, are customarily brought to evening meetings, and time to relax, certainly part of the daily routine, usually is spent in common game rooms and lounges. There is an old movie in Japan called *Susume Eiko-E*, which shows in quite rosy hues what is sought in this dormitory setting. In the movie a fictitious manager of the farm team who has had a poor season must face his responsibility for the team's failure. The manager acknowledges to his players that he has not been successful in training, and he apologizes. He accepts his having to leave and announces that he will be going back to his home, a small town in the provinces, there to rededicate his life by undertaking the teaching of small children. The players rise in tribute to their departing manager, put their arms around each other's shoulders, and begin swaying back and forth, singing the words of an old military song:

Both you and I
Are blossoms on the same cherry tree;
So we flower together
And together we die.

Now I must admit that I did not fit this ideal quite so perfectly. In fact, Mr. Takemiya has often said that Mr. Horiuchi, Mr. Shibata, and I are the three bad boys in the history of the Giants. I was also, according to Mr. Takemiya, a very messy person, someone incapable, it seemed, of keeping a clean and tidy room. How do I explain this alongside the honest assertion that I indeed tried as hard as I was able in those days to compete for my place on the team? I have no decent explanation other than the constant war between weaker and stronger, which I have already mentioned but which was not so neatly balanced in my thinking then.

It is true that I kept a fairly messy room. I was not so proud of the fact. Yet I was very new at this sort of life. With my first money, I bought a record player and records. I kept many magazines and books around. Even in those days, I was fond of mysteries, Western as well as Eastern. Anyone who cared to look—including Mr. Takemiya— could see a litter of Ellery Queen and Alfred Hitchcock anthologies (in Japanese, of course!) lying all over the place. People who are kind to me say that my messy room was the result of my not having any space for the many gifts fans regularly sent me. Yes, I got gifts from fans—fruit, rice cakes, mementos—but it was I alone who could not figure out a good stacking arrangement.

My sense of other people wasn't what it might have been either—and I know that led to trouble. I was through all of this "Mr. Take It Easy." My room, like my poor batting, just was not something that was going to get me down. I think if I had been hitting up to par, things might have been different, but not hitting yet remaining in a good mood was not the best way to get along in the dorm. Some of the other players began to get angry at me, believing that my good cheer was really indifference—which it never was—and so cards, phone calls, gifts, laughter became sources of annoyance to them.

One day, apparently, Mr. Takemiya decided to take all this out on poor Mr. Ito, my roommate. As Mr. Ito later reported it, Mr. Takemiya took him aside and told him that because he was three or four years older, the condition of the room, my slovenliness, everything was *his* responsibility. He, having the benefit of years and a college education, was even more to blame than I, who was, after all, still wet behind the ears. This was a serious charge to level at someone, and it was offered, remember, by Mr. Takemiya, whose sternness and temper were never to be challenged.

Mr. Ito took this reprimand with utmost respect and seriousness. He certainly had no intention of burdening me with what he had gone through, but he could do nothing less than tell me exactly what had taken place. I felt terrible. I could not bring myself to say anything. It was one thing if I had to pay for my own mistakes; it was quite different if someone else did. Mr. Ito, though, was a person of good cheer and understanding. He later told the story:

"Mr. Oh did not answer. Not a word from him, just a very serious face. It was late at night. We went to sleep. Very early in the morning, however, I awoke to find him vigorously sweeping the floor. Only he was very bad at it; he didn't know how to sweep. He used these big, long strokes that simply redistributed the dust from one end of the room to the other. He was like a tiger trying to catch his tail and he couldn't do it. I lay there laughing myself silly."

In all fairness to Mr. Takemiya, I know that he did not view the condition of my room as the main problem. I was also able to "cheat his eyes" with respect to curfew, and this he could not stand. I must say now—and very clearly—that in those early days with the Giants I began to drink. Drink a lot. I don't want to be misunderstood, and at the same time I don't want to dwell endlessly on an aspect of my life that I don't consider that important, so I had best explain.

Very early on, because I suddenly had money and because the world was a flower opening to me, I discovered the joys of Ginza. Ginza is an area of Tokyo filled with cabarets, expensive bars, and Mah-Jongg parlors. If you have money and time, you can find virtually any pleasure you want in Ginza. For someone of my years, so limited in background and experience, you can imagine what it was like to find your way amid clubs where you could see yourself in mirrors on the ceiling, where the clink of glasses and the rustle of gorgeous kimonos sounded to laughter and pleasant music. I can no longer name the places and the times. There were so many! Walk down Ginza at night and you will see the clubs everywhere, their names traveling up the sides of buildings many stories high on marquees splendid in lighting and design. If I had it to do again and had the time and the money I had as a boy of nineteen, so limited in his contact with the world, I would surely take exactly the same plunge.

The names of the clubs, the particulars, are not so important. What will it be tonight, Snow Girl or Baby Face, Ballade or Club Miyuki? No matter, the drinks were good, the women beautiful and elegant and witty, the cigarettes foreign and expensive.

Of course, I was not just another nineteen-year-old kid discovering Ginza. In the first place, young people rarely get to experiment there. They don't have the money. In the second place, I was a ballplayer, and a Giants player at that, well enough known even then to have to watch myself. And so I did. I drank mainly beer in those early days and, because I was doing so poorly on the field, never "drank with a big face." (In my country, "drinking with a big face" is a form of showing off, allowable if you're a big shot.) Instead, I stayed in the dark corners of bars and drank until I felt good. Also, because I was one of the few young men around—remember, it took money to frequent these first-class bars in Ginza—I did not have to pursue women. I was something of a favorite among the hostesses. They enjoyed my company and I enjoyed theirs. We played like the children we nearly were, silly games and flirtations, singing together, sharing our drinks and stories and youthful pleasures.

I never took a drink to avoid life or to discover what was missing in it. I drank always for pleasure, because it made me feel better and easier. I believe that a batter in a slump might sometimes help himself with a drink or two instead of further torturing himself over what he's been doing wrong. Many years later, I kept a notebook by my bedside to jot down different thoughts I had on batting. One night I woke up and wrote this: "There are three ways to get rid of a slump. One is to drink and change the feeling you are walking around with. Another one is to get involved in some sort of hobby so you can forget for a while. The third is just to practice and practice again. In order to get rid of uneasiness, the first two ways should be considered. The last way sometimes deepens the feeling of uneasiness. However, the first two have nothing to do with progress. If the monster called slump requires improvement in technique and skill then there is only the road of practice and practice and practice. . . ."

I practiced in those days—even as I drank. I drank again and again. I practiced again and again. I took it easy again and again. I worked myself to the bone again and again. I maintain to this day that my problems on the field, though they were surely made no better by drink, were not principally the result of drink either.

Later in the spring of that first year, I came off the bench as a pinch hitter and, to the chants of the crowd, struck out yet another time. Something seemed to snap within me. My spirits dropped, and I could not seem to pick myself up. Mr. Kawakami took me aside and told me that in his first year things had got so bad he even thought of quitting. If I was thinking like that, he urged me to change my mind.

"Please do practice hard," he insisted, "and please do not worry about striking out so much. Hit a lot at Tamagawa Grounds and above all, be patient."

I did exactly as I was instructed. When we were in Tokyo, I tried to make sure that I took three hours of practice at Tamagawa before going to the ball park for another three hours of work before each of our games. In mid-June, after a hard road trip, I was joined at Tamagawa by other players on the team, including some of the veterans. The weather by now was hot and sticky, and Mr. Kawakami thought that extra practice at that time might be unwise. But he later told a reporter that he granted us permission to continue "when he rememberd how serious our faces looked."

Toward the end of June—June 26 to be exact—we had an important game at home against the Hanshin Tigers. Significant as this game was to the standings, it mattered even more in the eyes of the fans. It was "the Emperor's Game," the one game in our era that was to be visited by His Imperial Majesty, the Emperor Hirohito. Hirohito-sama stood at attention in a box reserved just for him. We all stood at attention, too, in ceremonies just prior to the game. The game itself, on a steamy, sultry Tokyo night, fit the occasion—so much so that its tenseness soon removed any thought I might have had of the Emperor's presence. This was the kind of game that fans call *tenranjiai* in Japanese, a game charged in its every play and every gesture with dramatic possibility.

Going into the last of the seventh inning, the Tigers led

us 4–2. I batted with one out and a runner on first in that inning. At one point in my turn, I checked my swing—and Mr. Kawakami trotted over to tell me that I mustn't do that again, that I was to swing fully and hard. I hit a 2–2 pitch into the right-field bleachers for a game-tying home run, a thrill for me, yes, but only one more game along the way.

This game, it turns out, was important for other reasons. It was the game in which the most famous home run in all of Japanese baseball was hit. In the bottom of the ninth inning, with the score still tied at 4, Nagashima-san won the Emperor's Game with a "sayonara" home run into the left-field stands (a "sayonara" home run, by the way, is just that: a home run that sends everyone home—a "bye-bye" home run in the last of the ninth or in extra innings). This home run marked the first time Nagashima-san and I both homered in the same game. We were later to be dubbed the "O-N Cannon," and our specialty was to be the "avec" home run (another one of our borrowed terms, signifying the hitting of home runs in the same game by pairs of players).

Yet with all the hard work—and the very occasional good result—my batting average, home runs, and run-production continued to sink. By the end of August, with our team riding high in the standings, my batting average fell below .200. I was simply unable to hit. Mr. Kawakami thought that the reason might be that I was putting in too much time running. This was certainly true. I was running a lot. But I don't think that was the cause of my poor performance. I was running only because I was usually hung over from the night before. I discovered in that first year that when I showed up at the ball park hung over, running and working up a really heavy sweat was a good way to clear my senses.

Though the Giants won the pennant that year, I wound up hitting .161. I finished the season with seven home runs, twenty-five RBIs, and many, many questions about what the future held. We were swept in four straight games by

My parents.

A Waseda High School southpaw named Oh. I learned some-thing important in this period about self-discipline. My old friends and classmates, though, still chafe about my irrational fondness for forkballs.

96

The Waseda cheering section at a game. The headbands and whistles are typical—as are the two dark military-style school uniforms. High school baseball remains a national passion in Japan today.

My wedding. There were many people and groups to satisfy in this traditional ceremony between a Japanese woman— who consented to marry as a Chinese—and a Chinese man who was a modern Japanese.

Training with Arakawa-san and an unidentified coach. Arakawa-san's early efforts with me sought to apply the Japanese psyche to an American game. We trained without letup for three years. In my first three years as a pro I floundered hopelessly without him.

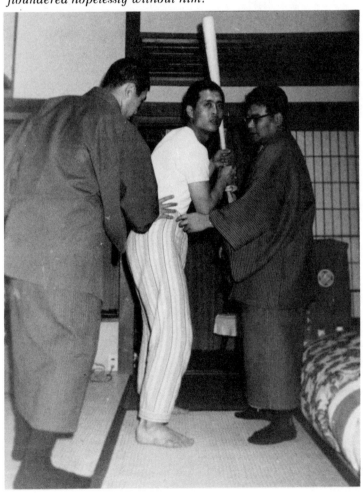

My traditional pose. I am practicing before a mirror here—as is customary among batsmen in Japan. The feel of tatami against my bare feet aided my sense of balance. Note the tilt of my bat.

Newsmen often wanted me to pose thus. I always felt comfortable in traditional costume, but in training I preferred few clothes, so I could sweat freely and so the handling of my sword and the movement of my body were one.

I am slashing a card here. Arakawa-san designed this exercise to test my ability to wait for exactly the right moment to strike. The card spins on a string. In the split second before it stops and twirls backward, you strike.

I am a contemporary Tokyoite, which means I am comfortable with Western ways, but I am most at home in traditional dress in a Japanese-style setting.

Slashing the straw dummy. This time, I severed the figure in a single clean stroke. Do you not see a power hitter here as easily as you do a swordsman?

Arakawa-san watches and instructs. He is my teacher always.

the Nankai Hawks in the Japan Series, a series in which I saw very limited action, striking out twice in the five times I came to the plate.

I didn't need anyone to tell me how badly my season had gone. I could think of little else. Yet, of the two decisive events in my life that followed, only one of them had to do with baseball.

Somewhere around the time of the Japan Series, I got a letter from one of my fans—a girl I had met briefly that summer at the Tamagawa Grounds. She had come there with a group of bicyclists, one of whom was a big Giants fan. I had signed autographs for them, but she was one of a number who had been unable to get one. "Come back tomorrow, and I'll sign more," I had said. She did. I remembered her for two reasons, really. The first was that she was very pretty. Very young and very pretty—a tall girl with large eyes, but only a junior high school student. She was also not really a baseball fan. When she wrote to me, her letter had none of the starry-eyed language of fans. It was straightforward and touching—and that December, I remember, I arranged to go and visit her at a resort in Shizuoka Prefecture, where she and her family had gone for a holiday. What I wanted most of all was just to get my mind off baseball for a day. And what happened there was that I got to drinking sake with her father and so stayed past the time of the last train back to Tokyo. As he later told it, he arranged with the resort management to find a room for me. There were no rooms available, so the management let me have one of their large banquet halls—a 100-tatami room. Sometime later, worrying that I would feel lonely in such a large room all by myself, Mr. Tadashi Koyae decided he, too, would bed down there for the night. When he slid open the *shoji* to the room, he saw me soundly asleep in the center of the floor, snoring so loudly that he decided I was a big enough man to take care of myself. He returned to his room. That was really all there was to this outing. There was nothing in it—including my big sleep—

that signified much of anything. The fact was, though, that the young, pretty girl who struck me with her straightforwardness and her interest in things other than baseball was later to be my wife. Seven years passed before we got married, and in the beginning, at any rate, I never saw that first evening as more than an evening's respite from baseball.

The other decisive event of that winter struck me far more directly. Around the beginning of December, the newspapers suddenly heralded the signing by the Giants of Fumio Kitsugi, a Waseda University graduate and one of the biggest college baseball stars of the season. There were two things about Kitsugi that immediately made me take notice. One was that he was a home-run hitter, the leading home-run hitter in the Big Six University League. The other was that he was a first baseman. The Giants' thinking could not have been clearer. I was shocked at the time, although I shouldn't have been. The first law of professional baseball is its absolutely remorseless competition. The world of baseball is a world of winners and losers, that's it, and my place on the Giants, after only one season, was from that moment in obvious jeopardy.

My friends all urged me to accept this competition with the college graduate. "Beat the King of Jingu Stadium," they urged. This was certainly a good slogan, but almost from the end of the season I had taken another: "Work Harder Than Nagashima-san." What I had found principally in the year that had just passed was that the Giants' biggest star worked as hard as anyone. It wasn't enough to work as hard as a big star. In my position—a not very successful rookie—I had to work harder. The signing of Kitsugi only underscored this fact. From the earliest days at Tamagawa, then, I tried to work harder.

Mr. Mizuhara announced that there would be no decision on who would be the Giants' first baseman until after the finish of our exhibition season. As if to keep both Kitsugi and me aware of the situation between us, we were sometimes asked to do things like pick up practice balls together on the field.

All that spring I was in a good mood for the competition. And the competition between us, no matter how easygoing each of us seemed to the other, was awful. Kitsugi, in fact, was a far more powerful hitter than I was. I watched him hit balls again and again over the wall in left field at Miyazaki. There was an automobile repair shop just beyond the playing area there. Kitsugi rattled the walls of the building like a drum beat—which sounded simultaneously in my own head.

Most fortunately for me, the most serious flaw in my batting style had not yet become clear to others. And somehow I got through that spring without this flaw being exploited. Kitsugi and I opened the season alternating at first base, but soon I was doing well enough to play on a regular basis. As suddenly as our rivalry came to life it was ended. Desperate practice and fighting spirit paid off. The coaches were finally convinced that I had "awakened at last." This, it turns out, was far from the case, but competition with Kitsugi made it seem so. I owe to him a very real lesson: that a man should have a good rival. He saved my career even in the throes of the awful struggle between us.

My performance in this second year was certainly better. I played in more games and hit a respectable .270, with seventeen home runs and seventy-two RBIs. I was strengthened by what I had to go through just to stay with the Giants. Yet, I was far from feeling easy. I knew that no matter what my performance level was, I still had not "found myself." All of the hard work and all of the competition could not ease the sense I had that something important still was missing—though, for the life of me, I could not begin to say what it was. In the meanwhile, the pressure of maintaining a good playing level had been terrible, and the demands in terms of hours and concentration left the easy side of my nature with a big thirst. I frequented Ginza just as regularly, finding, in the dark corners of the very best clubs I knew, the ease and pleasure that were so necessary in this time. "Is young Oh going to throw away his life?" I could not answer such critics sensibly, yet I knew that I was not throwing away my life—that I had found a way to bide my time and in the process discover a world I never knew in growing up.

The one person on the Giants who might put a stop to my comings and goings was Mr. Takemiya. No matter how adroitly I dealt with others who might be curious about my wanderings, Mr. Takemiya required something more. He grew increasingly suspicious of me with the passage of time. I ultimately had to figure out a good tactic to relieve him of the growing sense that I really was "cheating his eyes."

When I went out, intending to be back the next morning, I began carrying a toothbrush in the pocket of my pants. The real difficulty had been getting back to my room early in the morning without being noticed by Mr. Takemiya. Our dormitory, in the early morning hours, was hushed. The slightest sound attracted his sensitive ears.

Our house was located in Maruko-Bashi and was very old. Its wooden floors squeaked under my feet no matter how carefully I tiptoed. It was impossible to get safely back to my room without producing these damning floor sounds. So I learned early on not to try anything really sneaky with Mr. Takemiya. Thus the toothbrush. I cannot count the times I did it now, but it served me well. I can still see it. As soon as I tiptoed into the dormitory I popped the toothbrush into my mouth and walked on to the washroom, no longer caring about the squeaks and moans under my feet. Mr. Takemiya invariably rushed out of his room with a look that can only be described as Triumph Over Evil on his face.

"*You!*" he would splutter, taking in the toothbrush and the sleepy look on my face.

"Early bird, eh?" he would say at long last, watching

me go, the fierce mask of righteousness melting into a stupid stare. Usually I mumbled some sort of incoherent reply. And every once in a while, unable to resist, I turned bright:

"There's an old saying, you know, the early bird catches the worm." The look on my face was demure and sweet.

"Aha! Aha! Well, uh, aha!" Mr. Takemiya would mutter, and he would slowly go back to his room, shaking his head. In the washroom, I concluded my performance by making sure that I gargled as loudly as I could.

Mr. Takemiya, in his own way, made my life more enjoyable!

Of course, I was not spared anything by this. I might have drunk myself into oblivion or not—I would still have been faced with the fact that I did not really know what it was to consistently hit a baseball.

In my third year, my performance fell again. I hit only thirteen home runs, my batting average fell to .253, my RBI total from seventy-one to fifty-three. What was worse was that by now I was fully known around the league. Other teams knew how to pitch to me, and no matter what I did to adjust, sooner or later my weaknesses were theirs for the picking. *"Oh! Oh! Sanshin Oh!"* It crossed my mind more than once that I had gone as far as I could go in professional baseball. There was no regimen of additional work, there were no magic formulas to save me. I took an infusion of ginseng to strengthen my body before every game—I did this throughout my career—practiced with as much devotion as ever, but all the while my fighting spirit grew more and more discouraged.

I moved back home that year. Living with my family meant it was easier to get in and out at night after our games, but that brought its own problems, too. My father and mother nagged me regularly about staying out. "Why are you smoking and drinking and carrying on?" they would say as I stood there bleary-eyed, wanting only to get to sleep. They pointed out to me that I was doing harm to my body—no matter what else I thought I might be accomplishing. I never argued with them, because I really did know they were right. My father, too, was a person who always believed it was a crime to argue with a person. I may have been spared as a result. At any rate, there was no serious problem at home—any more than there was in the sweet world of Ginza. The problem, ever deepening, was on the ball field.

My father, sensing my feeling fully, reminded me often of some things he knew of the world: that it was important not to be a nuisance to others; that it was wrong to try to reach the top, because you have to be bad to others as you go along; that it was nearly impossible to be true to yourself without being useful to others. He never suggested to me that I leave the world of baseball, but I was always conscious of the offer that had been there from the start.

What would have happened if I had left baseball then? Perhaps I would have lived as my father did, simply and honestly, apart from any public scrutiny. There is something in me that longs for such a life and will to the day I die. But my business was baseball, a world of competition, of winners and losers. There was no avoiding that. I accepted that knowing full well that I had won a place in this world and just as easily might lose it before very long.

I loved my father with all my heart. But he could not teach me how to hit. No one, it seemed, could do that. And that is what I longed for most.

Chapter Six

Whatever understanding I have of Fortune is based on my coming together in this life with Mr. Hiroshi Arakawa. If I had met Arakawa-san only that one time when I was a boy, I would still have owed him a debt I could never repay—at least as far as my baseball life went. If I had added to that first meeting the second, where he allowed me to see a film of Don Larsen's perfect game, I would perhaps have come away with the sense that Arakawa-san was one of those distant, shadowy figures sent to us in this life almost without our knowing it—to offer a modicum of advice, to make sure that good opportunity is sometimes steered our way. Or if a business card with his name on it had been the last chapter in our relationship, I might have felt some permanent measure of luck for having had his good opinion at that time in my life when baseball was a new world. But all of these episodes are nothing compared to what followed. In the spring of 1962 our manager, who now was Mr. Kawakami, looked around for a new batting coach. He wanted someone who would be available full time for the team and, more specifically, who would be able to help me. His choice: Arakawa Hiroshi.

Mr. Kawakami knew nothing about my past relationship

with Arakawa-san. His choice was based strictly on baseball, because Arakawa-san's theories on hitting—at least the ones that were exclusively technical—most nearly coincided with his own. But, as it turned out, Mr. Kawakami summoned Fortune directly into my life. Arakawa-san taught me everything I know. All that I have ever accomplished I owe to him. What is best in me is only what I have been able to draw from his teaching. And as for him? If I may be bold enough to say it—Fortune provided for him, too. For Arakawa-san's dreams were very soon to be realized in a pro baseball player named Sadaharu Oh.

In all fairness, I must take the liberty of warning you: Arakawa-san is deeper than my knowledge of him, and hence you may wind up getting only an incomplete picture of him. To this day he is always a step ahead of my seeing. Twenty years after we began working together, my thoughts of him are almost hopelessly run together, so that the end of our relationship is the beginning and vice versa. What do I honestly know?

For one thing, Arakawa-san is a purebred city dweller, Tokyoite to the core. He is down to earth, sophisticated, nasty, sweet, cunning, simple, puzzling—and educated. He went to Waseda Sojitsu, as I did, and then on to Waseda University. His learning, though, comes from somewhere else.

He became a pro ballplayer after college, playing for the Orions in the Pacific League throughout his career. He was not much as a player. Perhaps because of that he became a student of the game. He certainly wound up knowing far more than the gift of his body permitted.

He is not a physically imposing man—in fact, in later years, I think he rather enjoyed this. A Western friend of mine mistook him, in his plain black trenchcoat, for a sickly Catholic priest the first time he saw him. But in those early years, he sometimes complained—because his playing days were not so far behind him. He also reacted oddly when certain players could not carry out his instructions. I can still hear his voice muttering in that strange, mocking sing-song, "If only I had been a little taller, a little heavier. . . . "

He was—and is—a devotee of Zen. He began studying it to help himself as a ballplayer, and the road has long since carried him from discipleship to mastery. But if he was ever a priest, he was an odd one. He teased me once: "The goal of Zen is to become void of desire, but can a man attain such a high goal? What a baseball player looks for is how to get a base hit—how to smash the ball—and the farther the better. How can a pro ever be void of such a desire? I'll bet you not even the monks themselves can be totally void of desire. They'd want to live if they were on their deathbeds."

He taught me, as he did others, without benefit of text-book, master plan, or anything even approaching curric-ulum. Sometimes I suspect he made things up as he went along. Regardless, he was, for me, the essence of what it is to be a Master.

Naturally, I was full of anticipation that spring of 1962. I arrived at Tamagawa with my spirits already uplifted, be-cause I hoped Arakawa-san would be able to help me. The first days of training came and went, and I did not see him—but that only increased my sense of anticipation. Soon he would be there, and perhaps I would at long last begin to make some headway.

I finally met Arakawa-san again on February 1, 1962. As I did regularly in training, I had first completed my running, done full sets of calisthenics, and had a long period of throwing and catching. I had gone to the toss-batting area and was well into my routine when I became aware—even without seeing him—that Arakawa-san was standing there watching me. I tried not to let on, but unconsciously I in-creased the tempo of my swinging, wanting to impress him from the outset. Toss batting, by the way, is a favorite Jap-anese form of batting practice. It involves a batter and one other person who sits a few feet away and, underhand, tosses balls one after the other, which the batter smashes into mesh netting directly in front of him. The purpose of the drill is to get the batter to step and hit as consistently and with as little interval as possible. Timing and intensity of spirit are necessary to perform this well. I had worked up a good soaking sweat and was under the impression that I had done quite well when I finally concluded my swings. I turned and found Arakawa-san glaring at me. There was little I could see that suggested anything like satisfaction.

"Terrible!" he said suddenly, after a moment. There was no greeting, no handshake, nothing beyond that one word. In fact, his face was the mask of a devil, not a guardian angel. I did not know how to reply. He continued to glare at me. Then:

"For God's sake, you should be playing with a much bigger ball. Why don't you try basketballs?"

I stared at him in disbelief. If I had been able to think of anything to say, I don't know if I could have got it out anyway. I simply stood at attention. His voice suddenly dropped, and his eyes twinkled ever so malevolently:

"I hear you're really something with the ladies at night. A real batsman in Ginza, eh? Maybe you left your big stick in one of those clubs!"

"What?" Perhaps I was getting shock treatment. No doubt I deserved it. And it was my duty to receive whatever Arakawa-san was going to dish out. I waited for more. Instead, he turned on his heel and walked away. That was it. He was gone.

I was dumbfounded. I didn't know what to do. All day I awaited his return. But he did not come back. I waited through the next day—and the day after. But it was as if he had only been a one-time apparition, an instrument of some subtle, fiendish torture whose purpose I could not begin to fathom. Four full days passed before I finally saw Arakawa-san again. In the meantime, my peace of mind deserted me. I could barely bring myself to eat. And at night, most ominously of all, I found that I could not sleep.

More than anything, that should have told me that I was in store for something.

On the fifth day Arakawa-san reappeared. By then my nerves were gone. When I saw him striding forcefully toward me like some evil gnome, I cringed. God knew what awaited me at this point. He stopped a foot away and barked:

"If you really want to make it as a pro, you will do exactly as I say for three years!"

I stared at him and nodded. Strange to say, I was grateful simply to see him again and have him willing to say anything at all to me. As the saying goes, "A drowning man grabs for straws."

That day he announced that my night life was over. Good-bye to all of that absolutely. Finished. Gone. Out. And also, no drinking and smoking. Just like that. Over and done with. He watched as I took this in. He must have seen the perplexity on my face, because his expression suddenly softened.

"Don't worry," he said comfortingly, "it's more important to do things than to brood over them."

Training began that day.

When Arakawa-san joined the Giants, his instructions, as far as I was concerned, were simple. He was to develop me into a player who hit twenty home runs and batted .280 a year. Simple. Elementary. Nothing mystical about it. So I listened carefully to him in these first days, wanting to do anything he said in the hopes that I would quickly improve.

The core of Arakawa-san's theory of hitting, if I may be technical for a moment, is called "downswinging." There are other theories. Ted Williams, for example, is an advocate of uppercutting, and Charley Lau teaches batters to try for a level swing. But in Japan the dominant theory today is downswinging. Arakawa-san once explained this theory, roughly, as follows:

"Have you ever seen a person trip and fall? He always

holds out his arms straight in front to protect himself. This is an instinctive movement. Movements that are made like that—without thinking, on the spur of the moment—are absolutely without extras. The same thing applies to batting. The bat head should swing over the shortest course possible to meet the ball. A pitch travels across a distance of over sixty feet at speeds approaching ninety miles an hour. The time involved is less than half a second, which means the ball will be by you before you can say yes or no. Therefore, the tip of the bat, which starts out above the strike zone, must travel the shortest course if you are to have any hope of hitting the ball. That is what I mean by downswinging."

My big weakness was that I had a "hitch" in my swing. This hitch grew more, not less, pronounced with time, so that in the beginning of my fourth year as a pro, it was very deeply ingrained.

Arakawa-san's theory of downswinging was well suited to meet this problem. All that was really required was to cut out the "extras" in my swing. If I learned to bring the bat head across the plate in the most direct line, my hitch would automatically be gone. So I thought of this in my time in the batting cage and during our special batting practice, when hitting was done under simulated game conditions. The results were mixed. Sometimes I made good contact, other times I didn't. I, of course, understood the problem only too well. Bad habits are easy to fall into and hard to break. In the worst cases they are never broken. To say that my hitch was a bad habit is somewhat misleading, because I was so imprisoned by it that there seemed to be no good habit I might substitute for it. I can only describe the sensation of this habit, not really its effect:

Once more I see the pitcher winding up. My bat is held high over my shoulder. I see the ball coming well enough; I hear it coming. My bat pulls slightly back. Even without Arakawa-san's instructions, I know there is not an instant of time to waste if I am to have any chance of making contact. But just at this very moment, just when the bat should now whip forward, there is this awful, absolutely uncontrollable second swing backward as though the bat has a life and a power of its own.

In other words, this was a problem that was beyond my will. No desire I had to change could bring change about. Arakawa-san and I talked about this between my training sessions. I agreed with him that much practice was required, and I put in as much time trying to improve as I humanly could. But when would there be a result? No way really to tell.

One night in Miyazaki, Arakawa-san came to me and said, "I think maybe the problem is with your stance. Maybe we should try something new. Really new."

"Such as?"

"I don't know yet. You see, your hitch is so strong that you accept it as natural. Therefore the stance we adopt to overcome it must not allow this 'natural' movement of yours to occur. All that I've been able to come up with is this."

Arakawa-san at that point assumed a batting position from the left side, then carefully raised his right leg so that he was standing on one foot.

"You see," he said, "standing in this position, if you hitch, you will fall flat on your ass."

I stared at him, unable to reply. There was a twinkle in his eye. Was he up to something, trying to poke fun at me? I did not know. He must have seen the look on my face, because he began to laugh.

"It's all right," he said. "It was only a suggestion."

He had no other suggestions. Perhaps it was his intention at that point to show me that there was no magic cure for my problem, that I was stuck with it until I figured out a way to combat it myself. At any rate, the search for answers continued.

One night Arakawa-san said to me that the real problem we were facing was to apply the Japanese psyche to an American game, and that for me this was especially important because of my lack of willpower. It was at this point that he first acquainted me with his theories about Zen. I was very absorbed in what he said. Recently, I had read Yoshikawa's *Miyamoto Musashi*. My imagination had been stirred by this account of a legendary samurai who overcame the chaos of his own heart by disciplined training and simple living to become the greatest of swordsmen. Though Musashi was a man of the past, he was an ideal, a model of what real accomplishment was all about.

Arakawa-san told me that he had become absorbed in studying the Noh drama. It had been developed in the fourteenth century, he said, from religious sources and folk myths, and is characterized by its highly stylized acting, unique vocalization, wooden masks, and elaborate costumes. He had felt for a time there might actually be a way to fruitfully apply some of this to baseball. He thus had read through the *Kadensho* (a book on the theory and practice of Noh), written by a man named Zeami, a prominent Noh actor. He had read it over and over again, searching for any clue that might relate the psyche of this traditional art to baseball. The problem, he said, was that the movements might be too stylized. I, too, looked into the *Kadensho*, trying to ponder its meanings—a fact that Arakawa-san noted with satisfaction.

"Hm, you know, you remind me of Takezo." (Takezo was the young Musashi before he disciplined himself in training.)

"I do?"

"Yes. There may be hope for you after all."

Soon after this, Arakawa-san abruptly removed me from all efforts to make sense of the *Kadensho*.

"Time to move on," he announced very forcefully one day.

"What do you mean?"

"Kabuki!"

Arakawa-san apologized for changing sources so rapidly, but as he explained it, my problem was so absorbing that it required constant study. Answers therefore did not come neatly packaged. From this task of ongoing study, which he said took up all his time away from the baseball field, he had come to the conclusion that Kabuki, another theatrical form, might be more useful to me. The movements in it, he said, even though more exaggerated than those in Noh, are delicately balanced on the transition from "motion" to "rest." I was to meditate on this constantly and seek to apply the image as best I could whenever I strode to the plate. Meanwhile, Arakawa-san said, he would delve into all the literature he could on Kabuki in an effort to further this line of approach. He watched me intently whenever I was in the batting cage to see what I could make of this new image. What I made of it was really the desire of my heart to follow it. I tried as hard as I could to improve with this suggestion of Arakawa-san's—but my performance at the plate still showed no particular change.

One day—or, rather, late one night—Arakawa-san confronted me as I was about to retire. "A discovery!" he said. He was waving a book in his hand. It was by yet another actor, the well-known Kikugoro. The celebrated performer had disclosed in his book that he had tried to incorporate Aikido into his own training. Specifically, what he had sought from Aikido was the idea of *ma*, the space and/or time "in between."

"This," Arakawa-san said, was the "essence of what we are looking for. All that remains is to apply it. Now you may wonder how this is to be done? Here we have a chance, because we have a living example to learn from."

He had me read a chapter of the book. This excerpt told of Kikugoro's visit to the great Aikido Master Ueshiba Morihei Sensei. Kikugoro waited around and waited around until the Sensei would speak to him. He asked, "Sir, what is *ma*?"

To this, the great teacher coolly replied, "If that's all you've got to ask me, you must be a lousy actor."

I was puzzled. I handed the book back to Arakawa-san,

with no idea as to what I was supposed to have drawn from it. He could barely contain himself.

"Can you imagine a guy saying something like that to Kikugoro!"

I nodded, still uncomprehending. "So?"

"So, the Sensei is a living master. He is there for us as well as for Kikugoro. We will go to him."

When we got back to Tokyo, we took our first trip to the *dojo* together, seeking the wisdom of Ueshiba Sensei. Twenty years have passed since that day, and I know now what I did not know then. Ueshiba Sensei was not only a great master of Aikido, he was its founder. Through his own study of all the ancient martial arts, principally in the uses of the sword, he had distilled those old forms, their essential movements, into this new art, Aikido, weaponless self-defense. People all over the world traveled to see him. Among those who knew, he was a living connection to the legends of our history.

His *dojo* in Shinjuku was an unpretentious wooden structure attached to his living quarters. Beyond the opened sliding panels of his windows, trees were visible, their spring branches delicately touching an old-style gabled roof. The *dojo* was rather small, perhaps twenty tatami, its simple wooden walls decorated sparsely with a paper calendar and some sayings written in brushwork by the Master. With all that I didn't know about Ueshiba Sensei that first day, it was very much like walking into yet another new world.

Arakawa-san and I, as any other students, sat at the far edges of the room, on our heels in the proper position, toe touching toe. All of the fledgling warriors wore combinations of white or white and black blouses with *hakama*. Ueshiba Sensei alone was dressed in a full-flowing black kimono. The time I first saw him, he was approaching eighty. His appearance and manner, though, were vigorous. He had a long, wispy, snow-white beard and moustache along with bushy white eyebrows. Severity and kindliness both seemed etched into his features. He looked more like a fifteenth-century village elder than a master of the martial arts—that is, until he began to perform the movements he had perfected over a lifetime. The beauty and power of these movements were astonishing. Trained athletes or dancers could not easily have duplicated them. They were the fruits of unparalleled accomplishment. When he finished his session, we spoke to him. It was Arakawa-san's turn to play the straight man.

"What is *ma*?" he asked, deliberately echoing Kikugoro. But the Sensei answered him differently.

"*Ma* exists because there is an opponent."

"I understand," Arakawa-san said. This seemed to jibe with something he was thinking. He took me by the elbow.

"You see," he said to me, "in the case of baseball it would be the pitcher and the batter. The one exists for the other; they are caught, both, in the *ma* of the moment. The pitcher tries in that instant of time and space to throw off a batter's timing; the batter tries to outwit the pitcher. The two are struggling to take advantage of the *ma* that exists between them. That's what makes baseball so extraordinarily difficult."

The Sensei looked at us both as if we were crazy men. His eyes seemed to darken as he turned them on Arakawa-san. He remained silent for a moment, then said:

"I will tell you something, you're a lousy teacher!"

I tried not to smile as I saw Arakawa-san lower his head, bowed with almost the same words that had been heaped on Kikugoro. And yet—I couldn't put my finger on it exactly—there was something a little too predictable in all this.

"You see, you're no good when you're thinking of *ma*," Ueshiba Sensei continued. "*Ma* is there *because* the opponent is there. If you don't like that situation, all you have to do is eliminate the *ma* between you and the opponent. That is the real task. To eliminate the *ma*. Make the opponent yours. Absorb and incorporate his thinking into your own. Become one with him so you know him perfectly and can so be one step ahead of his every movement. . . ."

This was the fundamental idea of Aikido itself, within which *ma* was only one of a number of important concepts. Arakawa-san bowed respectfully to the Sensei, and we were soon on our way.

And thus began the first really intensive phase of my training with Arakawa-san. Although I did not understand exactly what he was leading me to, I trusted him. I believed that Aikido, as Arakawa-san promised, would help me, although I did not actually practice it. This I was forbidden to do because, I was told, "injuries and martial arts are one and the same."

"How can I learn then?" I asked.

But Arakawa-san would not even consider it. "I can't afford to let you get hurt," he said. "I'll go through it myself and learn what is necessary, and you'll have all the information you need passed on to you. Perhaps you should go to the *dojo* and observe. You may learn things for yourself."

I then went to the *dojo* whenever I could, sometimes with Arakawa-san, sometimes without. I learned rather quickly that he had been a regular there for some time, that none of this was really new to him. He had, apparently, begun taking lessons there around 1960 with both Ueshiba Sensei and one of his assistants. He was absolutely scrupulous in his attendance, never missing a class whenever he was in Tokyo—and he was absolutely devoted to his Master. This became painfully apparent to me when I was a spectator. I watched Arakawa-san suffer manhandlings that would have left a weaker person gathering the remains of his own carcass. And this he always did in the best of spirits—and with the deepest sense of respect for what he was being taught. There is an atmosphere in the *dojo* that is very hard to convey to anyone not familiar with the setting—but it involves a sense of courtesy and respectfulness that is too often not duplicated elsewhere in life. We Japanese make much of fidelity to form, but in the *dojo*, respect and veneration for your teacher live in your spirit. For, after all, you are there in ignorance as one seeking enlightenment. You may, as I was, be there following your own First Mind (the first and strongest longing you have for a life path). Even as I watched him get battered, my sense of belief and trust in Arakawa-san grew.

"I've come to think that there is something more important than *ma* between yourself and the opponent," he told me one day. "How shall I put it? It is really more a question of how you coordinate your five senses. Put differently, it's about fully controlling the movements of your own body. Winning over yourself rather than the opponent."

I tried to understand everything Arakawa-san said to me. It was hard. There are things, after all, that words can never explain. But he was always patient with me. Many of our talks took place in his car as we went back and forth from *dojo* to home or from home to stadium—and whenever he saw me grow confused, he would invariably stop the car and begin gesturing out whatever concept he was trying to explain. Once, we got out of the car entirely and, in the middle of the street, enacted the *ma* of the batter alone, incorporating the doubts and desires he inevitably had to contend with in facing a pitcher.

"So you see," he said to me, with traffic whizzing by us, "even if you've got your timing right, it's no use if your body doesn't fully respond. You've got to coordinate your mind, your body, and your batting skill."

These theories were quite interesting, but the problem, of course, was how to apply them. Try as I might, the fog that had plagued me through three years of pro ball would not lift. While I coordinated things in my mind, my muscles just would not go along. I wondered whether Aikido would really do any good. Our first league games in April came and went, and I had little to show for it. At the end of the month, I had managed to hit only two home runs.

One day I went to the *dojo* early to watch the trainees practice. Arakawa-san was to join me later. When he arrived, I was absorbed in watching what can only fairly be described as a spectacle. On the floor for the better part of half an hour was Ueshiba Sensei—a man who stood barely five feet tall—throwing off big, hefty trainees one after the other, as though they were bags of feathers. They came at him in twos and threes and seemed to go flying in sixes and sevens. It was incredible! Or it was all prearranged.

Arakawa-san insisted it was absolutely genuine, that Ueshiba Sensei was demonstrating a basic technique to escape from multiple attackers called *Yamabiko no michi*, or the path of an echo. Even though Arakawa-san had seen this before, he was just as impressed as I was when we took our leave that day.

"Can you believe it, Oh?" he said. "How can it be that there can be so much strength in a man?"

I obviously had no answer.

"Of course it was not strength we were witnessing today, but the extension of power. Today," he explained, "we have had the most amazing demonstration of the use of *ki*. We saw what the spirit-power in a man extended beyond himself can accomplish."

But the word *ki*, as I understood it then, had both a good and a bad connotation. I suggested that to Arakawa-san.

"Of course," he said. "There is an old saying, 'Sickness comes from *ki*.' That means that you will get sick if you think you are sick. Likewise, you will be strong if you discipline your mind to think you are. Don't you see? Make use of an opponent's strength and yours will be doubled. What Ueshiba Sensei did was in the words of his oral instruction:

> *Many enemies*
> *Surrounded me*
> *In attack.*
> *Thinking of them as one,*
> *I do battle.*

This is what we have just witnessed. The moment you are able to draw another's *ki* to that which you extend from yourself, you have more power than you could ever have imagined yourself to have."

What was Aikido anyway, I wondered? Was it a mental activity or a form of the martial arts? By this demonstration there seemed to be no doubt what it could effect, but theory and practice when it came to baseball were almost impossible to reconcile. How could I begin to do in a batter's box what Ueshiba Sensei did in the middle of the *dojo* floor? Rather than feeling elated at what I had just seen, I felt even more confused than I had in the past.

The real problem, of course, was that I just was not hitting. With all the training and the thinking and the good efforts of Arakawa-san to improve me, I was doing as poorly as ever. It was doubly frustrating because, for a while, as we approached the opening of the season, I had begun to look a lot better in batting practice. I had even begun to receive some compliments on my form. But with game conditions and a championship season, it all began to crumble—just as in my first year.

If I have made Arakawa-san seem a bit too esoteric in all this, I have done him a great disservice. He was first and last a baseball man, and all his thoughts, no matter how far-ranging, were anchored in the simple but elusive task of finding out how a batter hits a baseball. Arakawa-san has forgotten more about the art of hitting than most people will ever learn in their lifetimes.

Now it is not totally impossible for batters—even very good ones—to sometimes hit with a hitch. Regardless of what you may have heard, even some big-league batters hitch and get away with it. The point is that if a batter hits with a hitch, he must have very quick hands or successfully guess what a pitcher is going to throw in order to compensate for the defect. I had always had a clear enough image of where my bat should meet an incoming pitch. I had a good eye and fast hands. Arakawa-san worked as diligently as he could to exploit these assets. A correct downswing meant less time required to meet the incoming pitch. So our work in the batting cage, in toss-batting practice, in swinging before a mirror, always had this improvement in my technique as its goal. The hope was that in time I would get over my hitch and move on.

Because I had quick reflexes, I could still manage to hit outside pitching. But, increasingly, I could not handle inside pitching. If my timing was thrown off in the least, I was simply lost whenever I was pitched in tight. To make up for my hitch, I committed myself too soon, and if a pitcher was on to me, I was cooked. After three years in the league, the book on me was pretty well established. "High and tight, low inside, set him up with change of speed and finish him off." It was an awfully repetitive book, but it worked. I tried desperately to compensate. With Arakawa-san's help, however, I reached the limits of what I could do. Where could I go from here?

April turned into May. For a while, I thought I might find a way out. Toward the end of the month, I hit four home runs in ten days, but in June I stalled again. For the first time in a regular season game since I had joined the Giants, the coaches had decided that I should bat cleanup. Perhaps it was too much for me. I homered early in the month in a game against the Taiyo Whales, but then everything seemed to go—no home runs, few hits, many strikeouts. My spirits decayed with my batting form. I found myself back at square one, as though I had learned nothing. I went for bad pitches, missed good ones, was hopelessly tied up by tough ones. I simply didn't belong in a pro lineup. Accordingly, I found myself not playing more and more. And however badly I felt, it turned out Arakawa-san felt worse.

He came up to me one day in practice and stood there watching for a while.

"Getting sick and tired of yourself, aren't you?" he muttered. I hadn't heard this tone for a long time.

"Big man. You belted seventeen home runs during your

second year. It was a license to go drink and fool around in Ginza, and so you never bothered to learn the game. Now look at you. We've been practicing for months, and what's it got you? A handful of home runs. Big deal. I really believed you could be a good hitter. Instead you're a goddamned bench jockey."

I couldn't believe my ears. Oh, it was true enough that I had fooled around and loved easy living. But I had made a sincere effort and faithfully—heart and soul—thrown myself into the program Arakawa-san had set for me so I could improve. But, apparently, all efforts had been in vain.

"You are beyond baseball," Arakawa-san growled at me, by which I think he meant I was beyond his help. Then, looking me straight in the eye, he said suddenly and accusingly, "Why the hell can't you get rid of that goddamned hitch?"

Of course, I had no answer for him. He paused for a moment, then turned to leave.

"I will take the problem to Ueshiba Sensei," he said, and walked off. I waited for him that day, but he never came back. The next day he seemed even more depressed than before. I asked him if he had seen the Sensei.

He said, "Ueshiba Sensei says I'm not teaching you right. . . . That's all he had to say to me."

And so, from that day forward, training became a strain rather than a joy for us both. Every day, a little after noon, I took a cab from my parents' house to Arakawa-san's place in Toshima Ward (I still did not have a driver's license then). I practiced swinging at his house until just before it was time to go to the ball park. We drove to the stadium together, usually having little to say to each other, and then, after the game, we returned to his house. I practiced swinging the bat some more, and we reviewed the details of the day's game. Then I went home by taxi alone. It was the end of June.

One day we had a game against the Taiyo Whales. I remember the day was cloudy with a threat of rain. I was in the lineup that afternoon, but after striking out my first two times up I was benched once again (as is traditional in Japanese baseball with a player who is having a poor game). I felt humiliated and lost. The idea of becoming an important hitter seemed like a faraway dream, a piece of arrogant nonsense. For the first time in my life, I felt sorry for myself. I can still hear my own wretched inner monologue: "What is there that's left? All that training, including Aikido. People are supposed to be rewarded for their efforts. . . . Didn't the saying go like that? Lies! All lies! Look at me. Hopeless. Stupid. Clumsy. Hung up on a backswing forever! Even a confident man like Arakawa-san has given up on me."

Rain began that afternoon by game's end, drenching the area. It was one of those soaking, late spring rains that seem to make Japan a nation of mountain fogs and forlorn seascapes. Left, right, left, right. The windshield wipers of our car punctuated the monotony of our drive home. With all my heart, I wished Arakawa-san would speak to me, but he remained silent. Only the windshield wipers sounded in my ears.

I sat beside him looking down into my palms. My hands were coarse. The calluses on them hurt my face every time I washed. My hands, like my soul, were worn out and unable to help me. We reached Arakawa-san's house, finally. We got out of the car and began walking toward his front door. I suppose he didn't have the strength to invite me in. At any rate, when he didn't I was glad. Both of us felt the same. Sick and tired of the whole damned thing.

I stood alone in the rain, and then all I could do was go back to the sidewalk and hail a cab. There was none on the streets. The rain was beginning to pelt. I pulled my jacket tighter around me.

A cab finally appeared. I signaled for it, but it drove on past me—even though it was unoccupied. Another—and then another. Perhaps I had turned invisible. No. Cab drivers didn't seem to want to get their seats wet, and I was soaked to the skin.

Arakawa-san had told me that the philosophy of Aikido

was "agape," or love. I thought about this now. The objective of Aikido was to strip oneself of opposition, to reconcile oneself with the universe. The enlightened one merges with the universe, loses all sense of struggle with it. In enlightenment, time ceases to exist. There is the universe, which is everything—sorrow and joy, gain and loss—and there is you. Unfortunately, there was also me, languishing in the rain, struggling hopelessly against myself.

But agape does not struggle. It has no foe. And struggle only carries one further from enlightenment. A man who cannot be in accord with the universe—no matter what it brings him—can only be destructive. He will never reach enlightenment. And what was I? A man seeking to use whatever skills he could—from the ball field to the martial arts—in order to compete for victory. I was locked in struggle, far from agape. Perhaps I'm being defeated by my own success-seeking heart, I thought. And in that moment I knew that I had lost because of the struggle within.

Just then a cab appeared and stopped for me. I climbed in and gave the driver my address, then slumped in the back seat, wet and cold, miserable with what I now knew. I knew I could no longer go on, and I thought for the first time of what my life would be like without baseball. I was too tired to think about it. I thought of what it would be like having to tell Arakawa-san and my manager and teammates, and I put that aside, too. I watched the rain.

We'll be rained out tomorrow, I told myself. That made me happy for a moment. What a welcome relief it would be to wake up the next day and be able to stay home. I began to think of all the things I could do around the house, and I began to feel easier. No practice, no game, no brooding. I was a loser, and I had a day off coming. What I determined then and there was that I was going to get a good night's sleep. The rest could wait. When I got home and got into bed, I was asleep before my head hit the pillow.

"Get up! Get up! What's the matter with you, you'll be late!"

I thought I was dreaming. I fumbled for the alarm clock.

The clock said twelve, and I was unsure whether it was midnight or noon. But it was my mother's voice, my mother calling me.

"Get up! Get up! You're late."

"We're rained out, Mom," I moaned.

"My God, how you sleep! What are you mumbling about?" She pulled the curtains, and the room flooded with light.

As long as I live, I'll never forget how lovely that day was. The sun on the sidewalk was like the first sun of the world. I have never seen such a sight! I stared like a man who has taken leave of his senses. My mother certainly was startled, because she prodded me to get a move on. I was late for the game! But I wanted nothing more than to drink in this sudden perfect beauty. There was a particular way the pavements shone with the rain of the night before; the color of the sky was so pure. I wondered, If Fortune had first put me in the way of Arakawa-san, was it not Fortune also at work in this moment? Not Fortune in any sense I had known before, but Fortune as a trickster, glazing my eyes and soul with the romance of things, so that I would be blind to the certain sorrows that awaited me. What was my answer?

The rain glistened on the pavements. The noon sun warmed the world. The sky was a painter's curve of blue.

"Get a move on, don't be so lazy! Move!"

Yes, I had to move, I had to leave, what choice had I? The beautiful aftermath of a storm. But you see, if it had rained that day, I would never have become a top batsman. For it was out there, under that lovely blue sky, just an hour or two away, that the idea of hitting on one foot came about.

I changed out of my pajamas, quickly dressed, and hustled out of the house. I jumped in a cab that raced on to Arakawa-san's. He was waiting for me out front, pacing rather nervously, but his manner was surprisingly serene.

"You're late," he said, smiling.

"I'm sorry, I overslept."

"Good," he said.

"There's no time for practice."

"Good," he repeated.

We got into his car and sped toward Kawasaki Stadium, arriving there after the gates had opened and the fans had already begun entering the park. We made our way to the locker room, where my teammates, unable to take practice, were still congregated. The field, it turned out, was in bad shape from the heavy rains, and the grounds keepers had their hands full trying to get it ready. In fact, the game almost certainly would have been called if any team other than ours was playing that day. The Giants regularly attract the largest number of spectators in Japan. Our home games are always full, and our road games guarantee good crowds for the other teams. The Taiyo Whales were not about to lose a full house to sloppy field conditions.

With everyone waiting around, Mr. Kawakami decided to use the time for a coaches' meeting. This is a traditional occasion in Japanese baseball anyway—coaches' meetings, team meetings, meetings with management occur in one form or another almost daily—so I did not think much of it. But later, when Arakawa-san emerged from the meeting, I learned just how fateful it was.

The meeting, in large part, was about me. The pitching coach, Mr. Bessho, who, after all, was responsible for the well-being of our pitchers, was concerned that my lack of hitting was making life extra tough. "What the hell is being done with Oh, anyway?" he demanded to know. How could his pitchers win when they were being undermined by my nonhitting? This ignited the rest of the coaches.

"He's supposed to be hitting .280!"

"He'll never hit .280."

"He's supposed to be a twenty-home-run man. He'll be lucky if he gets ten."

And so it went. There was no defense to be made, said Arakawa-san, who had felt the heat more than anyone. When he found me later, he was both angry and agitated.

Something had to be done—and done quickly. A couple of jobs seemed to be hanging in the balance.

"Look," he said, "it's time we faced up to something. That hitch of yours looks like it's here to stay. We are going to have to get a little extreme, I think."

"Extreme?"

"Very," he said. "Remember one day in Miyazaki we returned from camp and I had you take different poses with the bat in your hands? Do you remember?"

I vaguely remembered trying to experiment with different batting poses as a way of getting myself to stop hitching, but I didn't remember specifically what Arakawa-san was referring to.

"The one-legged one, remember that? The one where you bring your right foot up and hold it there?"

"Yes, yes." It came back to me.

I was at first not sure Arakawa-san was really being serious. Perhaps this was just another bit of shock therapy to make a point. But, no, he was quite in earnest. He picked up a bat and coiled himself into the pose to demonstrate.

It looked *so* peculiar. I could not imagine how a batter could survive more than a few seconds in such a position, let alone react to any kind of pitch. But what I saw in front of me was a man standing on one foot, who told me, as he stood there, that the time had now come for me to try that in a game.

I didn't know whether to laugh or cry. I sat there bewildered. Arakawa-san winked and smiled. And continued standing on one foot.

I was miserable. Why was he playing with me? What was he trying to do? I finally decided that all this was just an attempt to psych me up for the game, so I tried as politely as I could to shrug it off and gear my thoughts to the afternoon's work. But Arakawa-san did not budge. Only now the smile left his face. I turned, finally, and began to go off toward my locker.

"*Oh!*" he called; his voice snapped like a whip. I turned around. He was glaring at me.

"I order you to do it."

I stood frozen for a moment, terrified. All I could do was bow my head.

And thus commenced the biggest gamble of my life. The tens of thousands of fans in Kawasaki Stadium witnessed my first attempts at "flamingo batting" in the game that followed. I had no chance to try it beforehand, because the team had omitted batting practice; even in the on-deck circle before my first at-bat in the game there was no chance to do anything but kneel and wait.

"Batting for the Giants, number one, Sadaharu Oh," boomed the loudspeaker. I approached the plate, stepped into the batter's box, and then assumed my pose. The crowd buzzed, then chattered, then hooted and roared as the first pitches to me were thrown. With the count two and two, I flicked out my bat and hit a clean single into center field. The roaring of the crowd suddenly dropped away. I was standing on first. The first trial was done.

I came up again two innings later, and this time the crowd was ready for me. They whistled and stomped and called out to me as I moved to the plate. When I coiled myself into the flamingo position, they roared—I didn't know whether they were enjoying this or viewing it as an insult of some sort. I tried to concentrate. I held my leg as steady as I could. I took one pitch. Then, on the next pitch, an inside fastball, I stepped forward, bringing my curled leg forward and toward the mound, snapping my bat through in the shortest possible arc. I hit the ball on the sweetest part of the bat. It rose on a low trajectory and kept going, far over the right-field wall. I circled the bases, wondering how in the world I could ever have done that standing in that position. But who was I to argue with Fortune, who had indeed smiled on us that day?

"Yes," Arakawa-san said, beaming with satisfaction, "yes. You have passed the 'dog-lifting-his-leg-at-the-hydrant' test. Now all that remains is for you to become what you secretly are."

Chapter Seven

Two days later I hit my first home run flamingo style in Korakuen Stadium. The crowd in our home park had some forewarning of the new style that I had adopted and so was not as surprised as the fans in Kawasaki Stadium. Still, they were not going to be easily impressed. I was batting lead-off that night, and I did not connect until the sixth inning—in a game we were to lose to Hanshin. *"Oh! Oh! Sanshin Oh!"* was in my ears when I came to bat before the home run, and the destruction of the chant amid cheers was music I longed for. But I knew what the fans knew also. Each time I swung the bat successfully, I had luck as much as skill going for me. The truth of the matter was that I felt so unbalanced that anything might have knocked me over.

Several days after that first experiment with flamingo hitting, Arakawa-san and I were driving along in his car. His spirits, like mine, had picked up considerably. This day, though, he seemed a little distant, lost in his own thoughts. At one point, he began mumbling.

"Well, what do you say, shall we try beating Babe Ruth?"

I didn't reply immediately, because I assumed he was talking to himself. But after an interval of silence, he said,

"What do you think?"

"What?"

"Shall we try beating Babe Ruth?"

I laughed. I didn't take this seriously, but I was happy to see Arakawa-san enjoying himself.

"You think this is a joke; it's not. We can beat Babe Ruth."

When I realized Arakawa-san meant it, I felt foolish. Babe Ruth is as much an idol in our country as in America. A boy in the provinces here is as likely to know when and where he pointed to the center-field bleachers as a kid in Kansas. A baseball player growing up in Japan will be no more likely to pattern himself after Babe Ruth than a baseball player seeking a model in America. I shrugged off his suggestion. Arakawa-san, though, drove on in silence.

I mention this because I realize now, twenty years later, that from the start one of Arakawa-san's basic strategies was to plant in my mind goals that I might never have striven for on my own. At any rate, in the summer of 1962 my first and most immediate target, which Arakawa-san understood all too well, was simply to stand upright without toppling over. In fact, I wasn't even sure I wanted to go on with it:

"Are you really encouraged by this one-legged batting?" I asked Arakawa-san.

"Oh, I am always encouraged by good results."

"You mean to continue it?"

"Good results are good incentive."

"I am therefore to continue hitting on one foot?"

"You are. It is imperative that we understand the meaning of what it is to hit on one foot."

We were able to continue with our experiment, however,

only because it was successful. There is no doubt that Fortune smiled on us in this period, because there was no sensible reason for my being able to defy gravity as I did. The odd thing was that I understood this, along with Arakawa-san and our media, who, with less kindly intentions, labeled my new style "scarecrow hitting." In fact, I, who had been a schoolboy unable to fulfill his promise, had now matured, according to our commentators, into "The Scarecrow." Who was to say they were wrong?

There is a nursery rhyme about scarecrows in Japan. In a country where rice is a staple, sparrows have always been regarded as pests because they so easily damage the crops. Scarecrows are used to frighten the birds away.

> *The one-footed scarecrow stands in the rice paddy.*
> *Why does it stand there*
> > *with a rainhat over its head*
> *When the sun is shining brightly overhead?*

Scarecrows are something that man created in his own image to protect his harvest from the birds. Scarecrows were given only one foot because they have no need to walk. You see, a gust of wind can level them, a tug at their sleeves and they are gone, these fierce protectors, these helpless men of straw! Yes, I was a scarecrow on one foot.

Arakawa-san knew better than I what my charmed life as a hitter was all about. I not only believe he was ready to deal with it, I also have become convinced that it was his ingenuity that led me to the moment where I had no choice but to get up on one foot. There is a saying we have in our country, "One or eight," all or nothing—and Arakawa-san had certainly convinced me that I had reached that extreme in my career.

I do worry that people might mistake Arakawa-san for some strange practitioner of the occult. He is much too down to earth, very conservative and modest in his lifestyle, one for whom spiritual philosophy leads inevitably to life practice. When he told me that I was to understand what it meant to bat on one foot, he did not mean that I should go off somewhere and contemplate my navel. His meaning was hard, hard work. The difference was that now that I had come to this gamble of last resort, I also had reached a point where Aikido had become absolutely necessary rather than merely complementary to what I did. Without Aikido, I would not learn to stand on one foot, I would not "understand" it.

The problem, both of us knew, was gaining balance. This is what our work focused on for the remainder of the season. If this sounds like a technical problem, it is. But if it is thought of in technical terms alone, it will be misunderstood. The most obvious thing to say about standing on one foot in order to hit a baseball coming at you at ninety miles an hour is that it requires as much belief as technique. In Aikido, though, belief and technique are one.

One of the first things a student of Aikido learns is to become conscious of his "one point." This is an energy or spirit-center in the body located about two fingers below the navel. While many martial and spiritual arts make use of this center, it is essential in the practice of Aikido. Aikido, which means the Way of Spirit Harmony, requires tremendous balance and agility, neither of which are possible unless you are perfectly centered. So much of our early work was getting me to pose simply with the one point in mind. I would get up on my one foot and cock my bat, all the while remaining conscious of this energy center in my lower abdomen. I discovered that if I located my energy in this part of my body I was better balanced than if I located it elsewhere. If I located my energy in my chest, for example, I found that I was too emotional. I also learned that energy located in the upper part of the body tends to make one top-heavy. Balance and a steady mind are thus associated with the one point. In Aikido you inevitably deal with both the strategy and the psychology of combat. *Uke* and *nage* are the names given to attacker and defender. Aikido takes into account the action of both. If the attacker, for example, is mentally ahead of the defender, his tactics will probably be successful. The defender, not really being prepared, will react instinctively, bracing for assault by bringing his shoulders up in a protective manner—thus shifting his balance away from the center of his body, where strength and agility must be concentrated. So this problem of *uke* and *nage* became a basis for exploring what it was to stand on one leg facing a pitcher.

Aikido is different from other martial arts in the clear distinction it makes between the directing of energy and the gathering of strength. Even Judo, which relies on ex-propriating the movements of an opponent, rests on a lot of pushing and tugging. There is no particular emphasis on the spirit-energy that directs strength. Aikido, though, as its name suggests, is about the projection of spirit-energy, or *ki*. It is the most spiritual of the martial arts.

The notion that one use *ki* in action is really the simplest of ideas. But seeing it employed, as I did, in the thick of battle, with bodies flying this way and that, can be deceptive. As Arakawa-san told me, "The same *ki* that is available to a Master like Ueshiba Sensei is available to anyone. *Ki* is universal energy." One day in the *dojo* Arakawa-san and Ueshiba Sensei demonstrated something. Ueshiba Sensei took a long wooden pole and held it before him in the ready position of a swordsman. Arakawa-san took a baseball bat and hit the sword as hard as he could. The pole in Ueshiba Sensei's hands did not move at all. It was as though Arakawa-san had hit the side of a tree.

"You have seen focusing of energy," I was told. "This is what achieving balance can do."

As long as I had this fatal hitch in my swing, I could not begin to think of using *ki* in my batting. But posing on one foot, having eliminated the hitch, the goal of using *ki* did not seem so far-fetched—if I could learn to steady myself enough.

Earlier in the season, when we had simply been trying to overcome my hitching habit, Arakawa-san had had yet another discussion with Ueshiba Sensei about the problem. The Sensei, not being much of a baseball fan, had cut the talk short.

"Look," he said, "the ball comes flying in whether you like it or not, doesn't it? Then all you can do is wait for it to come to you. To wait, this is the traditional Japanese style. Wait. Teach him to wait."

With this new pose that could be secured only by gaining real balance, the notion of waiting became the means to an end. Arakawa-san became intrigued then obsessed with the idea. All that he knew about baseball, all that he had ever studied and thought about, seemed to flow into this one idea.

"This will be easier said than done," he told me, "but we will learn how to wait." He had me reread *Musashi*, reminding me that it had been Musashi's great task to learn the secret of balance through waiting. Waiting. This was the key. In waiting, said Musashi, one learns the "Immovable Self-Discipline," the ultimate aim of which was to "acquire the Body of a Rock."

"The Body of a Rock!" The image entered my mind as simply as a bird alighting on a branch. If I could not take seriously the idea of pursuing Babe Ruth, the goal of perfecting what was in my own body seemed entirely natural.

We worked on exercises in concentration that would enable me to wait. All of Arakawa-san's training, all the hours we had spent talking and reading mattered now. Because so much of what we did then was geared to the mental side of the game, it is hard to describe. Concentration, like everything else in Aikido, is both a spiritual and a physical term. Its goal is the unity or harmony of all forces that are employed. Mind, body, technique are one in Aikido. This oneness is the expression of nature. And so from the start Arakawa-san enabled me to understand that our work was not to triumph over natural forces but to become one with them, to discover that what was in and outside my body were part of a single force even when they seemed to be divided in opposition.

"This business of standing on one leg," Arakawa-san purred, "we discover is a matter of life and death. Accordingly, when you step into the batter's box, you may never do it casually. Too much is at stake. The center in your lower abdomen prepares you for any contingency just as if you were a warrior awaiting the moves of a deadly opponent. Likewise, when you are good enough to have mastered *ma*, you bring your opponent into your own space; his energy is then part of yours. Together you are one. This is what concentration can bring, why it is so crucial. So you must locate it properly, in the one point, and be conscious of it at all times, even when you're walking down the street or sitting at a meal. Once your concentration is thus focused, you automatically begin to see things better. In a state of proper concentration, one is ready for anything that comes along. Even a baseball hurtling toward you at ninety miles an hour!"

I thus discovered, in standing on one leg, that concentration, maximum concentration, is something natural to *ma*. It is necessary to reacquire only because somewhere in our long history we have forgotten it.

Because I continued to hit, my confidence increased as I went along. I began to see how important it was to be united in mind and body—as the samurai were—if I was to be more than a mediocre hitter. Hitting a baseball is a matter of timing. How simple that sounds—but how difficult. All the craft of pitching goes into throwing off the batter's timing. On one foot or two, what difference does it make if a batter's mind says "fastball" but his body somehow reacts to a change of pace? If your body is not as one with your mind, you are lost. And no amount of strength you put into

your swing will help. You can tell yourself anything, but it is something else to join what it is you know to the snap of your wrists and swing of your hips.

What Arakawa-san and I both knew was that my batting on one foot was meaningless as long as I felt unsteady. We were both blessed by Fortune that good results continued to come from my new pose. But it was more a gift of time than achievement. Time to practice, practice, practice. Time to learn what it "meant" to be balanced on one foot.

I practiced with a mirror. Over and over again, I stood there under Arakawa-san's watchful eye, trying to pick up things in the position of my body as I swung. I stood on my left leg with my right leg in the air. Sometimes I saw myself as a dog at a hydrant, and I laughed myself off balance. Or I would stand there and see my leg, after a minute or so, begin to quiver, and would wonder why God permitted scarecrows to hit home runs! Most often, I scrutinized myself as though I were a pitcher. I kept imagining how I would throw this one-legged fellow off balance: *He's ready for the hard one, I'll throw him a terrible forkball. He's looking for a curve, I'll throw him one that jumps over his bat.*

My objective at the time was to root myself as powerfully as I could. I did this by imagining *ki* power as a fat iron bar that ran straight down from my kneecap through my toes into the ground. Rooted thus, I would take my swings again and again. I don't know how many swings I would take in a single training session, but there were surely hundreds.

I would simply pose this way, too, and whenever I was in the *dojo* working along with Arakawa-san, I would have my balance checked by a slight push or tug on my arm. Some days I felt that I was improving; other days I would seem to be as unbalanced as before. If I truly were an iron bar, I would be strong enough not to be bent by anyone. I confessed this to Arakawa-san.

"Well, what kind of bar have you turned into?" he asked.

"What *kind*?" The question seemed absurd. I laughed. "I don't know."

"You must. Concentrate."

"Well . . . " I forced myself to visualize the image I had created. An iron bar is after all an iron bar. Eventually I described the bar as a straight line from the knee through the top of my shoe.

"Very good," Arakawa-san said. "Now you say this bar is fat?"

"That's right."

"You don't need to make it fat. *Ki* can be thin, too. But take your image seriously. Now, an iron bar can be bent. You know the wrestler Takamiyama?"

He was referring to a popular Hawaiian-born sumo wrestler. I nodded. Everyone knew Takamiyama.

"In his demonstrations of strength, he bends iron bars," Arakawa-san said.

"Yes?"

"Yes."

"What are you telling me?" I asked.

"I'm telling you that you must make yourself into a bar that cannot be bent."

And how was I to do that? By envisioning this bar not as a straight pole but as something like a gymnastic bar attached to supports at either end. The ground, the earth, instead of being a passive receiver, was also to be seen as an active support. Thus no amount of opposing strength would be able to bend the bar.

And so we continued, trying to incorporate this new image of a parallel bar that was my own *ki*, looking for the strengthened balance that was fundamental for my new pose. Slowly, day by day, I was able to increase the time I could stay steadily on one foot. The one foot was now an iron bar joined or fused to the iron of the earth. I could feel myself grow more secure. My confidence increased not only because I was having good results at the plate but because I saw tangible progress in my employment of *ki*.

I often get the feeling that when people ask me about the use of Aikido in baseball, they are looking for a secret source of strength. It does not matter how many times I suggest that this is a wrong-headed approach, the question keeps coming up. So I had best be as clear as possible before I go any further. *Aikido and the use of ki power have nothing to do with strength.* How to show this?

During this period, several of the Giants players who were also interested in Aikido used to make occasional visits to Ueshiba Sensei's *dojo*. These players became somewhat more involved in the actual exercises than I did. Sometimes when they were by themselves, they practiced one of the elementary throwing techniques of Aikido on the tatami floor. The movement employed is very swift, very graceful, and most effective. It is called a *tenkan* movement, which denotes pivoting (as opposed to the *irimi* movement, which involves thrusting). The use of *ki* in this movement enables *nage* to harmonize with the *ki* of his attacker, *uke*, to join his movement by this pivoting movement and, by so doing, much in the manner of a vortex, add unbelievable centrifugal force to the act of throwing. The actual throw involves nothing more than the placing of a single finger in the small of *uke*'s back, and the fall is as complete as the felling of a tree! It is a most amazing thing to see, and it has absolutely nothing to do with the employment of physical strength. A child might do it easily.

A more vivid example occurred many years later when a team of American all-stars came through Japan and some of the players expressed an interest in my one-legged batting. Among these stars were Pete Rose, Rod Carew, Mike Schmidt, and "The Bull," Greg Luzinski. Arakawa-san, wanting to explain my form to the all-stars, got Luzinski to help him illustrate. With the assistance of an interpreter, he said, "I'll show you how Oh manages to bat on one foot. I will hold out my arm horizontally; you try to bend it."

"The Bull" told us later that he thought the interpreter had not translated the request accurately. Arakawa-san is just under five and a half feet tall and had to look up to Luzinski when he talked to him.

"Are you sure? What will you do if I break your arm?" Luzinski asked.

Arakawa-san smiled and replied ever so softly, "Let's worry about that later. Try it. See what happens."

At first, Luzinski was a little tentative with his strength. The arm did not move an inch. He smiled sheepishly, looking around at the small circle of people who had gathered to watch.

"Well, all right," Luzinski said, "here I go." He now tried with all his might. He turned red from the effort. Nothing! Arakawa-san's arm remained rigid and motionless.

"Fantastic!"

"Oriental magic!"

"What strength!"

The foreign pressmen were very taken in by this seeming feat of great strength. But it was not that at all. It was the use of *ki*, in a rather elementary way. Luzinski used strength, but Arakawa-san used *ki*. If you are dubious, this is an exercise you can try for yourself. No prior knowledge of Aikido or *ki* is necessary.

To do this, get a partner, someone in the room with you, a friend, anyone, and instruct that person to hold his arm out rigidly and with all his might resist your effort to bend it at the elbow. Unless this person is very, very much stronger than you, you will succeed in bending his arm. Now instruct this partner to hold out his arm again and, instead of having him contract his muscles in a pose of strength, have him imagine that power flows from a point below his navel in a direct line to his shoulder and then through and beyond his arm, beaming outward from his fingertips through the wall of the room you are in. Make sure you instruct your partner to keep his hand open (rather than clenched in a fist) and to consciously forgo all thought of using great strength to resist you. The chances are that you will now have no more luck in bending your partner's arm than Luzinski did when he tried this with Arakawa-san.

At the all-star break that year, even though I had hit five home runs in the half month preceding, there was not much enthusiasm for my new style among either the players or the press who gathered during the week for the three games that traditionally make up our all-star play. Impossible to gain effective balance, many of them said, while others noted that I might be able to hit the fastball using such a stance but that change-of-speed pitching would certainly do me in.

I was not at all sure at the time that my critics were wrong. But what mattered most was that my manager, Mr. Kawakami, who could have called a halt to this experiment, allowed it to continue. He noted the improvement in results, saw immediately that my hitch had been eliminated, and was most encouraged by the way I now shifted weight during my swing. For Mr. Kawakami, this had been a sore point. I had not "seen" well with my hips, and as a consequence I had been shifting weight poorly when I moved from my back to my front leg.

I took it as a kind of blessing that I was allowed to go on with our work. Results were of course important, but the real test was whether or not my "understanding" would grow enough.

Arakawa-san and I continued to work on this image of the bar—that was my *ki*. We worked before mirrors, in our locker room, at his home, whenever and wherever we had time. Sometimes I used a bat alone, sometimes I worked without a bat, sometimes I used a wooden pole and Ping-Pong balls—making sure that my every move flowed from the one point.

More specifically, I learned rather quickly that all my weight and all my *ki* had to be concentrated on the inside of my left sole from my heel to a point of emphasis in the middle of my big toe. If I transferred my weight from the right to the left side of the sole, I would topple over. This may sound too fine. But it is crucial. Try it out for yourself. You cannot last a second.

With this inside sole placement, I could project my *ki* down through my toe into the earth, anchoring myself ever more firmly. Over the next weeks and months, a row of blisters formed and then callused over as I grew accustomed to the pose. But even as the base hits continued to come, I knew something was still missing. I could finally balance on one foot very well. I had increased the amount of time I could securely hold my pose from just a few seconds to well over a minute. But standing on one leg was not all that was required of me. I really did have to find a way to deal with the problem of timing. All the talk in the world about *ki* and *ma*, of harmonizing oneself with one's opponent so that you are both one, does not take away from the fact that pitchers are the wiliest of foes. They move the baseball in and

out, up and down; they work the magic of curves and drops; they change speeds, paint the corners of the plate like expert calligraphers. To beat them, to harmonize with them, I first had to become the panther as it crouches in readiness for its prey, I had to be the snake as it breaks from its coil, the wolf ready for the rabbit. I had to be ahead of, not behind, my opponent's thinking.

"What is missing," Arakawa-san told me one day, "is the other support. You have a parallel bar in the earth. That is only one support. What do you have above?"

Far from being an absurd question, this was exactly to the point. What should I have answered—"the sky"? Yes, that was the logical reply. Earth below, sky above—but if one extends that correct analogy, the solid support of the earth is balanced by an insubstantial opposite of air! Clearly impossible. Applying such an equation to the problem of one-legged hitting, there would be no balance at all!

"You are too awkward at the plate," Arakawa-san said. "You can hit a pitch if you know what it is that's coming. But your reaction time is still much too slow. Your bat is fast when you're ready, slow when you're not. In a real life-and-death struggle with a sword, you'd be a dead man many times over by now."

What was missing?

It was simple to figure out—if only I cared to concentrate.

The key, he pointed out, was my bat.

Of course! Obviously. I remember for a time making some sort of picture for myself of my arms and shoulders as a balancing support, but I had completely overlooked the bat.

"Look at yourself in the mirror," Arakawa-san said to me, "look carefully. The lower part of your body is fine. The upper part looks very impressive, too. But looks can be deceiving. Describe the position of your bat."

I gazed in the training mirror and saw myself there on one foot, as comfortable as a flamingo now. I held my bat back, cocked off my shoulder. It seemed strange. Not the pose but the position of the bat in such a pose. It didn't match. Suddenly it seemed to me that this very traditional manner of holding the bat was precisely what made it seem strange.

"Exactly," Arakawa-san said, "you are not using the bat. The bat is the other end of the bar!"

What a discovery that was! I found very quickly that by moving the bat this way and that, my sense of balance was completely changed. I suddenly came to realize that until then it had been only the lower part of my body that had been balanced. However it might have looked in the mirror, the upper part of my body was just so much dead weight.

If you scrutinize my batting form, you will surely observe something peculiar in the way I hold my bat. This is what I learned—what I was then about to discover. I learned to hold the bat high over my head, with the tip pointed back toward the pitcher. This tilt back toward the pitcher cannot be too extreme, because it will do as much to damage balance as no tilt at all. But if the bat was properly angled, I was perfectly balanced. If you visualize a tightrope walker you have seen in the circus, you will get the idea. As he carefully treads across the wire, he holds a long pole to balance himself. The angle at which I now learned to tilt my bat enabled me to achieve the same effect. By holding the bat in such a "peculiar" position, I was able to balance the upper part with the lower part of my body, thus ensuring that my power was truly concentrated.

And so, finally, I stood ready on one foot. My pose was no longer the effect of simple shame but of hard work. It wasn't a matter of luck anymore when I stood on one foot and stepped forward to hit a baseball.

The weight that I rested on the inside of my left sole and toe was swiftly transferred to the right foot and toe as I uncoiled and once more touched ground. Power explodes in that instant. The explosion lifts the ball high and deep into the air! The tilt of my bat whipping down and around allowed me to achieve the maximum amount of strength I had in my body at the moment of contact!

If I seem now to speak without any sense of contradiction in my progress from failure to achievement, please be assured that it is only the interference of memory. I look back and see that there was a day of accomplishment, a day of "understanding." But until that moment there was only faith that tangible results might be achieved. And afterward, for a long time, results and faith seemed confused to me, so whatever I accomplished was always undermined by the fear that I could not continue it.

I also worry that I may be doing a disservice to Arakawa-san by presenting him simply in the light of my undying gratitude. He was never a magician from another planet but a man of earth like myself, caught in his own longings and uncertainties. He was thirty-one years old when our

149

training together began, and though he was surely wise beyond his years, he was still young enough to dream and doubt.

Once during this first year of our training, we were riding along in his car. It was late at night, after a game, and our work had not been going well. I was gearing my mind to a hard training session at Arakawa-san's. Instead, he turned to me and said:

"I think we'll skip training tonight and go to Ginza."

"What?"

"Yes. That would be nice. What do you say?"

"Are you serious?"

"Of course. All work and no play is no good. Besides, I think it's time we allowed you out of the cage for a bit."

And so we took our first of many trips to Ginza together. I must admit it is hard even now to keep other images of my Sensei clearly in mind. There is just some way that Arakawa-san and Ginza will always seem completely incongruous to me. And, yet, I believe that even here he had something important to give me.

Arakawa-san was never meant for alcohol. I can still see his face turning bright red from just a drink or two, sweat glistening on his brows and forehead. One night we got drunk together. Our spirits were light, the atmosphere gay. I leaned across the table and stared at Arakawa-san, who was being waited on by a couple of attractive hostesses. It was obvious that he could not hold his liquor, and I realized that he might soon be in trouble. I could not help smiling.

"You may be my master in the batting cage," I said drunkenly to him, "but I am your master in Ginza!"

Arakawa-san gave me a heavy, owlish look and then burst into laughter.

And so the 1962 season came to an end. And what had been accomplished? By year's end, I had not only improved my batting form, I had achieved previously unimaginable results. Our training enabled me to hit thirty-eight home runs, twenty-eight of them coming after July 1. I raised my

batting average to .272 and my RBI total to eighty-five, both career highs. Most important, I won the home-run and RBI titles for the Central League that year. I cannot begin to say what joy this brought. I cried over this. I remember the feeling of my swollen eyelids! And I remember feeling also that these titles had nothing to do with me! It might have been different if Arakawa-san had been merely a batting coach whose advice in the future I could have accepted or rejected as I chose. But
he was so much more now. I could no more choose my way with him than I could with my father or brother. I received no particular praise from the Master of the Arakawa School that year. I accepted that. I knew he had his reasons.

"Think of it this way, Oh," he said to me. "Gain and loss are opposite sides of the same coin. It is best to forget them both."

It turned out that Arakawa-san had all the while been making his own plans. These had little to do with my having won a title or two. His mind was already in the future.

"You are ready now," he said, "to truly acquire the Body of a Rock."

I suggested that this was what I had been striving to achieve all season, but he replied that there was far more to what we were doing than simply gaining balance.

"Immovable Self-Discipline comes only when you master the use of *ki*. And this you have only just begun to do."

To that end, he said, we were now going to turn to the use of the Japanese sword.

Chapter Eight

It is not possible to explain this next phase of my training—which lasted for two years and which began almost immediately after the end of the 1962 season—without first saying something about the Japanese sword itself. It is a touchy subject in my country, because it is immediately associated with militarism, which has meant so much suffering to ourselves and to others in this modern period. But the sword has a deeper tradition than modern militarism, which is why it has survived in the consciousness of the Japanese people over all these years. Musashi sought an all-embracing Way of the Sword. As Yoshikawa had written about him, "The sword was to be far more than a simple weapon; it had to be an answer to life's questions."

And so in the handing down of the sword from one generation to the next, the master swordsmen and the disciples who followed them were also handing down an approach to life. That approach certainly involved the Way of the Samurai and hence the potential for military misuse. But it also involved the samurai devotion to discipline, a devotion whose silent companion is Zen and whose end is the training of the spirit.

The sword itself has undergone almost no changes in design, material, or shape in fifteen hundred years. It looks and feels very much like the sword of the Nara period or, later, of the Tokugawas. The art of making a sword is still very much the same today as before; fine swords possess an almost mystical hold on some, while others cherish them as works of art. During the Occupation swords and swordsmanship were outlawed by the authorities, but it was no more possible to outlaw these symbols of consciousness than to outlaw consciousness itself.

Because the Way of *Budo* is so deeply associated with the sword, it is almost impossible for a Japanese to pick up a long sword without knowing that he has hold of far more than a weapon. A gun, for example, can be held in the hand with no sense of its destructive power. A man can fire a gun and be almost oblivious to what he has done. He need not take responsibility beyond holding up his hand. It is the gun that does the dirty work. It cannot be so with the sword. The sword cannot be used effectively without the complete training of the swordsman. And when the matter is life and death, the training cannot be merely physical. It must also involve spirit. It is personal. The first position that a samurai swordsman is taught is one in which he faces his enemy directly. This is called the frontal position. His back and front feet describe a triangle as do his arms, tapering forward from his shoulders. But in this first position it is the mind of the swordsman that counts. He must stand there, perfectly patient, concentrated to the point where no pressure, no fear, will distract him and where his very composure will draw the opponent forward to make the first move. The sword is thus an extension of the swordsman, the weapon no more—and no less—than the person holding it.

I was not then—and am not now—attracted by the cult of the sword. It is not my Way. I came to it only because I wanted to learn how to hit a baseball better. When I finally bought a Japanese long sword, I didn't dally over what kind. It was a cheap one, and I have never gone through any rituals in keeping or using it other than in making sure from time to time that it was cleaned. But from the moment I first held a sword in my hands, I think I understood something of its personal character. I felt the demand it placed on me for a certain kind of approach. Life and death. You can hold a baseball bat with no such sense of focus. The difference, I learned, was a crucial one when it came to practice.

Within ten days or so of the season's end, Arakawa-san had enrolled us at the Haga Training Center in the Kanda area of downtown Tokyo. The correspondence of sword and bat, I was soon to learn, was no matter of fancy as far as Arakawa-san was concerned. The batter swinging his bat was best off if he was most like the warrior wielding his sword. This had to do with the actual techniques of swordsplay as much as in gaining the desired spirit. The way in which a warrior swings his sword can be directly transferred to the technique of a batter at the plate. Even more so, it turned out, for a home-run hitter. Above all, in the Body of a Rock, with the Immovable Self-Discipline that lay behind it, were the attributes of a warrior I might now gain for myself.

From late November through early January, we went to the Haga *dojo*—every day for fifty straight days. We had to leave our homes at five in the morning to get there in time for the training sessions. The training was hard, and the weather was cold. On the wooden floor of the *dojo*, winter's cold came up between the highly polished floorboards. I was always aware of cold creeping up my legs.

The atmosphere of this kind of *dojo* is very tense. You cannot avoid the sense that very serious, concentrated efforts are required here. Imagine it for yourself. Setting out from home when it is still pitch dark. Driving through still-deserted streets, the fish markets and bread shops barely stirring, the slow heat of the car warming numb limbs that are not yet fully awake—and then a hall full of *hakama*-clad students, odors of old varnish and floor polish, the ritual of gathering that sets a tone for what is to follow.

You cannot enter such a *dojo* without observing very traditional rules of etiquette. These have been developed over centuries, and they serve to remind the student of what it is he is undertaking. In entering or leaving a *dojo*, the student bows first to his teacher and then to others present; one bows also to one's opponent, at the beginning and at the end of practice; neither hats nor smoking are ever permitted; when practice equipment is laid out on the floor before the student, one always walks to the rear rather than the front of this student. If walking in front of a student is necessary, then this is done with an accompanying bow and gesture of the hand; the position on the floor of beginning and advanced students is carefully defined; one always awaits the instructions of the teacher; if a piece of one's armor comes loose during practice, the exercise is immediately stopped. And in Haga Sensei's *dojo*, this important variation was also included: Katanah practice is done with wooden swords. Haga Sensei, however, demonstrated all techniques with a real sword—so the effect was at all times powerful and convincing.

There are many ways in which the use of the sword parallels the swinging of a baseball bat. The attention to details of positioning one's feet, gripping the sword, shifting weight, turning one's hip, extending one's arm, the manner of cutting, all are suggestive enough even if they cannot be applied with complete exactness. But it is a basic mistake to look at that which is merely technical in this work. The phrase "merely technical" is almost incomprehensible, because it cannot be separated from a generating spirit. You cannot work technically with a sword without also being engaged spiritually. What is technical combat without the will to fight? It is possible only at the level of sport. It has little or nothing to do with real conditions. So when I speak of this or that cut, please understand that I am talking about something that surely involves positioning but which includes something far more essential.

There are a number of basic movements in *ken no michi* called *suburi*. These involve patterns of footwork and the movements of the sword from the ready position into different attack and defense modes. Basic strokes with the sword can come from directly overhead, or to the right or left side. In each case the positioning of the body will be different, the shifting of weight will be different. Obviously, those *suburi* that involve swinging from the side or from above the shoulder on one side to a position crossing a lateral plane are most directly applicable to the act of swinging a baseball bat.

The gripping of the sword, though very different in the placement of one hand over the other, is also important for a batsman. In the holding of a sword, the traditional placement of fingers around the *tsuka*, or grip, of the sword enables the swordsman to hold his weapon tightly against his palms while at the same time maintaining relaxation in the hands. This is accomplished by the way in which the fingers tighten around the handle. The forefinger and the thumb of the top hand are held loosely, in a guiding rather than gripping position. In holding a bat this is also done, keeping in mind that a reversal of hands is involved and that relaxation of the forefinger and thumb is desirable in both hands. This alternating of loosened and tightened fingers accomplishes not only required power and suppleness but also prepares one for the basic cutting technique involved in *suburi*.

For a time, I consciously prepared myself by gripping my bat as though for *suburi*. I first paid attention to my bottom or pulling hand. I gripped the bat finger by finger: ring finger first, middle finger next, then pinky. I would feel the pressure of the bat against my palm, then I would loosely curl my forefinger and thumb above; next, I would repeat the arrangement with the top hand.

There is a special maneuver with the hands in *suburi*, which a student of the sword must learn before he can become accomplished. This involves a kind of twisting of the hands at the moment of cutting, and it is very hard to describe and to master. The way we are taught to visualize this is to think of wringing out a towel just at the moment of fullest extension of the sword. In fact, the beginning student of the sword will often be asked to use a *hachimaki* (a cloth headband) gripped in both hands to effect this movement, which requires both relaxation and firmness. The student will be asked to think of wringing out a wet towel, and when he understands what his hands do to accomplish this he will then seek to employ the same movement in the swinging of the sword.

For Arakawa-san, this movement of twisting was crucial, because it meshed perfectly with his theory of downswinging. The twist in *suburi* occurs almost naturally as a result of swinging the sword in a hard downward movement. At the end of such a swing, the hands inevitably seem to move in this twisting manner, but it is important nevertheless to make sure this happens with as much decisiveness as possible, because it determines the kind of power delivered in a blow.

For Arakawa-san and me the question was where to apply this twisting. The most obvious answer pointed to the moment of impact. But Arakawa-san maintained that twisting at the moment of impact was not what we were looking for. To illustrate this, Arakawa-san designed an exercise in which we set up a figure of wet straw—a scarecrow!—and the object then was to swing in such a manner that we would be able to cut the figure in two.

"You try this," he said to me one day, as he positioned the strange-looking straw dummy before me. At the time this did not seem like much of a challenge. I felt strong. As usual, I was stripped down to my shorts so I could sweat freely and so Arakawa-san, following advice he had picked up from Kikugoro, could observe the movements of my muscles. I was every bit as much the warrior as I could be. But I was hardly a master swordsman. I followed Arakawa-san's instructions exactly. I picked up my sword and took my pose. The morning light glinted against the steel blade. I concentrated hard on what I was about to do. The man of straw wasn't about to run away or to attack me. It stood there silently, giving me all the time I needed to strike the fatal blow.

With my right leg in the air, I swung the sword as I would a bat. It felt right. The straw flew in all directions. I gazed at the fallen foe in triumph. Arakawa-san, though, screwed up his face as though he had just eaten something unpleasant.

"What have you done?" he asked.

"Killed it," I said.

"No, no. Describe it. Just what it felt like in your hands."

So I traced the movements for him. When it hit the figure, the blade of the sword almost flew out of its hilt. The blade bit into the straw with such ferocity that it left a slightly unpleasant vibrating sensation running through my hands. The sword had cut the figure on a slightly upward arc, but the wetness and thickness of the straw—designed to simulate the density of a human body—had prevented the cut from going completely through.

Arakawa-san nodded, then said, "Just as I thought. You have not really accomplished twisting."

He took the sword from my hands and faced the second figure we had set up.

The blade gave a gleam. . . .

The next moment the figure was in two.

"That is twisting," he explained, "You will notice how perfectly suited it is to downswinging."

I was very impressed but also rather puzzled. I had surely thought my downswing was correct, that my good hitting through the last part of the season seemed to bear this out. But when I looked at the figure of straw that I had cut, I could see that my stroke, though I delivered it horizontally, had left a track that went upward. My downswing, I thought, guaranteed a horizontal swing, and so it had. But there was this upward cut staring at me like a piece of incriminating evidence.

Most existing theories on hitting tell players to twist or "pop" their wrists just as they make contact with the ball. Using a sword, I discovered that if I did that, I would never be able to cleanly cut a straw figure in two. The secret to such a stroke—and to an addition of unbelievable power—was to twist my wrists *after* contact was made, during the follow-through. In following through, if the downswing was correct, the twisting occurred naturally—rather in the

159

manner of a fireman holding out a hose—with one's arms fully extended.

"Try it again," Arakawa-san said. I did it over and over again until I, too, could cut the figure in half with a single swing of the sword.

"Another thing," Arakawa-san said. "You mentioned nothing about the sound a sword makes. Listen."

He took the sword and made various *suburi* with it. Each time he swung, the sword made a low whistling sound.

"The reason you didn't mention sound to me is because you heard none," he explained. "When you swing the sword correctly, it makes the sound you just heard. When you swing it incorrectly, it makes no sound at all. In the future, this will be a way for you to check on what you're doing."

As I have mentioned, you cannot be "merely technical" when you swing a sword. If it is possible to fall into the habit of a harmless game when you repeatedly swing a baseball bat, that can never happen with a sword. The feel of a sword in your hands will prevent this; the knowledge of what gleams on the edge of the blade compels your attention. It is also impossible to swing a sword without in some way risking injury to yourself. A slip, an off-balance move, going too far in a follow-through, and you run the very real risk of slashing yourself. Practice with the sword demands intensity. As your mind must be concentrated when you face an opponent, so, too, your practice must include this mental effort.

Because I had been studying Aikido for some time, I understood what was demanded. I also had the good incentive of holding two titles. As *ki* was so crucial in learning how to gain balance, I now could apply this to the work I did with the sword. To truly follow the way of the sword is to learn how to direct *ki* power through your body into the sword itself. Power travels the length of the sword as you swing it. The sword, in the hands of a true warrior, is the extension of his own spirit.

So I swung the sword—and the bat—again and again

and again. Arakawa-san said our goal was to get an exact repetition of these swings. It is obvious that any kind of athletic technique demands repetitive ability. This is what separates the amateur from the professional. So much more so does it separate the warrior from the brawler. It was Arakawa-san's contention that if I took three hundred swings, the chances were almost certain that each of those three hundred swings would be slightly different. The goal, he said, was not  three hundred or three thousand swings in a day but three that were exactly alike.

The reason it was so hard to accomplish such a task was that the repetitions could not be just mechanical. Repetition as Arakawa-san meant it was a unity of body, mind, and technique—a goal of Aikido. In the swinging of a sword this meant the merging of the swing itself with the attitude behind it. It sounds easy to say, but it is very hard to bring off. Are there two moments in time that are exactly the same? This is what the swordsman seeks; this is the impossible goal that Arakawa-san pursued.

During this time he was reading and absorbing many different books. Ueshiba Sensei's book *Zen and Swordsmanship*, a Western book called *Zen in the Art of Archery*, the *Gorin no sho* of Musashi were just a few of the works he sought to incorporate into his own understanding of hitting a baseball. In all of this the sword had now become the key.

In swinging the sword over and over again, Arakawa-san sought not only a pattern of motion but also one of behavior. *How* did I swing the sword? Musashi talked about the difference between cutting and slashing. You can kill an opponent by slashing at him, but one trains to cut him, to concentrate all one's mental and physical energy into this single effort, which is the cut to the bone. It is an attitude of deadly thrusting as well as a technically correct handling of the sword. So I could not swing either sword or bat in a lackadaisical fashion. Each swing had to be all or nothing. Because I would have four or five hundred at-bats in a season, the need would be there to put all of myself several thousand times into this act of swinging a bat. And each time the consequence, as far as my own spirit was concerned, had to be decisive.

Gorin no sho, Musashi's farewell treatise on swordsmanship, means Book of Five Rings. These rings are analagous to the five rings of the human body: head, left and right elbows, left and right knees. We approached these rings of the body as checkpoints of my stance. Spirit and mechanics could not be separated. In the positioning of the head, it was vital to ensure that the opponent would be seen with both eyes, that the longest possible sighting of the ball would occur. It was important also to be able to look at a pitcher in such a way that he would not be frightened and at the same time so that his spirit-energy or *ki* could be led. One of the practice techniques in Kendo is called *metsuke*. This means the focus or point of observation. In this exercise the swordsman is required to deeply observe his opponent and to do so in a flash—because in battle one simply can't count on an excess of time. The student is taught to make this observation as though with two sets of eyes: one that will take in his opponent's eyes— the eyes mirroring what is in the spirit, the other paying attention to the opponent's body. Because this two-layered vision is seemingly impossible (it is very hard to perfect), the instruction most often given is to look at the opponent as though he were a distant mountain. Musashi called this a "distanced view of close things." It was important, he said, that in doing this one made sure not to move the eyeballs.

The position of the elbows and knees is also crucially important in almost all the martial arts. The position of elbows and knees determines the ability to concentrate power. In Aikido, as in Kendo, the basic focus of power is in the description of a triangle by arms and legs. If the position of the driving elbow in a swordsman—or batter—is too far from the body, it is not possible to form a good triangle with the torso. The position of the knees, as well, is fundamental in being able to

secure proper balance located near the one point. So while I never studied these matters by name, as Arakawa-san did, I followed his instructions with absolute fidelity.

Our routine that winter was the same throughout: the predawn drive to the center in Kanda; several hours at the *dojo*; the rest of the day and far into the night practicing at Arakawa-san's house, trying to apply what had been learned to the main problem of hitting a baseball. I went home only to grab a few hours of sleep.

I had all my meals at Arakawa-san's. Thinking back on it, it was a wonder that Mrs. Arakawa could put up with my constant presence in the house. Often we did not finish our work till nine, ten, or later.

Arakawa-san, I know, deeply appreciated his wife's patience and generosity—as I did. He would try to explain: "These days most workers don't like to bring their work home. That's as it should be. But it's only the lucky ones, the ones with talent, who can afford to leave their work behind."

Mrs. Arakawa made delicious meals. She'd listen to her husband speak while she set the table and brought out the food. "The others, myself for one . . . since I'm not talented," Arakawa-san went on, "must bring their work home. I have to cut down on sleep, and I have to think of improving Oh's batting day and night. It's enough to try the soul of any wife, I know, but I'm lucky that way. . . ."

Mrs. Arakawa laughed and gently shook her head at these loving explanations, making sure I understood as well that I was indeed welcome in the house. Through all of this, the one thing that was utterly beyond me was how Mrs. Arakawa seemed to know—know exactly—when to start cooking. Because invariably at the time we quit, the freshest, most wonderfully prepared hot meals would be just arriving at the table.

I felt it almost an impertinence to ask about this, but finally curiosity simply got the better of me. I had to broach the matter with Arakawa-san. The explanation was roughly as follows: we practiced upstairs. Mrs. Arakawa could hear my right foot landing on the floor when I took my swing. She began to distinguish the sounds after having listened to them for so long.

"She can tell how you're doing by the sound you make," Arakawa-san explained. "She can tell exactly where we are for the day, you see." When the sound from upstairs was of one kind, she'd delay preparations; when it was another, when the rhythm was good, she would know it was time to begin.

"My cooking is not magic," she explained to me laughingly one night. "It is because after all this time, I, too, have learned something about the art of one leg!" This particular grace of Mrs. Arakawa's went deep into my consciousness. It imbued my training with a feeling of welcome and well-being. Arakawa-*nabe*! What a source of nourishment! Years later, Mrs. Arakawa told me that on the day I retired she would cut her beautiful long hair. It was her way of letting me know that in her deepest feelings she, too, supported and encouraged me in my work. My debt to Arakawa-san is also a debt to Mrs. Arakawa, to a couple who opened their home to me and gave me support in life that sustains me to this day.

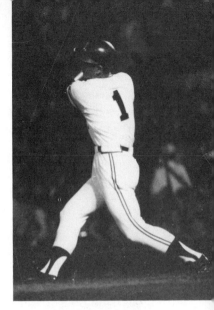

Because so much of the work we did now was both arduous and repetitive, there was a danger, at least in Arakawa-san's mind, that I would look for excuses to ease up. I only learned this later, but at the time it accounted for little variations in our routine that I sometimes wondered about. One of these variations was Arakawa-san's leaving the house in the middle of a training session. Sometimes he would be gone for a few minutes, other times for longer. One day he was absent for over three hours. He never explained why he was leaving or offered any apologies when he got back. Recently, he confessed to a mutual friend that it was all a strategy to test me, because he knew what a divided person I was when it came to working hard. I wish he had told me. I might have set his mind at ease. Although Weaker One and Stronger One are permanent parts of my personality, Stronger One definitely had the upper hand then. Those days were exciting and alluring. I loved batting and working!

The value of repetition, fundamental to any Zen practice, is understood on one level by anyone who has ever tried to learn a musical instrument or to gain a skill of any sort. Skill is improved by repetition. There is no avoiding it. In swordsmanship, this improvement in skill is understood in most particular terms. Repetition of cutting and defensive strokes for purposes of practice is called *kirikaeshi*. It is essential for the student to learn. A Kendoist learns that as an attacker he gains ten virtues by these repetitions; to the defender *kirikaeshi* gives eight virtues. These virtues are specifically associated with improving technique, the strengthening of arms and wrists, the accomplishment of agility and the ability to deliver ever more powerful blows, improvement of eyesight, dexterity in the palms, and the better focusing of balance in the waist. I did not have the terminology to go with the work I was doing, but I understood it in my body and in the occasional sunlight of Arakawa-san's seductive words of encouragement.

"There is something about you that does remind me of Musashi, you know," he told me one day. On another day: "Set your mind on Babe Ruth. You are going to beat him, you see." And then again: "You have the body and spirit that will enable you to play till you're forty."

Still, Arakawa-san was not sold on my willingness to work. As far as he was concerned, a certain amount of ingenuity was required just to make sure that I stayed at it. One day, after a particularly strenuous session, he announced to me:

"Expect reporters and photographers tomorrow. They'll be doing a story and taking pictures of our session."

I could not very well say "no" to him then—or any of the other times he brought in the press to observe my training—but I was most uncomfortable. For one thing, camera flashes were distracting. For another, I trained in my underwear and sweated freely. I wanted to train that way, true enough, but I didn't want people photographing me in my underwear, sweating like a hog. Still, the photographers came. They took pictures of me swinging the bat and the sword; they recorded me for posterity looking more like an Indian fakir than a professional baseball player. They even brought along a fifth- or sixth-grade boy one time and had him hang off one of my arms as I was standing on one foot—an illustration for the mass dailies of how I was progressing in my efforts to become balanced.

Why did Arakawa-san need to do this? He wasn't the least impressed with my discomfort.

"What's the big deal? You think it's such a bad idea to show everyone how well balanced you are?"

On another occasion he suggested slyly that having our opponents worry about what I might be accomplishing was also very much in our favor. What he held back was his primary purpose: by scheduling reporters and photographers—in advance—to cover our training sessions, he was making sure I would do nothing to escape daily work habits.

Because Arakawa-san forbade me any kind of combat in my training, he was forced to find other means to challenge me. The challenge of an opponent is, of course, the ultimate test in any martial arts practice. In baseball, just as much as in Aikido, success against an opponent is fundamentally bound up with timing. Our goal, "acquiring the Body of a Rock," literally meant having the discipline to wait. This implied far more than balance. To train one's entire being to hold back from the tricks and feints of a pitcher, no less than from an enemy with a sword, is finally the single most important step in harmonizing one's *ki* with the opponent's. *Ma*, the interval or distance between you, is eventually that which you rather than the other create by the strength of your waiting.

Arakawa-san designed an ingenious method to overcome our self-imposed limitation. One afternoon toward the end of that winter's training, he got up on a chair and very meticulously tied a piece of wet paper attached to a long string to a beam on the ceiling. The paper swayed to and fro. The string and the weight of the paper caused it to move this way and that. Every so often, the swaying paper would stop for just a fraction of a second. In that instant, Arakawa-san said, I was to slash at the paper with my sword. If I hit it right—that is, only in that split second

167

when it was perfectly motionless, I would shear the paper in half. If I waited just an instant too long or started too soon, the paper would be knocked away or would cling to the blade. By this rigorous demand on my sense of timing I simulated the challenge of an opponent.

So I took my pose before this sliver of swaying, twisting paper. I could feel my irritation grow as it swayed and swayed and swayed. It was an effort to keep calm, to hold my concentration steadily in my abdomen. So much time seemed to pass. I could now stand coiled comfortably on one foot for over three minutes. But I barely gave this a thought. I was no longer striving to achieve this. Everything was now suddenly poured into this single act of waiting. For waiting, I understood in this moment, far from being something passive, was the most active state of all. In its secret heart lay the beginning and the end of all action. In it lurked the exact moment to strike. The paper was suddenly still. Or I somehow sensed that it would be, *just an instant beforehand*, so I was able to start my swing and sever the paper just as it came to a stop.

"Yes, Oh, *yes!*" Arakawa-san said. I was perspiring and almost breathless from the effort of concentration. It is many years ago now, but I remember what a sense of accomplishment I felt when I first performed this exercise. It sounds much easier than it is—just as the idea of hitting an off-speed pitch in baseball sounds easier than it really is. In both instances, the test of reflexes is supreme, the act of waiting fully engaged. Months of training had gone into this moment. I could not have accomplished this without all that had gone before. Over the years I have tried to explain this to other players, that is, what a challenge the exercise really represented. Some players, expressing curiosity, have tried it for themselves. They discovered what was really involved. The exercise simply cannot be performed correctly—that is with perfect ability to wait— without hair-trigger ability to swing and control enough of one's stroke to cut through the paper on a straight rather than a hooked line. The requirement of controlled waiting, the danger of lunging and missing and, hence, of injury is so great that Arakawa-san and I have nearly always insisted that the paper be hung with no movement for those players who have had no previous training with the sword but who have wanted to try the exercise. Very few have been able to simply cut through the paper, no less at the correct angle.

Beginning with the spring camp in 1963, the triangle and the circle became the focus of our attention. In all the martial arts, but especially in swordsmanship, the triangle is, as I have suggested, elementary. But transposing this to hitting a baseball from a one-legged pose could not be accomplished as long as the struggle to achieve balance was taking place. We could do this now because we were finally able to pay attention to the swing itself.

In Japanese swordsmanship, when you bring down the wooden sword to hit your opponent's mask, the points connecting the two arms and the body form a triangle. The same is true in golf when a player readies himself to hit a shot with a driver. The triangle in both cases is drawn at exactly the point where power is to be concentrated: the opponent's mask in the case of Kendo, the little white ball on the tee in golf. In baseball it is the point where bat meets ball, which the batter normally visualizes slightly forward of the plate.

With the ability I had acquired to wait, I now could move my contact point somewhat farther back. This in turn gave me slightly more time before I had to commit myself. I thus wound up being able to see an incoming pitch till the last possible moment.

In Aikido the power expressed in the forming of a triangle is reinforced by the adding of a circle. Drawing a circle by some movement of your body is the easiest way to exert power. I don't mean to make this sound so mathematical, so imagine, if you will, a deadly struggle in which one person thrusts forward with all the power he can muster while the other, one split second ahead of him in his thinking, moves in circular fashion to the side and around, carrying the force of the attacker's thrust within his own circular movement. The two strengths have become one, the power contained in the movement doubled. One thus exerts unlimited power by annulling the opponent's strength and by appropriating it in the circular motion of the batter bringing his bat around and into the ball. It is counter-centrifugal power, but it is based on the same principle of joining the opponent's force to your own. The exact second of impact is therefore crucial. I had now reached the point where I could make contact harder and more precisely than I ever had before.

Chapter Nine

I began the 1963 season right where I had left off the previous one. In the fourth game of the new season, I got my first home run of the year in a 17–2 onslaught against the Hiroshima Carp. Two days later, still in Hiroshima, I got another, and then, when we returned to Tokyo, I added seven more home runs in a matter of days. The half month of play in April ended by my hitting as many as I had in the first three months of the previous season. Through May, my home-run batting, if not my overall hitting, remained steady. But then, at the beginning of June, I went into a slump.

The word "slump" itself is one of those magical words among baseball people. A slump in hitting is second only to a slump in the economy in generating so many inches of imaginative column space a year in daily newspapers. In my case, however, there wasn't much to figure out. With good results coming right away, I had begun to believe that the kind of daily training Arakawa-san and I had been doing was no longer quite necessary. Though I continued to work hard, I began more and more to confine myself to the daily routines that any responsible professional puts himself through prior to a game. I found, also, that the effort of batting on one foot was so demanding, so strenuous, that I did not want to keep it up. I believe that Mr. Kawakami and perhaps Arakawa-san himself hoped that I would finally settle into a more orthodox way of hitting—but at any rate I allowed my own wish to do that to influence what I was doing. I came down onto two feet again, hoping, mistakenly, that I had learned enough in matters of technique and spirit to sustain me no matter what form I used. But this was not to happen. Above all, I saw that I was in jeopardy of losing the titles I had won the previous season. My titles were also in jeopardy because Nagashima-san was having a simply outstanding year in every department. Toward midsummer, press, fans, and teammates alike were buzzing with the possibility of his becoming a Triple Crown winner.

After a few weeks away, I finally returned to Arakawa-san, full of shame and apology. I bowed to him, palms to the floor, and begged him to forgive me.

"*Onegai Shimasu*," I said in the traditional manner of student supplicating master. Arakawa-san, for his part, neither chastised me nor said anything to make me feel worse than I did. This was his way then and always—whenever he was faced with sincere apology. His answer to me was simply to get back to work. I was very frank about what I wanted. I knew I had no chance to win a batting title or even one for RBIs.

"I want to win a home-run title, at least," I said.

"Yes," he said with a smile.

I believe that my going to him then in that way may not have been all that easy for him. Arakawa-san, whatever our relationship, was also batting coach to the Giants. Among the pupils who now regularly sought his advice was Nagashima-san himself. Everything about him suggested that his own motto was to establish himself once and for all as the number-one player in Japan. My motto then was only to keep pace with Nagashima-san and pass him in home runs.

"A slump, you see," Arakawa-san explained, "is a mysterious word only because it is misunderstood. In reality, 'slump' is a very difficult word to define. There is no slump for a person who is trying hard every day to get better. When you almost get there, when you have almost achieved perfection, you may have what others will call a slump. But it isn't really that at all. Mass media says slump, but it isn't. There's only one answer to your slump now—let's do it again!"

And so we continued. Because my pose was so difficult to maintain, I had to practice it every day. We did not talk about the absolute need for me to bat this way. The possibility of one day returning to an orthodox method was neither discussed nor ruled out. The only point now was that if I wanted to continue one-legged batting, I had to train for it much as if I were a long-distance runner or a classical musician—with daily workouts to strengthen and sustain the resources needed for proper performance.

"It may be that we are discovering that this business of one leg is for keeps. That all or nothing means just that. But that is a problem of the spirit also, you see. You will have to determine the rightness or wrongness of such an idea. One way or another, it will be your choice."

And then he added in his most confiding tone, "I will tell you this—you have the chance to be a Triple Crown winner, do you know that?"

I couldn't really believe that. I knew if I really worked hard and obediently I could keep pace with home runs and RBIs, but I wasn't really the kind of consistent hitter who would be likely to win a batting title.

"Not this year," said Arakawa-san, "maybe not for the next few seasons, but soon enough. I think maybe when you're lazy you are really telling yourself you can't be that good."

I had nothing to say. Arakawa-san knew me all too well. There was beneath everything I did in baseball this gnawing sense of fear that I would let down or be unable to play up to what I had previously done. I wish I could have said at that point that miserable success-seeking was a thing of the past, but that wasn't so. To do well meant that I had to do well again. The joy of the present moment in no way relieved me of fearing that I might not be so lucky in the future. The answer, I knew, lay in having to extend myself beyond any desire to take it easy, to be absolutely unremitting and persevering in holding down this natural "other" in myself who more than anything craved easy living, good times, release from labor. *Amae* is a Japanese word for affection, softheartedness, tender feeling. Without it, life is false and hollow, and yet it must be struggled with so that you are able to move. *Amae* warms your heart. It also enables you to work twice as hard to overcome all those siren songs of laziness.

And so we resumed our work on a daily basis. I could no longer say it was fear or love of the game or even the presence of Nagashima-san, but I seemed to put more and more of myself into what I was doing. It was not so much a question of hours but of feeling. I wanted to swing the bat, I wanted what standing on one foot brought to me. More and more I came to see that when I stood on one foot, my sense of things changed. On one foot, I became hungry for hitting. On two feet, I was just another hitter. I loved the contest between myself and the pitcher, the struggle of wills that, miraculously, could be resolved in this unity of movement that was the home run.

I found in the course of this season, particularly after I resumed my daily training with Arakawa-san, that my capacity for intense work reached the point where even he wondered about its beneficial effects. One week during the summer, for example, I caught a cold. It was bothersome, but that was all. One afternoon, after running out a double, I had a coughing spasm standing on second base. It must have worried Arakawa-san, because afterward he told me he was concerned about my physical condition. He suggested that we might now begin to cut back on such hard work. But I knew I was all right. And anyway, I was not about to let up. I joked with Arakawa-san. "You know about *ki*. If you think disease, you'll be diseased." At the beginning of August, I went into another slight slump, but I was out of it by mid-month and on the way to my best year ever.

The press at this time had largely acknowledged my play and for the first time had begun to use the phrase "O-N Cannon," describing the home-run combination of Nagashima-san and myself in the middle of the Giants' order. Still, my goal for the season was only to retain a portion of what I had won the year before. I reached season's end with forty home runs, surpassing Nagashima-san in that category to win the title. I failed to recapture the RBI crown, although for the first time I knocked in over a hundred runs. More important, I raised my batting average over thirty points to .305, and most important of all, I began to have a growing sense that I might after all be a good hitter as well as a good power hitter.

I was sorry to see the end of the 1963 season. Not only had I done well but our team won the Central League pennant and then the Japan Series in seven games—games in which, incidentally, I hit a series career high of four home runs. Instead of feeling glad to have baseball behind me, I was hungry for more. Sometime in that season, I cannot pinpoint it exactly, I woke to find that my heart was on fire. It did not matter if I went to Ginza or put away a whole bottle of scotch and a few beers in a night, I always woke clear-headed and on fire for baseball. I had reached the point where I simply lived to hit. How can I say it without sounding foolish? I craved hitting a baseball in the way a samurai craved following the Way of the Sword. It was my life.

The relationship between Arakawa-san and I had changed now, too, subtly but surely. We were not only student and master but also friends who, on a team where division between players and coaches was strict, had to pick our social moments. The man sitting across the way from me in the bar was usually quiet and serene as a Buddha, the fearful devil in his eyes completely gone. I realized he seldom got mad—and that was very different from me. One night we were in a sushi bar in Roppongi. We happened to meet a famous actor there, Mr. Akutagawa. We somehow got into an argument about technique and artistry. I was drunk enough to give a lecture on the subject while Arakawa-san smiled and faded into trance-like silence. Mr. Akutagawa, I think, belittled baseball. Or at least the way he used the word "craftsman" (as opposed to "artist") made me think so. Anyway, inexperience and fire singed my pride, and rather than become belligerent, I stormed out of the establishment. The most distressing part of all to me was that I could not explain why baseball was more than a game. I believe that was what Mr. Akutagawa was really denying. For me it had become everything. It contained all I knew about interpersonal relationships, all I knew about winning and losing and being oneself; whatever I knew about the world outside baseball, I somehow was learning from baseball itself. I cared for little else. Because I have always consciously sought to have what I do rather than what I say speak for me, I have had many people convinced that I was some sort of secret truth-seeker. This was never so. I never thought like that. I played baseball because I loved baseball. My heart caught fire at the idea of hitting—more hits, more home runs, more strength to overcome adversity.

Arakawa-san and I went to a geisha house in Kagurazaka one night. Even in such a pleasing setting, I'm afraid my spirit was all too visible to those expert in seeing.

"What's the most important point in hitting?" our geisha asked.

I was unprepared for such a question and could not bring myself to answer. Arakawa-san, knowing me so well by now, smiled and replied to the geisha by asking a question of his own:

"What's the most important in dancing?"

The geisha discreetly raised her kimono, revealing her foot. She pointed to her right toe. By this she indicated that balance in dancing was everything, and that in the shifting of her weight, she moved from point to point, from the big toe on one foot to the big toe on the other. Yes! Of course! That she was talking about dancing faded from mind as I saw that this secret of centuries-old geisha dancing was allied somehow with the way of one-footed batting! Baseball was with me wherever I went. There was simply nothing else!

Our training was by no means completed. Although I now understood that the secret of standing on one leg was standing on one leg and that waiting meant being able to wait, there was more. What I had to do now was to bring to completion what was already alive in my feeling. In the course of two seasons' work with Arakawa-san my confidence and my prowess in hitting had really changed. But if you look back over my record, you will see that in those two years, even with the added number of home runs, I hit more doubles than in any two years of my career taken together. The reason for this, according to some critics, was that I tended to hit too many line drives. I did not get the kind of lift on the ball that a traditional American home-run hitter would get. Still others suggested that even though I was physically big for Japanese baseball, I was still not *that* big. If there was a place of doubt about myself as a home-run hitter, it was there. The Giants had briefly been in spring training with the Los Angeles Dodgers in 1961, and I had seen Frank Howard, one of the most gargantuan power hitters ever. Howard attacked a ball with a wonderful sense of aggressiveness—something I was more and more able to do now myself—but his enormous size and strength made copying him impossible. If that was what it took to be an authentic home-run hitter, I really never would match up. But as I had no way of being transformed into a physical giant, I was left with what I was.

Arakawa-san's answer for this phase of our training was a particular aspect of swordsmanship called *Iai Nuki*, or the art of withdrawing and replacing the sword.

Iai, according to those who know, is the most spiritual part of sword training, because in order to gain mastery of it, one's mental state has to be perfect. You position yourself in readiness. Your opponent does likewise. In this moment of ritual preparation, the outcome of the battle itself is decided. The strength of your spirit must be just that much faster than the impulse of your opponent. There is a popular Japanese movie called *Seven Samurai* that illustrates this very well. In one section of the movie a group of townsmen are looking around for a samurai to help protect their village against marauders. They come across a crowd of people in a field who have gathered to watch a warlike, very belligerent man challenge the swordsmanship of an apparently nondescript man who seems to want no part of the action. The belligerent one, looking every bit like the fiercest samurai around, finally induces his smaller opponent to a mock battle with wooden swords. With a lot of swaggering and a great roar, the large one assumes the most intimidating pose imaginable. Meanwhile, the other, with perfect composure, takes his wooden sword and steps back and then into the triangle of the frontal position, and remains as motionless as a snake hypnotizing a frog. With the first panicked rush of the larger one, the slight swordsman makes one, simple, swift movement and then turns and walks away. The belligerent one bellows out that he has won or that at least it was a draw. The slight warrior, played by the wonderful actor Seiji Miyaguchi, will not acknowledge this and so is challenged again, this time with a real sword. Many in the audience believe that an unfair fight is about to take place, with the smaller man in immediate peril of his life. In fact, it is exactly the other way around. An old samurai in the crowd lets us know, if we have so far failed to understand, that for the belligerent one, the fight is already over. What follows is a repetition with deadly steel of the mock battle that preceded it. The concentration and lightning-like use of *ki* by the smaller warrior results inevitably in the killing of the one who looks like but is not a real samurai.

In *Iai*, Arakawa-san pointed out, the action is from the wrist to the tip of the sword. You must project *ki* power in this focused way, sending it from this last outpost of your body into and through the sword.

Because *Iai* concerns itself exclusively with this first moment, two things are absolutely essential. You must assume a perfect attitude of readiness. You cannot fake this in any way. This moment is possible only if you have mastered certain of the technical requirements of swordsmanship. Yet these technical aspects are meaningless without the other necessity—the ability to wait. Technique and spirit are thus completely dependent on one another. The quickness of unsheathing and striking with the sword is tied to sureness of mind in a single motion of eye, hand, and body.

There is also in *Iai* a mechanical adaptability to hitting a baseball—particularly for hitting home runs—that cannot be overemphasized. The art of *Iai* is essentially the art of withdrawing and engaging the Japanese long sword. This traditional sword is so long that it cannot simply be withdrawn from its scabbard in a single upward motion of the arm and wrist. In order for the sword to fully clear the scabbard and become instantly an attacking weapon, the swordsman must turn his hips as he withdraws the sword. This motion is almost exactly identical to a batter's turning his hips forward as he hits a ball. In *Iai*, though, there is this addition. With the rotation of the hips and the dramatic weight shift involved, there is also the stroke of the sword itself, a lightning-like cutting motion performed by the wrist driving forward and upward. Wrist action in batting conventionally involves the turning over of the wrist. This motion of *Iai* is different and accounts for the ability of a downswinger to make a cut through a figure of straw or a swinging card that will be a straight line drawn at a slightly upward angle. As it turned out, it would also enable a one-legged batter not only to hit a ball hard at the moment of impact but also to send it flying upward into the air.

Another close parallel in baseball to this motion of *Iai* is obviously the batter's follow-through. Most theories of hitting say this should occur naturally, the inevitable result of everything that has gone before. This is allowing momentum to continue without any interference. But in *Iai* the motion of hips, extended arm, and wrist demands the powerful release of *ki*. In the follow-through, all of one's spirit is projected from the wrist into the tip of the sword and beyond, so that the moment of impact is like an explosion that continues to the very end of the follow-through. In Japanese there is a special term for this continuation of spirit in delivering a blow. It is called *zanshin*, and it is meant to remind one that it is, after all, life and death that ride outward from one's hands.

It is most curious, but all of this training, all of this minute attention to detail, rather than complicating hitting for me, seemed to make it simpler. What I or any batter hoped for was to go up to the plate and hit. No more. But what I was coming to see was that this seemingly simple act was forever being interfered with by one roadblock or another. If it was a mechanical problem or a mental one, it didn't matter; the result was always the same. Performance sometimes rose or fell, but the act of hitting remained unnecessarily complicated.

"You see," Arakawa-san explained, "the better you hit, the less reason you have to think. After all, isn't the goal of Zen to achieve a void?"

I am not sure if he was poking fun then or not, but his words were very soon to become prophetic.

I think I knew that 1964 was going to be a special year even before the season began. One day when I went to Arakawa-san's for training, I assumed my pose with the sword and methodically began my swings. I had taken only three swings that day—normally I took hundreds—when

Arakawa-san suddenly stopped me, a look of pleasure glowing on his face.

"That's it! That's it! You've done it," he said excitedly.

"Done what?" I asked, puzzled.

"It has taken all this time," he said triumphantly, "but you have just performed three identical, perfect swings. There is no more to do for today than to concentrate as hard as you can on remembering what it is you have done. You have finally understood. That is all I can say. You must accept this now."

And so this strange day ended then and there. I wondered what I had really done that I had not done before—but trusting Arakawa-san as I did I knew that it was important. I tried to follow his instruction, to remember these three swings. But all I could think of was that I had made these swings with the sword intensely and fully. That was all. The motion and the feeling were one.

At the beginning of the 1964 season something else occurred that marked a real change in my career as a hitter. I began regularly to use a handmade Ishii bat. This bat has a machine-made equivalent, but there all similarity ends. Mr. Ishii himself made my bat, according to what he personally knew about me. He made this bat as carefully and as skillfully as if he were a master swordmaker. As the goal of the swordmaker was to provide the individual samurai with a sword that was matched to his particular spirit, so Mr. Ishii consciously sought to match the bat he made for me with his perception of who I was. I had used Mr. Ishii's bats from time to time in the past, trying and rejecting many and never settling on any one model until suddenly, with the beginning of this 1964 season, Mr. Ishii gave me a bat that I "knew" was right for me. When he finally evolved this model, I knew it as clearly as if I had been waiting all my life for it. I came to trust Mr. Ishii's bat as I trusted my own hand. Once this particular model was placed in my hands, I never needed to test any of the replacements or check out any aspect of the bat prior to using it. I trusted

Mr. Ishii absolutely. To most people, rightfully so, a baseball bat is just a baseball bat. But this is not Mr. Ishii's approach. As far as I know, there is not another batmaker like him in the world.

Mr. Ishii is now over eighty years old. His connection with baseball goes back to the beginning of the century. As I did, he went to Waseda Sojitsu and, it so happens, was a member of the Sojitsu team in 1914, which played in the first Koshien ever.

Wood is an obvious prerequisite to everything he does. In Japan, until Mr. Ishii came along, most hardball bats were made out of a wood called *toneriko* from a tree located in the central and northern sections of the country. But there is a peculiarity to baseball played here that is not duplicated in other countries. We distinguish one kind of hardball from another. Until children are close to physical maturity, the baseballs they use are, though the same size as regulation, somewhat softer. At this level, where "soft" hardballs are used, a different kind of wood—*tamo*—is normally employed in batmaking. It was fairly well known that *tamo* actually was a livelier wood than *toneriko* to use for the "hard" hardball. The only problem was that *tamo* could not withstand much contact with an actual hardball without splintering. Mr. Ishii discovered how to overcome this.

First he had to locate a special kind of *tamo* that was found only in the wildest and most remote parts of Hokkaido, the northernmost area of the country. He employed a partner, a man named Satose, whose job it was to make expeditions to these areas of Hokkaido solely to find the right wood. Any kind of *tamo* simply would not do. Mr. Satose was on the lookout for a variety of *tamo* called *yachidamo*. And this wood has both a male and a female variety, too. The difference is important. Male *yachidamo* has a long, straight, parallel grain; female *yachidamo* has a wavy grain. Mr. Ishii always selected male *yachidamo* for me. This search for the correct wood, for the absolutely perfect grain, involved also a perception of souls. Trees, like people, were the possessors of souls, and Mr. Satose's search was therefore to match the "soul" of the tree with the "soul" of the batsman in readying the wood. As everyone's style and power were different, Mr. Ishii believed it was important to find the particular kind and cut of wood to be used. The deepest of Mr. Ishii's secrets was that each of his bats was handmade for individual batters.

Once the wood was selected, the problem for Mr. Ishii was how to extract the water and air from it. This he accomplished by subjecting the shaped bat to steam and fire on a specially designed rack.

From the time I first settled on the bat I was going to use, I have never changed style. Mr. Ishii has since made hundreds of bats for me. Every one of them, handmade, looks exactly alike—and to the naked eye you could not tell them apart from machine-made bats. Yet I would be able to tell the difference easily—even if I were blindfolded. Mr. Ishii's bat has a nice thin grip, giving it good bend in the hands, but what distinguishes it from all others is the particular sound of the bat when good contact is made with the ball. There is no sound like it I know. If I were walking by a park in early spring, and I stopped off to watch a team of boys play baseball, and I saw a batter swing at a pitch and heard the sound of the bat making contact, I would know if that hitter was using one of Mr. Ishii's bats or not. What he placed in my hands in the spring of 1964 was a sword I used until the day I retired sixteen years later.

Our first game of the season that year was on March 20 at home against the Kokutetsu Swallows. In the third inning I hit a two-run homer on the way to a 3–1 Giants victory. Two days later I hit two more home runs, including the first "avec" home run of the year with Nagashima-san. By the end of March I had seven home runs. And by the end of April, thirteen. On May 3, against the Hanshin Tigers at Korakuen Stadium, I homered four times in the same game—in the first, fourth, sixth, and seventh innings. Three of the home runs were almost as far as I could hit a ball. I hit one to dead center field, another to right center, and two more far into the right-field bleachers. Press and fans were thrilled with the feat. For myself, there was only this continuing fire to hit.

The day following the game against the Tigers was a scheduled day off. I was sorry. It meant no chance to hit in a game. But on May 5 there was something new to contend with. The Hiroshima Carp, our next opponent, had devised a defensive alignment—just for me. The Carp management, after studying videotape and computer print-outs of my hitting, determined that I pulled an excessive number of my hits to the right side. They decided that the logical thing to do was to employ an "Oh Shift" to stop me. The shift was similar to but slightly different from the "Williams Shift" first employed by Lou Boudreau in America. When I came to bat in the first inning, I watched the Carp players arrange themselves with the third baseman standing directly behind second base, and the shortstop pulled over to the position normally occupied by the second baseman, who, in turn, had moved to an outfield position between the right and center fielders. The right fielder stood almost directly on the right-field foul line, the center fielder was in the normal position of the right fielder, and the left fielder was moved far over toward center. The entire left side of the field from where I stood to the outfield wall was empty. (In the Williams Shift, the left fielder was positioned about thirty feet beyond the infield in left center field.)

The challenge in this was as simple as the picture that greeted me. Hit to left field. From that day forward, critics have maintained, as they did in America with Ted Williams, that I could have hit .400 any time I wanted if I had chosen to go to left field. I did not, and not really because I had no interest in hitting for average. To do so would have meant altering my swing. I believe that's what the Carp management was really hoping to accomplish by this Oh

Shift. It was a psychological challenge as much as anything. At any rate, my answer to the Oh Shift that day—and thereafter—was to swing as I always did, to keep the contest of hitting between myself and the pitcher standing sixty feet away. In the seventh inning, I answered this new Oh Shift by hitting a 400-foot home run to right field.

Arakawa-san and I had reached the point where there were no tricks in what I was doing. And consequently no tricks used against us would get in our way. Nothing could stop me from hitting. I longed to hit as a starving man longs for food. The ball coming toward me was a rabbit, and I was a wolf waiting to devour it. I attacked a baseball as though it were no longer a question of hitting it but of crushing it totally. The home runs rocketed off my bat almost as though a power beyond my own was responsible. I was fascinated by the runs I got all by myself. My head, my mind—quite literally—became a void. I went to the plate with no thought other than this moment of hitting confronting me. It was everything. And in the midst of it, in the midst of chanting and cheering crowds, colors, noises, hot and cold weather, the glare of lights, or rain on my skin, there was only this noiseless, colorless, heatless void in which the pitcher and I together enacted our certain, preordained ritual of the home run.

I hit fifty-five home runs in a 140-game season that year. I continued to study with Arakawa-san on a daily basis. His answer to the Oh Shift was clear.

"Well," he said at the time, "our response will be to hit the ball so hard that the speed of it will scare off the fielder even if it goes straight to him. Better yet, *Iai Nuki*! We'll concentrate on getting the ball flying, because they can't position fielders up in the sky! We'll make them long for ladders and magic beanstalks, which aren't yet a part of the game. Our goal is Babe Ruth!"

For the first time, the idea didn't seem ridiculous. But it was hitting as I did and the change in the way I was regarded by my opponents that opened this strange new door of possibility. On August 9 I hit my forty-second home run of the season against a pitcher on the Taiyo Whales who was used exclusively to face me, a tactic soon used by other teams in the league. On August 20 a pitcher on the Tigers, Mr. Kakimoto, told his teammates that he had found a secret way to pitch to me and that I would not be able to hit him at all. When I faced him in the game that followed, he walked me intentionally with no one on base!

The home-run record for one season until then was fifty-one, by Makoto Kozuru of the Shochiku Robins in 1950. I tied that on August 27 but then did not break the record until September 6. My final home run came on a rainy closing day at Korakuen Stadium on the twenty-third. At this season's end, everything in my life, including my own outlook, had changed. The door of possibility had opened. I walked through, never to go back. This was not unadulterated joy as far as I was concerned. For I discovered in this most amazing season of my life that achievement and recognition were not necessarily the same thing. While I had made an all-time Japanese record in a sport beloved by our people, I was confronted immediately by the fact that 1964 also happened to be the year of the Tokyo Olympics. And as the Giants had not won the flag, excitement over my record was more than eclipsed by interest in the Tokyo games. Also, as far as Giants' fans were concerned, my record was a record. It had nothing to do with popularity. No matter what I did on the field, it became absolutely clear that Nagashima-san would remain the number one Giants' player for as long as he played. The big baseball news that fall was Nagashima-san's marriage. Nagashima-san, in fact, had become so popular in this time that fans universally referred to him as "Mr. Giants." I could have hit seventy-five home runs and I would have remained well within the shadow of his popularity. In its own way, this absence of popular recognition was as significant to me as hitting fifty-five home runs. For I vowed to myself in this peculiar mid-zone of disappointment that I would deal with the question by making records. Let Nagashima-san or anyone else be the darling of the fans; I would win respect only by what I did on the field. I vowed then and there to go after every record that was open for me to challenge.

And there was one other matter. I had finished my third year of work with Arakawa-san, exactly what he had asked of me when we first began together. He told me now that I not only reminded him of Musashi, I also had his capacity. I initially took this only as praise. But he meant something else by it as well.

In his thinking, I had progressed through a number of the four stages of martial arts training on the way to mastery. The first of these stages is called *gi*, or the stage of technique; this is followed by *jutsu*, or skill; the third stage is *gei*, or art; the final stage is *do*, or the Way itself. Arakawa-san believed that I had attained the third stage of *gei* just before the Way. And because of that, he believed that he had given me what he could.

"Musashi said that he looked up to the gods and Buddha but that he would never rely on them. That is what I mean by your sharing his capacity. Musashi led the life of a swordsman."

What Arakawa-san was really telling me in praising me was that our work together on a daily basis had come to an end.

Chapter Ten

I began the 1965 season as if I had learned nothing. I was very confident in my abilities, and as a result I did not use my time away from Arakawa-san all too well. At the beginning of the season, I had a stretch in which I failed to hit in thirty-five consecutive at-bats, the longest hitless streak I ever experienced as a professional. Fortunately, even though Arakawa-san and I were no longer working together on a daily basis, he was still the team's batting coach. I went to his house, asked his forgiveness, and resumed training with him until I was concentrated again.

Although I could not really agree with Arakawa-san that I had attained *gei*, or art, I believe I had actually accomplished *jutsu* in our work. While maintaining consistency would always present a problem to me—as to any professional athlete—I had come to believe that at least in terms of acquiring skills I could now begin to work on my own. My challenge, though, had become, without my ever seeking it, much broader. As my performance improved, my standing on the team changed. I was no longer a player with interesting possibilities, still in the shadows. I was a prominent player now, if not as popular as Nagashima-san, one on whom the team depended as much for performance.

While this new challenge to be a leader seemed at odds with any private desire to perfect skills, it was actually not the case. Yes, my goal was to do with records what Nagashima-san couldn't. But things were never quite that simple. I realize now, almost a quarter of a century after I first met him, that after Arakawa-san there was no more important person in my baseball life than Nagashima-san. I believe he is a key to what I evolved into as a player.

And yet he was as far from me as Arakawa-san was close.

To this day, I wonder who he really was.

My own answers are now, as then, so limited, my questions, even today, so active. Learning to play *with* him was everything.

Shigeo Nagashima was a kind of baseball genius who comes along once in a lifetime. Though I spent almost a quarter century as his teammate, it is difficult even now to talk about him. I am not sure I ever knew him.

If I were merely to mention his records, it would say a great deal. Nagashima-san joined the Giants a year before I did, the "Golden Boy" of the Tokyo Big Six university circuit, where in one season he compiled the second-highest batting average in the history of collegiate baseball. He was an instant star, a dominant player from the day he put on a Giants' uniform. In his professional career that followed, he succeeded in winning six batting titles, five RBI titles, and the home-run crown twice. He was the league's Most Valuable Player five times, a perennial all-star selection at third base, a lifetime .305 hitter who hit 444 career home runs. And yet records don't begin to tell the story of this very strange and wonderful player.

I have always believed from the day I first met him in Tokyo Station that Nagashima-san had a "mysterious part" that accounted for the tremendous hold he had on the imaginations of people in our country. It is this part that makes me think he had genius as well as great talent. With it, Nagashima-san revolutionized our game.

The best way I can think of to describe this "mysterious

part" is to recall the oneness he had with fans and players alike. Nagashima-san was the kind of player who seemed genuinely to depend on the support of fans. When the game was on the line and the fans were wild for a hit, he always seemed to rise to the occasion. It was as though he allowed the fans to lift the level of his game. If ever he was in a slump, everyone in the park would be aware of it; there was a way Nagashima-san carried himself that seemed to draw everyone into his own trouble, so that there might be help and comfort to get him through.

Nagashima-san had the ability to make a routine play look like a great one and a great one merely routine. If the fans seemed to hang on his every move, he seemed always to be perfectly tuned to what they were feeling. If they wanted to roar with approval—he would provide them with a moment; if they wanted to laugh—he would find a way; if they needed, somehow, as a collective body, to express the poignancy of things—he would concentrate that longing and draw it into his own person.

A genius, it is often said, usually has a side that is quirky and arrogant. This was not the case with Nagashima-san. He was the most natural of men, a hard worker and easy-going at the same time. Emotional to the point of seeming almost dependent, he always had a way of being totally captivating. With reporters and the media, he always had the right words to go with looks that everyone agreed were handsome and dashing. In the clubhouse he did little things that seemed invariably to endear himself to his teammates. Sometimes he would put two socks on the same foot or start to the field wearing someone else's uniform shirt— and hence someone else's name—on his back. He always did these things in such a way that everyone knew they were happening. There were explosions of affection and emotion around him wherever he went.

But in spite of all this we were never close. In the twenty-five years we have known each other, we never spent a social evening together. We never had a drink together, save at an official function. We never had a heart-to-heart talk about anything.

I believe some of this undoubtedly had to do with the differences in our personalities. As outgoing as Nagashima-san was, I was inclined to stay within myself. As easy as he found it to say the right things in public, I found it difficult. Where Nagashima-san seemed to love the stir around him, I wanted to be seen only for what I did on the field. I sometimes appreciated the fact that baseball caps had long bills, because there were days when I came to the ball park not wanting my face to be seen.

A team of course is composed of different individuals. There is no need for teammates to be friends; in fact, there is something about being teammates that can make friendship not especially desirable. It is hard, for example, to be perfectly objective with a friend. But the fact that Nagashima-san and I were so different, and yet were so prominent on the same team, gave rise to speculation that we did not get along. This was never the case.

In my first years with the Giants, whatever differences there were in personality between us simply did not matter. He was a star, *the* star, and I was a very ordinary, struggling player, barely able to hold on to a starting position. But beginning in 1963, when I won the home-run title for the first time, my position on the team began to change. Then what we did in tandem became as much a part of the Giants' story in these years as what we did individually. Together, as the "O-N Cannon," we hit home runs in the same game 106 times. With Nagashima-san hitting from the right side and me from the left, we were an extremely potent combination. Beginning in 1965 and going through 1973, the Giants won nine consecutive pennants and Japan Series championships, a feat unparalleled in professional sports anywhere. Nagashima-san and I were a pair throughout.

There is a saying in Japanese: *"Ryou yu narabi tatazu* [Two heroes cannot coexist]." Over the years, feeling between myself and Nagashima-san grew more remote. It is said that brothers sometimes fight bitterly. Nagashima-san and I never argued in even the slightest way—because we were so distant from one another. In a sense, we did become rivals. But the term may be misunderstood. We were not like Musashi and Kojiro, for example, who were predestined to fight each other to the death. We were also teammates, great teammates even as we were rivals.

Nagashima-san and I sometimes played golf together, not as two friends, but as members of the same organization on company-sponsored outings. When we played in the same group on the fairway, we invariably bet on the outcome between the two of us. We bet on the overall match, on each individual hole, and double or nothing on one selected hole, often the ninth. We barely spoke as we played, and each of us played to win.

Sometimes we played Mah-Jongg in the same group (Mah-Jongg, by the way, is the favorite game of Japanese baseball players on the road). I occasionally got by because my abacus training enabled me to rapidly handle numbers in my head. Nagashima-san was not so good at Mah-Jongg.

I never knew what to call Nagashima-san. In a way, the different names I used for him at different times are a kind of capsule history of our relationship. When I was a rookie with the Giants, he was so commanding a figure that it was completely inappropriate to use any sort of informal address with him (at least so I thought). Later, as our positions more nearly evened out, I began to call him "Cho-san," as everyone else did (this was a play on his family name and thus became a nickname). Then he was, to everyone, "Mr. Giants." Later, when he became manager of the team, the remoteness between us was pronounced enough so that I could refer to him only by title, "Mr. Manager." Today, he is Nagashima-san only.

Nagashima-san was the first person in Japanese professional baseball who believed the sport was really for the fans. And in his manner, he made over our game. When he took ground balls, for example, he would be sure to step forward, right into the ball, always aware of the fans. Making a difficult play look easy was something he consciously tried for. And as the fans craved it, so he was able to do really showy things with balls that were easy to play. I am not making light of this at all. Nagashima-san was, in his way, teaching us something about the difference between our game and American major league baseball. Until Nagashima-san, we thought of baseball as somehow for the players. Even the design of our stadiums reflected this, the fields always being laid out with the sun at the players' backs but in the fans' eyes. In America, where the game is more for the fans, the layout of most fields is the opposite, with the players having to fight the sun while the fans are given all comfort in viewing the game. Where did Nagashima-san, who did not play in America, learn all this? It was inborn. The world of baseball is a world of power. But Nagashima-san had something beyond power—this mysterious part, which compelled people to him and which, in my envy and admiration, I think of in glamorous terms.

Nagashima-san once said baseball was a game for sunlight. In my heart, I took exception to this, and it became a point through which I could chance my rivalry within teamwork. Baseball, for me, was a game for good and bad weather, demanding equal devotion in rain and cold and darkness, in the dog days of August and the hand-numbing days of March. If the only answer I had to Nagashima-san's popularity was records, it would not be one but many. This or that single accomplishment would never change anything. What I could do, out of my own nature, was to play not for a day or a season but inning by inning, as hard as I could, under any and all conditions, till I was forty years old or beyond.

Change came very slowly for me, playing day in and day out in the only way I knew. While we did not win the pennant in 1964, we did win in '65—and the Japan Series afterward—the first of our so-called "V-9" record. The year before, when we had failed to win, I remember going into a bar in Shinjuku, and some of the patrons there commiserated with me, even though I had just had the very best year of my life:

"Oh-san, please be sure you help the Giants win next year so you can be Japan Series winners," one of the patrons said.

"Next year, Oh-san. Please make sure next year!"

Of course they were right. Something was missing even though I had made a big record—and it didn't have to do principally with Nagashima-san's wedding or the outcome of the Tokyo Olympics!

In 1965 winning turned out to be far better than losing, but the year was very difficult for me. I did not yet fully appreciate that records and team play were not necessarily at odds.

In early July I suffered one of the only serious injuries of my career—a severe spike wound of the right leg that required hospitalization. Strangely enough, the injury occurred when I collided at third base with my old Sojitsu team captain, Mr. Tokutake, who was now a member of the Sankei Swallows. I did not miss many games, because the all-star break was coming up, but I played in pain for the rest of the year, the only such extended period in my career. Through the late summer and early fall, I was hitting as I had the previous year. Only now, for the first time, even though the Giants were winning the pennant, I had an outside chance to win a Triple Crown. Pain did not matter. I was leading the league in homers and RBIs, but marginally trailing Mr. Etoh of the Dragons for top hitter. Day after day through late September, the race between us tightened, so that on alternate days, even individual times at bat, we seesawed back and forth between leader and runner-up. The race got to me. I knew I was a power hitter, but I had never before been so convinced that I might win a hitting title. The Dragons, at this late stage in the season, played mostly day games, while we still played most of our games at night. So I knew what Mr. Etoh had done each day when I showed up at the ball park. The more certain it appeared that the pennant was ours, the more the race for the batting title weighed on me. I found that I could not sleep at night.

Mr. Etoh, too, I am told, suffered from our desperate race. Something of an odd fellow, the reports were that he used to walk the streets of Nagoya at night in a traditional kimono (kimonos are normally worn in public only on very special occasions), frequenting bars and drinking a lot. Nevertheless, Mr. Etoh won the competition between us. But the result was that my baseball hunger now included a big craving to add a batting title to any other records I might set. Two years later, Mr. Etoh, along with Mr. Naka of the Dragons, engaged me in a three-way duel for the title. The pressures again were awful. The race—I finished third this time—was not decided until the final day. It was only in the following year, when my chief competitor was Nagashima-san, that I finally won my first batting title. How ironic! Nagashima-san, who strove just as hard, sustained a serious injury to his left elbow in the midst of our competition, enabling me to win. I did not care that I had won by default. I was exultant, doubly so in that my first batting title came in a race with him!

In our run for V-9, there is no doubt that our manager, Mr. Kawakami, played a crucial role. I believe that very often we tend to place too much emphasis on what a manager can and cannot do. If a manager has talented players, he should do well; if he has poor players, he will likewise be bound by their performance. Mr. Kawakami, though, was undoubtedly the right man at the right time. Our team, through these years, was remarkably talented. We had powerful pitching led by Masaichi Kaneda, Kunio Jonouchi, and later Tsuneo Horiuchi. We had a bullpen ace named Miyata who was as regular as clockwork. In fact, his late-inning heroics in many games earned him the popular nickname "Eight-thirty Man" (our games, starting earlier than night games in America, are usually over by nine o'clock). Our defense was exceptional. Mr. Mori was a first-rate catcher. Mr. Kuroe at short and Mr. Doi at second were a great double-play combination, fierce competitors both, tireless workers. Mr. Shibata in center added tremendous speed both defensively and offensively. He was our one authentic base stealer, and his show was wonderful to watch. Whenever he reached first base, out came this bright red glove, which he slowly pulled onto his hand. Fans loved it, and opposing pitchers became unsettled at the sight of it! Mr. Takata, in left, literally created a whole new style of defensive play, using tremendous throwing power with a really aggressive understanding of the game to limit opposing teams' offensive tactics.

Nagashima-san and I, at the corners, were very reliable defensively as well as adding a power punch to the team. We were both physically larger than our teammates, and we were also able to use this advantage to the utmost. "O-N Cannon" gave us a decisive edge over other teams.

Mr. Kawakami knew his talent perfectly and used it fully by instilling in us a style of play that many people in our country named after him. "Kawakami baseball" was generally thought of as team-oriented rather than individual-oriented. But that really was not it. Of course Mr. Kawakami stressed harmony among us. He purified himself at a Buddhist retreat before he took over as manager. He did strongly emphasize that baseball was a game involving nine men rather than one. He stressed fundamentals such as bunting, moving runners along, correct positioning in fielding, and the like. And he backed up this approach with fines. If a player missed a sign from a coach, a fine of so many thousand yen; failure to run out a ball, so many more thousand; failure to sacrifice or bring in a runner from third with less than two out, you were poorer still. Mr. Kawakami was always a stern and exacting man.

But it was his approach to the game that distinguished him most. Play with greed for victory, he taught, and this he most peculiarly emphasized as an individual thing. One strove for the highest individual goals possible and did so relentlessly. There was never to be any letup, never any lowering of individual standards. We had an obligation to the team, but this obligation was best fulfilled by learning to use ourselves individually to the limit. When Mr. Kawakami taught us the correct strategy for defense against the sacrifice bunt, for example, he removed from our style of play the usual method of having the catcher signal to the charging fielders. He believed this dulled our aggressive defensive thinking. I grew to love fielding against the bunt precisely because there was this keen mental involvement in the action. In a completely different vein, he once confronted me toward the end of one season when I had grown tired and wanted more than anything to rest. Mr. Kawakami came to my house and spoke to me quietly but firmly:

"It's true there are only a few games left," he said, "but it is still your obligation to do your very best. This is the only correct attitude toward the fans. Your training of today won't necessarily produce good results tomorrow, but it is your obligation as a professional nevertheless. Because of who you are, your goals are the highest. So is your responsibility. Do the training."

Mr. Kawakami was not a "nice" man in the usual sense. Normally, his way was to have a team meeting when there were things on his mind. His desire for victory was the constant goal, and his focus was how fully each individual player was contributing even when there were no individual goals left for the season. He would scold anyone at any time. There was just this standard: that it be effective. Thus, when he spoke to me in private, it was because he knew that my nature would better take hard words that way. He scolded Nagashima-san, too, but nearly always in the clubhouse in full earshot of other players. With Nagashima-san, that was the most effective way. Other players could see that even a great star like Nagashima-san had to answer to the same demands as anyone else. Such clubhouse scolding never left any bad feeling—just as there was never resentment on my part at being spoken to so deeply in private. In both instances Mr. Kawakami, understanding the difference in our characters, demanded the same thing of us: that our advantage in individual talent be used always for the team. The rivalry between us was offset by a demand for leadership for which we both assumed responsibility.

I am at a loss, really, to speak of leadership, because it is such an individual thing. Nagashima-san and I led in very different ways, and I cannot honestly speak for him. But for myself, I perceived this in the way my role within the team changed over time. There was an incident in June 1968 that illustrated this very well. We were in Nagoya in the midst of a road trip, and we were not doing well. On this particular day we happened to have been rained out. The weather was uncomfortable, and with our fortunes dragging, everyone was feeling listless and dull. Nagashima-san and I decided to call a meeting to see if we couldn't lift our teammates' spirits. This led to the only time in my professional life when I hit another player.

We encouraged each other at this meeting to do our best. This applied as much to what we did off the field as on. To get back a good style of play we would have to make sure our condition was good. As we were grown men, we could not lay down humiliating rules beyond collectively promising to exercise self-control and to obey the curfew at night. This was enough.

A few people went out that night, among them, the young and superb pitcher Tsuneo Horiuchi. Aside from being a fine pitcher, he also had "a reputation." Many people thought he was cocky and arrogant and went out of his way to deliberately ruffle the feathers of his seniors. Yes, as I well knew, young people sometimes adjust in their own peculiar ways, but that was not the point. Horiuchi indeed returned that night before curfew—just before. In fact, he made a point of shouting when he entered the inn, "Here I am, I'm back, see! Made it in before curfew, you'll notice!" If we had been staying in a Western-style hotel, as we sometimes do these days, what followed might never have taken place. But we were in a *ryokan*, a Japanese-style inn, where there is no real privacy, where sliding doors and panels, none of them with locks, permit people to go from one area to another without inhibition or restraint. It is a building whose traditional design accommodates the very traditional sense our people have of belonging to a group. In such a setting, there are many verses but only one poem. At any rate, Horiuchi's shouting carried everywhere in the building.

If he had gone straight to his room, there most probably would have been no incident. But he stopped at a phone booth and made a call. The call went on and on. His voice throughout remained loud, sometimes assuming an affected and provocative tone, as though he was letting everyone within earshot know—which was everyone in the inn—that he didn't give a damn what people thought. At one point someone made a derisive clacking noise with his tongue. The atmosphere in the house had grown very tense, very negative.

My roommate and friend, Mr. Kunimatsu, got up and started to go downstairs to intercede. I stopped him. Mr. Kunimatsu was a coach, and I remembered an incident of a coach being forced to resign because he hit a player on his team. I could not allow this to happen.

"I'll go," I said. I went downstairs and waited by the phone booth as Horiuchi continued talking. We exchanged glances, but he was in no way feeling constrained. As I stood there, I felt I knew something about Horiuchi. He was a young player, and he already was an accomplished one. He knew what many young players had a hard time learning—how to win. He knew the world of baseball was a world of power, and he lived within this world as though nothing else existed. It was as though the notion that baseball games are also played by teams had never crossed his mind. So long as he could win, the rest be damned.

Horiuchi was too young to understand what he was doing. His manner and his look were disdainful. He had no thought whatever about his "bad" reputation. I waited and waited for him to finish his call. When he finally put down the receiver, I grabbed him by the lapels and dragged him to a large vacant room. This was a traditional tatami-mat dining room, and I remember a large table in a corner of the room reflecting a cold light off its highly polished surface.

I punched Horiuchi in the face as hard as I could. I did not stop. I assumed I was in control, but I was not. It was as though the pent-up fury of a lifetime was bursting forth. I pounded Horiuchi over and over again, oblivious to what I was doing. I had no feeling in my hands.

"He hit me so hard, I went backward in the air for over a meter," Horiuchi said later, but I have no memory at all of this. Nor do I remember how many times I hit him. I just know that I blindly beat him with all my might, blow upon blow, until he was crouching and whimpering on the tatami floor.

When I returned to my senses, I saw him there. I sat on a low table and glared at him, my eyes filled with tears. His face was bruised and misshapen.

"Do you understand why I beat you?" I said.

I beat him in order to convey my wish that he awaken. I wanted him above all to understand what I meant. He understood. How do I know? I revealed this story years later at a party in honor of Horiuchi's 200th big-league win. As he was the only person I had ever struck in such a manner, I watched him carefully as I spoke. He looked glad listening to my speech.

I want to add something here. I have no wish to be mis-understood. I consider myself a peaceful man. I don't look for fights, and I will go far out of my way to avoid them. But I have strong feelings about using one's fists. I have no guilt over what I did.

No one, except those with mental disorders, likes to beat

people. But people today are far too sensitive to the whole subject. There is a confusion in many quarters between beating someone to correct him and mere violence. When a person who has a responsibility to guide others becomes too sensitive or too confused about this, there is a strong chance that he will either refrain from beating or else do so with more ego than desire to correct. To hit someone without responsibility for them or with the single desire of injury is bestial and unforgivable. I hesitate to describe the kind of beating I gave Horiuchi as a "whip of love," but I believe such a term exists. My father used it once, I grew up with it in school, and it has been a bond between myself and others. If there is strong belief and genuine concern for another, it is possible to knock him down in order to make him stand up.

Times are changing; there is both more violence and more timidity in our world. There is growing danger of destruction and less concern for our fellow man. I will say it in the strongest terms I can: you have no right to hit another unless your feelings are so deep and your understanding so clearheaded that you actually know what you are doing. At any rate, I cannot imagine that I would have done such a thing in my first years with the Giants.

The Giants and I prospered together. In '65 and '66, after we won the Central League pennant, we went on to defeat the Nankai Hawks in the Japan Series. Through the rest of V-9—except for that final year when we again beat the Hawks—our fall opponent was the Hankyu Braves. In '73 we won the pennant on the final day, a thrill for all of us because the game meant the pennant for whichever team won. For the most part, we were simply unchallenged. We took the field knowing we were going to win. Other teams did not. Whatever advantage we had in talent, we also possessed the kind of confidence as a collective unit that separated us from everyone else.

Nicknames, gossip, publicity, popularity were never things I could control. But I could make records. That was always my answer. In each of these years I won the home-run title and the title for most walks, most intentional walks, most runs scored; except for those three years when I was chasing a batting title, I led in RBIs and total bases, too. And then, finally, in '73, the last of V-9, what I had been shooting for for six years came about—Triple Crown! How sweet that was! In fact, it was so sweet, I did not want to let it go. In '74, when our streak was broken, I set my sights on the Triple Crown again. There had been only one Triple Crown winner before me in Japanese baseball, and no one anywhere had ever won it back to back. While our team slowed, I pushed on. When I looked up, I had my second straight Triple Crown! Also, when I looked up, I saw Nagashima-san suddenly at the end of his playing days. Within one year of V-9, his wonderful skills seemed to desert him. The baseball story of 1974, according to a poll of newspapers, was not my winning the Triple Crown in successive seasons, but Nagashima-san's retirement.

There had never been anything like it. On the final day of the season, 55,000 people jammed Korakuen to say good-bye. And Nagashima-san responded by hitting two home runs against the Dragons. His play, from the first moment he trotted out on the field to the last moment of the game, was full of joy. He was presented with a bouquet of flowers, and with tears streaming down his face and nearly everyone else freely weeping as well, he said good-bye, urging everyone to continue supporting his team. Who could not have been moved? Even as I knew that more responsibility would now come my way, even though I sensed two Triple Crowns obscured in this moment, I wept, too.

Actually, it no longer mattered that Nagashima-san was—or was not—a rival. There was no contest with him. There had been none for years. I had long since come to understand that performance was the only measure of myself I had as a professional. My standard of competition was not set by Nagashima-san but by myself—and, of course, by

Arakawa-san. The goal he set for me, the thinking he demanded from me had, for years, reached across the Pacific. One year (1967) we spent some weeks in spring training at Dodgertown in Vero Beach, Florida. The previous autumn the Dodgers had toured Japan, and we had done quite well against them in our exhibitions. There was a period in that tour when I hit home runs in four consecutive at-bats in two games. On this one spring day the Atlanta Braves were in town, and Arakawa-san took Nagashima-san and me to the visitors' clubhouse to meet Hank Aaron. At that point Aaron had not surpassed Ruth's record, but he was the premier home-run hitter in all of baseball. He had over 440 home runs and was still clearly in his prime, and there was certainly talk that the career home-run record might be within his reach. We discussed some technical points on hitting. (Arakawa-san was most interested in knowing how he trained himself to wait. Aaron replied that he did so by measuring the pitcher's best fastball.) In the game that followed I had one at-bat and struck out. But by far the most memorable aspect of this experience was realizing that Aaron was not so big, physically. It therefore was not a massive body like Frank Howard's that enabled him to hit home runs. I was most impressed and said so to Arakawa-san, who all along had been maintaining that it was not size and strength that accounted for home-run hitting.

And what of Arakawa-san in this period? Though I had ceased to train with him on a daily basis at the end of the 1964 season, I still could call on him when I needed help. He was for me the support of 55,000. If my mind began to fill with thoughts and doubts, I needed only to reach out and say "teach me," and he would be there. If I could not figure out on my own what was going wrong in my batting form, he would be sure to pick it up for me. I had a habit of dropping my left shoulder, for example, that was almost impossible to detect on my own. Because he had watched me for so long, he knew the problem and would correct it by having me work hard on achieving a level hip movement during my swing. Arakawa-san was a friend as well as a teacher. He was all the while my guide and, quite literally, my protector, almost without my being aware of it. In the last weeks of the 1968 season, for example, we were in a struggle with the Tigers for the pennant. In mid-September we held a three-game lead over the Tigers and arrived in Osaka for a four-game series with them. The Tigers took the first two games of the series, so the third game was particularly intense. The Tiger pitcher that night was an American named Gene Bacque. Bacque, though he had been very tough on us in the past, was a friendly, joking sort, and I considered him my friend. While the game was still extremely close, Bacque had surrendered a solo home run, and again we mounted a threat by getting two runners on with no one out in the fourth inning. I came to bat. Now in Japanese baseball there is a custom that pitchers do not often throw "brush-back" pitches. A certain challenge—which a good batter will always adjust to—is minimized in our game because of this, but at any rate there is a difference between a brush-back pitch and deliberately trying to hit a batter—no matter what side of the Pacific you play on. Bacque, I think, was upset with himself. The first pitch he threw nearly took my kneecaps off. I dove to the ground, avoiding the pitch. The next pitch he threw sailed right under my chin, knocking me to the ground again. I was not angered by this, but I did think what Bacque was doing was foolish. I picked myself up and began walking toward the mound so I could have a talk with him. Before I got halfway there, both benches, in most uncharacteristic fashion, emptied. Players rushed the field. Leading the rush of our players was Arakawa-san! I couldn't believe it! Bacque was a huge, strapping fellow, and Arakawa-san barely came up to his chest, but there he was going for him like a small locomotive. Bacque threw a big, wild punch that bounced right off Arakawa-san's head. Players then seemed to engulf them both. When order was finally restored, Bacque walked off the field holding the thumb of his pitching hand, which, somehow, had been broken. Arakawa-san came away with a knowing gleam in his eye. As I walked back toward the dugout with him, I asked:

"What happened to Bacque?"

He smiled nastily. "Aikido!" he said between his teeth. My protector!

The following spring of 1969, Arakawa-san took me to visit Ueshiba Sensei on his deathbed. Our old Master had been ill with cancer for some time, and the hospital had let him go home to die. There was not much time left when we visited. We went to his house and *dojo* in Shinjuku once again. There was utmost quiet in the house now, and Ueshiba Sensei, lying motionless in his hard Japanese bed, was surrounded by several of his younger disciples. When we came to the bedside, room was made for us. Ueshiba Sensei's eyes were closed; he seemed to be asleep. But one of his disciples gently asked:

"Sensei, Sensei, do you know who is here?"

Sensei opened his eyes, which were very deep in his sunken face. He looked directly at me. There was a flicker of recognition.

"I understand," he whispered. He continued to stare at me. "You have good eyes," he said. Soon he seemed to be sleeping again, and we took our leave.

Arakawa-san—then and afterward—had a different memory of what had taken place. He was very moved and very thoughtful.

"Imagine that, Oh," he said, "Sensei telling you that you have the face of a Master." I was startled but said nothing.

"He saw this in your eyes, which always show the condition of the first mind. You see what power you have. In all the time I have known him, Sensei never once complimented me." There was no trace of envy in these words. In fact, he seemed satisfied in some deep way that was beyond the sadness he was feeling at the Sensei's impending death.

I believe Arakawa-san was still teaching me in that moment, though I did not quite know it. My position on the Giants had changed. I had gone from being a struggling young player to being a star to being a leader of my team to being a public man. Even more, through my struggle with Nagashima-san I had come to understand how important depending on myself really was and what a subtle but certain balance there was between what I personally achieved and what my team achieved.

I did not yet fully know what it meant to be on one's own. Nor did I really comprehend what it was to make myself useful to others. I was certainly full of my own power, young and strong. But beginning in 1971, I was forced to learn a new Way. One day, toward the end of the 1970 season, Arakawa-san came to me while we were on the road. His appearance was very somber. Even before he spoke, I felt something was wrong.

"I will resign," he said. Nothing more.

"When?" I asked. I was shocked.

"After this season." I waited for him to explain. Later I learned that his foster son was about to go into professional baseball with the Yakult Swallows and because of that Arakawa-san felt it would be a conflict of interest to actively work for an opposing team. Arakawa-san was shortly to accept an offer to manage the Swallows.

"Please stay," I said.

"I can't," he replied. That was the end of it. In my country a son does not ask explanations of his father.

The following season I truly was on my own for the first time in my life.

Chapter Eleven

It is a little peculiar to talk about "being on one's own" after so many years as a professional ballplayer. But I cannot think of a better term. At the beginning of the 1971 season I had certainly become a top player in Japanese baseball. Going into that season I had already hit 447 home runs, and Arakawa-san's early talk about beating Babe Ruth no longer seemed crazy to me or anyone else. I was not yet thirty years old, my health was excellent, and, barring serious injury, the best years of my professional life lay ahead. But when Arakawa-san left the Giants, I wondered what would happen. I had become a very public person, my face was known everywhere in Japan, and yet here I was feeling vulnerable and alone, a little like being a rookie again.

I have been asked many times over what kind of an effect public life has had on me. I wish there were an easy answer to give, but the only thing certain is the knowledge that you remain the same person—even if you are tempted to think otherwise. There are many ways in which having a public position affected me, for good and bad, but the most important was in having to deal with intensely personal and private matters out in the open. I was married at the end of 1966, for example, and many people aside from my bride and myself and our families had to be taken into account. The marriage of a prominent baseball player is a public event, and so the interests of the press, the Yomiuri organization (owners of the Giants), the Overseas Chinese Organization, all had to be considered. We were married in Meiji Jingu Shrine. There were over a thousand guests and a hundred reporters, and there were speeches from the Taiwanese ambassador and others not normally associated with private weddings. Mr. Kawakami, responsible for the well-being of his team, had important words to offer a player's bride:

"Please take good care of your husband's health so that he can work in good shape and be free of worry. At least make sure he doesn't get sick. Please take care of your own health, too. And last, make sure you are in good condition when you welcome your husband home. This is important."

For Kyoko and me, the matter was how to be with each other, not such an easy thing given who I was. Baseball was my life, though it was not hers. I was a Chinese and she was not. When my family formally proposed to hers, they asked if Kyoko would accept Chinese nationality—this was necessary. She and her family accepted. There was the matter of a press conference. The year before, when Nagashima-san was married, reporters trying to get an advantage over each other in filing stories handled matters badly. We announced our engagement two days earlier than we had planned, because we learned that one of the papers had gotten a scoop on the others. Kyoko had a pimple on her face at the time and was reluctant to appear in public, but she did nevertheless.

We fought a great deal in our early years together, though we loved one another and were good friends. Perhaps the public demands of the baseball world helped, because I think they enabled Kyoko to withstand more than she might have otherwise. She often referred to me as her "fourth child," because when I got home I demanded everything and could give little. I used to lie around the house naked as though paralyzed when all I really sought was to be briefly free of the pressures I lived with every day in the public world. If ever Kyoko was sick, or the children, or even myself, I could not remain at home. No room in the world of baseball as in ordinary life for such things. The overriding demand on a baseball player is that he give himself to the game, every day, one hundred percent. No other way. So, always, there was this dual phenomenon. Public pressure helped me as a baseball player; it actually became something I could use to help discipline myself. At the same time, it made a normal private life almost impossible.

Losing Arakawa-san was one thing, but losing him and being so prominent in the public eye was quite another. There could be no replacing him—one doesn't go from master to master. There was no one who knew me as a player as he did. In such circumstances I had to rely on myself, even if I could not figure out what had gone wrong. And things did go wrong. In 1971, my first season without Arakawa-san, though the Giants continued to dominate, I began to have my problems. I could not hit. Not as I had, at any rate. By mid-season, a slump of a few days became a slump of weeks and then months.

I had my own methods for getting out of slumps—and I employed them. I stood on my head, because that is a good position in which to restore proper circulation and clear thinking; I had a special bat drill in which I would hold my breath and take thirty very hard swings in succession—this fires the senses and raises energy. Likewise, I performed *kiai*, a method of shouting taught in many of the Zen martial arts; this is a technique that both aids energy and instills a renewed desire for victory. And most of all, I hit. I took additional batting practice over and over again. I trained every day on my own to make sure my pose was secure and my swing correct. I went to Tamagawa in the morning and worked there for a couple of hours before going to the ball park early in the afternoon to resume training for the evening.

In spite of poor results, I was determined to see this through. It did not matter to me that I had to make these efforts in the midst of crowds and media. The spirit of challenge is the same in the company of a thousand or one. To maintain this spirit you ask the inevitable question— "Why?" This is silent, never to be overheard. It seals you in the privacy of effort.

Why am I not hitting?

Why don't I make correct contact?

Why can't I further enhance my energy?

Do I lead a regular life?

Did I do this halfway?

"Halfway." The most hated word I know and yet so helpful, because "halfway" is not something you can discover at the end of a question. It is a whisper from the invisible world, the urging of the "other." "Halfway" must be challenged always.

Many observers of baseball say that you have to be hungry to play it. I asked myself if I was really hungry enough. It was true that financially I was no longer in need. My family was in good circumstances now. I was certainly not hungry financially. But I *was* very, very hungry for skill. Then the crucial question became:

Why do you do this?

Because I am hungry for skill!

I kept a bat and notebook at my bedside so that if I came out of sleep with an idea, I could practice it and then write it down. I also got in the habit of simply writing to myself to raise my spirits, as I was the one I had to depend on. It was then that I wrote about slumps and drinking, because I was determined to get out of my slump by making progress rather than by relaxing. On another page, I wrote:

"You are the number-one specialist at what you do in Japan, aren't you? Do you think you can keep up the position of number one doing the same thing other players do? Have there ever been specialists at anything who have been able to keep up without making extraordinary efforts?"

I was shocked that I could fall into a slump like this when my confidence was basically high, so all I could do was trust to effort and whatever time it would take.

I did not finish the year well. I hit .276, the first time since 1962 that I had been under .300, and I finished with thirty-nine home runs, enough to win the title again but the fewest, again, since my first year of training with Arakawa-san.

There was no one I could really share any of this with. On September 15 of that year, we were at Koshien Stadium playing our twenty-fourth game of the year against the Tigers. The Tiger pitcher, Yutaka Enatsu, was a fireballer. I had a hard time handling him in even the best circumstances. This day, he struck me out on my first three appearances at the plate. In the ninth inning, we were losing 2–0 when I came to bat for the last time. There were two men on and two out. When I reached the batter's box, the crowd, many of them filing toward the exits, responded with friendly laughter and a good deal of sympathy. What I was facing was a foregone conclusion. Enatsu stared in. He looked as enormous as if he had been leaning on me. Something gave way inside. I did not want to be sympathized with. When fans offer sympathy to a player, his day is over. Better "Sanshin Oh!" than this, I thought, and damn it anyway, where are they going? The game isn't over yet! Enatsu worked the count full by throwing a wild pitch, allowing the runners on first and second to move up a base each. His 3–2 pitch was a crowding fastball. I was ready for it and pulled it down the line in right into the first rows of seats. When I circled the bases, it was the only time in my career I ever wept over a home run I had hit. This home run, made in the worst of conditions, turned the game from defeat to victory and for me was a proof I ached for about the value of effort. I did not know it at the time, but at that moment I had reached the other side of my trouble.

There is a puzzling aspect to this period, concerning my relationship with Arakawa-san. He, of course, had not gone to another planet. He was the manager of a rival team also centered in Tokyo. Our paths crossed frequently, usually on the playing field, and sometimes, after a game, we went out together. I did well against the Swallows. Arakawa-san always maintained I did too well. At any rate, we limited our get-togethers to an after-game drink or two when we both were in the same place at the same time. I could not presume on him for more, and yet I never lost the sense that I owed him everything, because what I was as a hitter was what he had made me. He must have known what I was going through by seeing me at the plate—or at least by reading the daily batting statistics. Still, we joked and had good times, never discussing our changed relationship.

"How come you always hit home runs against the Swallows? Are you looking to cost me my job?" he kidded.

"I need all the hits I can get. Please forgive me."

Arakawa-san surely knew what I wished for—to have him at my side again. And I believe that he had very mixed feelings about no longer being able to coach me. Still, he could go no further than ethics and a sense of honor would permit. I could never presume on this.

One day, though, when we were scheduled to play the Swallows, I injured myself in practice. I twisted my knee, and it began to swell hours before game time. Word had spread, apparently, that I was in trouble and would not play that night. But I was in the throes of my slump and therefore in the midst of fully coming to appreciate what persistent mind meant. I was not about to sit down. I played that night and hit two home runs, but I went home directly afterward. I showed my wife what had happened and then went to get some rest. I did not know whether my injury was going to be serious or not.

Sometime after midnight, the doorbell rang. This was

certainly a strange time for anyone to be calling, but stranger still was the sight at the door. It was Arakawa-san carrying a small package wrapped in brown paper. I was dumbfounded.

"You, here! What a surprise!"

Kyoko stood in the background.

"I heard the rumor that you injured your knee. And even though you hit two home runs against us, I can't help wanting to keep you intact for better things. I brought you some horsemeat!"

"Come in, Dad," Kyoko said.

Horsemeat was an old peasant remedy for inflammations of any sort, and by its daily application a quick reduction in swelling was supposed to occur. Arakawa-san assured me of that, anyway. My injury would take a week at the very least to heal, and the prospect of missing a few games seemed inevitable. I followed his advice and applied the horsemeat that night and the next. To my surprise, my knee responded almost immediately. I missed no games at all, and in less than a week the swelling was gone completely. But how Arakawa-san had so accurately been able to define my condition has remained a mystery to me, though he swears there was nothing mysterious at all about it. Even more mysterious was how he came to get horsemeat at that time of night. "How did you do this?" I asked. "Woke up a butcher," was all he answered. Most important of all, he had signaled yet another change in our relationship. With this gift of speedy recovery, he had distinguished between me and the team I played for.

I eventually broke my slump, but in the very worst moments I thereafter met with Arakawa-san secretly, and he reviewed my work. We went through the seven steps of my form—fighting spirit, stance, grip, backswing, stride forward, downswing, impact—taking them apart and putting them together again. In each aspect, the little unnoticeable things that might have escaped my attention, Arakawa-san watched for, too. It was only a matter of time.

I was on my own then. And I had made it.

But Arakawa-san will always be my teacher.

When I came out of this almost year-long slump, in 1972, two important changes had taken place. One was that I played with a kind of steady fighting spirit that was stronger than ever before. The other was that Arakawa-san was no longer the manager of the Swallows. I learned one day when we played in Osaka that he had lost his job. This was most upsetting. But there is in my country an almost pathological fear of humiliation. To humiliate another is simply not tolerable, and so face-saving becomes part of the daily bread of our lives. If someone is fired from a job, a most humiliating turn of events, he is usually allowed to resign or go "on vacation." This was not the case with Arakawa-san. So our method of saving face became lightheartedness in which each of us kept from the other knowledge we both possessed. I called him immediately after I heard the news.

"Hello, Arakawa-san?"

"Yes, it's me."

"It's true you've lost your job?"

"Quite true."

"Congratulations! Now we'll be able to consult much more often!"

"Just what I needed to hear," he said. "If you hadn't hit so many goddamned home runs against the Swallows, I'd probably still be working."

I called my wife right afterward and told her what had happened. I wished I could have felt only sadness, but I was also truly happy that we would again be able to meet openly.

"Darling," I said to my wife, "have some *sushi* delivered to the Arakawa-sans. The very best ones, mind you."

I know Arakawa-san will forgive me any small selfishness in this. If it had not been for him, I would never have hit 868 home runs. He was the first person I phoned to thank when I broke Babe Ruth's and Hank Aaron's records.

On June 6, 1972, I hit my 499th and 500th home runs in Hiroshima against the Carp. By year's end I had added thirty-four more home runs, and at the end of the 1973 season, the year of my first Triple Crown, I was at 585, fifteen shy of being the first player in Japanese baseball to reach the 600 home-run mark. I no longer needed anyone to encourage me to think of records that were unattainable. All of Japan, it seemed, from high politicians to humblest rural people, knew where I stood—and knew, also, where Hank Aaron stood. At season's end, I was 130 home runs away from breaking Babe Ruth's record, but Hank Aaron was just two away.

My 600th home run came on a rainy night in May, the following year, against the Hanshin Tigers in Koshien Stadium, my old stamping grounds. By then Aaron had surpassed Ruth's record, and, as everyone let me know, the achievement of being the first to hit 600 home runs in Japan was a stop along the way. I knew as much, too. I was surely excited by what I had done, caught up in the fans' excitement.

"I'm going after eight hundred," I said then, feeling sure that if I remained healthy, it was within my reach. But there was something else I wanted to say, too, so that people might not get so excited about false displays of strength and love of power for their own sake.

"I don't necessarily have stronger arms than other players," I told one newspaper, "I've just learned to put my weight on the ball better than others." This was the simplest way I could put it.

In everything I did now I was visible. My ordinary comings and goings were reported on. What I said seemed almost as important as what I did.

Musashi's fame as a swordsman increased with each challenge he met and overcame. His incomparable spirit led to his technique, and his technique led him to fame. He became known from Edo to Kyushu, admired by shoguns and envied by rivals. But his way permitted him to remain withdrawn. He deliberately stayed away from the limelight, and he became known as something of an eccentric, preferring the life of a hermit to life in the court. For Musashi, this was quite acceptable, because it in no way interfered with his singleminded quest for perfection as a swordsman.

No professional baseball player can follow Musashi in this manner. The most reticent player, he who would take a vow of public silence, still does his work in the limelight, out in the open. Whether he wants to be or not, he is a public performer, and prominence in his craft means that the public will be with him wherever he goes. His private life will grow smaller with each feat of accomplishment.

I make no quarrel with this. It would be like complaining that blossoms come with trees. But learning to understand what this public dimension is, it turns out, is also a technical problem. A baseball player's life can be enhanced or ruined by the manner in which he handles public pressure. He must learn to use it rather than have it take him over. It is not easy.

The most obvious limitation of public life is the loss of privacy it brings.

As a public man I have certain obligations and certain boundaries. My family and I cannot be as free as we wish— even my children. Because I am away so much of the time, my three daughters have come to regard my times at home as special occasions. Our natural relationship is made into something of a treat—very nice because we can use so many hours in a row just to play. When my daughters were young enough, I'm sure I was the strongest and most willing horse-on-all-fours any children had. But sometimes my children wouldn't know me. When they finally began to watch me on TV, they saw someone other than their happy horse. My face in competition is dark and frightening. My children, not particularly understanding baseball, saw only this mask of a warrior that was their father. When I came home and wanted to play with them they held back. One day I picked one of my daughters up in my arms and she was frightened. For many years they were too young for explanations.

I have never been able to do things that others do easily every day. Everywhere I go in public, my face is known. I have never missed being able to go to turkish baths, for example, but I have always wanted to be able to go to ordinary public bars. There is an atmosphere that is warm and friendly about them. You can drink and sing and say good night with a light heart. I have always wanted that feeling. If ever I had walked into a public bar during this time in my life, I would only have caused a fuss and spoiled people's fun.

Once, at Christmastime, I was in an expensive bar in Ginza. I got a little high and put on a costume mask, a rather ridiculous-looking thing with a big nose, bushy eyebrows, and glasses. I suddenly realized that no one would recognize me in this, so I left the place with it on. I walked down a main street in Ginza, rubbing shoulders with people, exulting in this freedom of being able to walk where I wanted without at all having to be conscious of those around me.

There is only one real break from this public world that I have maintained over the years—and it means everything to me. Twice a year, once overnight, my old friends and teammates from Waseda Sojitsu get together. Sometimes there will be as many as forty-five or fifty who gather, a real school reunion; sometimes there will be many fewer. On our overnight meeting, we conspire to come together at an out-of-the-way *ryokan*. We arrive from many different directions, as anonymously as possible. Our names are already on the doors of the rooms we will be staying in. We are quickly out of our street dress and into *yukatas*, then a bath and dinner in our tatami dining room.

Once I reach the *ryokan* and draw on my *yukata*, I am no longer Oh of the world but just another fellow from Sojitsu. Sitting at dinner, we all are dressed and look the same. We are boyhood friends; we have nothing to prove and no airs or titles to explain. My old friends come from every walk of life. They bring with them many interests and many new things to talk about. We drink—and drink—and drink. We sing songs together, old *enka*, traditional Japanese songs, some funny, some sad, about common, everyday life. The following morning we play golf or walk in the countryside and take pictures like any ordinary group on an outing. The center of our party is always Mr. Iida, who years before was a reticent sort. But he has since acquired a wonderful flair for mimicry and singing, which we have all come to depend on.

Invariably, the high point of our drinking party gets down to one shared memory: the final extra-inning game we lost that kept us from going to Koshien. My friends all pick on me.

"You remember how that guy from Nichidaya-ku on Meiji hit a screwball off you?"

"How come you threw a goddamned screwball, what's the matter with you?"

"Had the game all wrapped up!"

"It was my best pitch."

"*Best* pitch?"

"Best pitch I could think of then!"

"But he hit it!"

"How come you threw him a goddamned screwball anyway?"

The public world of baseball both enlarges and limits one's contact with life. Because of baseball I have met people from all over the world, from many different backgrounds, whom otherwise I would never have known. But baseball is all-consuming. In twenty-two years there was not much time left over for other interests. I love music and tennis and books about Chinese and Japanese history, but I could only be cursory in my pursuit of them. My oldest daughters have begun using computers in school. I used to be good in math, but they are learning a language of math that is utterly bewildering to me, that seems to mark a hopeless generational line between their new world and my old one.

My everyday friendships really are not close as such but are confined to the socializing that is possible within the team. I prefer the company of senior members of the team, because to be with juniors means that I have to keep a caring eye out for them. Oh, we have our pleasures, we baseball players. But the point is, I suppose, that baseball is never far away.

The most difficult part of public life for me is relations with the press and media. I have nothing against them. They have a job to do, and no one can begrudge them that. Among them are many good acquaintances. But the tendency toward sensationalizing things is not healthy, and the power to create illusions is far too great. In order to make copy or to beat a deadline, stories will be filed that may have only marginal bearing on who people really are or what may have really happened. I suffered a good deal because of stories written about me and Nagashima-san, for example. I have also been portrayed in the media as someone I really am not. For years there has been a tendency to present me as some sort of saint. "Look at Oh-san," they say, "he's the model young people should follow. No one works like him, selfless to a fault, the epitome of one who gives all." I learned to work hard, that is true, but others in my profession do also. It is what we are paid for.

The press has told stories about how, when I had a bad year, I voluntarily went into the front office and asked for a pay cut! Well, not quite. I never asked to have my salary reduced. If I had a bad year, I took the attitude that I didn't deserve *more* for the following year, and I also took the position that I didn't want multiple-year contracts—not for any selfless wish to deprive myself but because I believe that making things too comfortable takes away the challenge. And everything I do, including salary talks, has only one goal—to keep my mind focused on the challenge.

Someone found out that I made visits to an orphanage in Hokkaido. Oh-san the saint again. Imagine this player with such a vast reputation going out of his way to visit poor unfortunates like that. Yes, I have visited this orphanage every year of my professional career, even when no one knew me. I visited at first because I believed it was important to follow my father's instructions and be helpful to others. I kept going back because I wanted to and because I knew the children looked forward to it. If I had been a .200 hitter, the press wouldn't have thought twice about it. Certainly, this had nothing to do with baseball. The only thing cameramen and writers accomplished by finding out about this was to make it harder for the children and me to play a game or two with each other before I left.

What you are in public and what you are in private can be very different. I have always been myself in public and have never wanted media or fans to take away an impression of me that was an illusion. My brother taught me very early to be discrete about revealing my feelings openly. I have ever since been careful about what I would and would not show in public. If I seem respectful of my opponents, it is because it is so; if I seem to care about my team, it is also true. But because I run the bases after a home run showing little emotion doesn't mean that I have effaced myself beyond feeling—I just keep things inside. If I go to the mound during a game to talk to the pitcher, it doesn't necessarily mean that I'm taking responsibility for lifting the spirits of my teammate. Sometimes I'll go there for the hell of it or because I'll observe that the pitcher is sweating too much from having taken too much water before the game—and I'll be there to yell at him for being a fool.

I care that the fans have a good impression of the game, and I also know that they like seeing only the ideal in their baseball heroes. This is a harmless need and really does not cost that much. It is much more important that fans and players have a bond between them that is mutually perceived and respected, because in it the game of baseball itself is preserved in a healthy state. My one quarrel with huge salaries in American baseball is not that players get paid too much (which may or may not be the case) but that fans become alienated in the process.

Appearances are as necessary in our game as they are in life. If everyone did absolutely as he wished, people would be wretched. In my country it is impossible to play just for oneself. Everyone wants to play that way—but you cannot show it. You play for the team, the country, for others. This sense of appearance is not false, even if it seems to go against individual feeling. Obligation also comes from feeling. If you go against this, you also go against yourself.

One last word on this subject. In terms of what I accomplished as a baseball player, public pressure has, in the end, been very beneficial. I think constant public attention made it easier for me to concentrate on baseball just because it limited all the other things I might have been doing. The eyes of the public, the standards of praise and shame always reflected there, gave "stronger one" an advantage over "weaker one" in my nature. Aside from whatever satisfactions of ego were involved—and there were those— public attention was something I learned to use, much as the sword and swinging card, to keep my eye better focused on the ball.

The end of the 1974 season was memorable for me in many ways. Most important was the second straight Triple Crown. But other things happened, too. Nagashima-san retired only to rejoin the Giants as manager following Mr. Kawakami's resignation. The end of 1974 was also when Hank Aaron first visited Japan. In November a home-run contest was staged between us at Korakuen Stadium, a contest which Hank won, hitting ten balls into the stands to my nine. At this point, Aaron had reached 733 career home runs, while I, playing in Japan, was at 634. He was forty years old then, while I was thirty-four, and I knew that I would probably surpass him before my playing days were over. There the comparisons stopped for me. He played in America and I did not. I knew enough of American baseball to know what his record meant. The Americans were better schooled in fundamentals, played more aggressively, were far ahead of us in speed, speed of outfield defense, and the power of their pitching. It was an honor to be on the field with this great champion, but I did not compare myself with him. His numbers, yes, his accomplishment, no. Winning the contest was important for many fans in Japan, and I tried my best to accede to their wishes. I might have won, but I didn't. The importance of my being there was in the fact that some people recognized that I played the game in a certain way, at a certain professional level. All along, that has been the secret source of my pride.

Chapter Twelve

When Nagashima-san took over as manager in 1975, there was big fever over my pursuit of the home-run record. When would I reach 650, 700? When would I finally catch Babe Ruth and overtake Hank Aaron? There was also very big fever over the fate of the Giants. For the first time in ten years we had failed to win the pennant in 1974, finishing a close second to the Chunichi Dragons. Because the Giants had been together successfully for so long, not many people realized that a time of rebuilding was at hand. I think our players may not have realized it either. We did terribly in 1975, worse than anyone expected. We finished last, an almost inconceivable turn of events, given who we were and given the expectations of Nagashima-san's leadership. There was such incredulity over this turn of fortune that even some political and economic writers began wondering aloud whether the fate of the Giants wasn't in some way a foreshadowing of national events. On the final day of the season, Nagashima-san led us from the dugout to stand before our fans and offer them a formal bow of responsibility.

For me, personally, the season was also difficult. I lost a consecutive game streak that year. Over several seasons, well into 1975, I had played in 648 straight games. I had pulled a muscle in my thigh during spring training, and it had never fully healed. Nagashima-san therefore often rested me for parts of games, allowing my streak to continue but conserving my strength at the same time. One day I did not start in a game against the Hanshin Tigers at Osaka. The game progressed and still I did not get in. The game went into extra innings, and at one point Nagashima-san turned to me and said, "Prepare to go in next inning." But there was no next inning. The Tigers won the game then and there with a "sayonara" home run, and my streak was broken. There was gossip afterward that Nagashima-san did this deliberately, but I never took it that way. A manager's job is always to use his players with regard for the team first and individual records second. It would be perversion for it to be otherwise.

But that might well have been a foreshadowing of the season I was to have. For the first time in fourteen years I failed to win the home-run title. It was a very sad time. A boxer is defeated in a single night, but this was a defeat that lasted many months. It was with me every day when I went to the ball park, and there was nothing I could do about it. Koichi Tabuchi of the Tigers won the crown that year with forty-three homers. I finished tied for third with thirty-three.

I certainly did not believe that I was finished as a player, or even that I was really declining. For the first time since I had begun alternating in third and fourth spots in the batting order, there was no "O-N Cannon." I may have been easier to pitch to than in the past. Also, our team was not nearly as intimidating. Davey Johnson, who joined the Giants that year, perhaps suffered more than anyone, because he was expected to fill the void left by Nagashima-san in the lineup. He did not. Many fans rode him with a chant that was a play on his name. ("J-son! J-son!" they called. *Son* in Japanese means loss.) I was reminded all too well of my own early difficulties, but that changed nothing. The year 1975 was just not a good one for the Giants or for me. When it ended, however, I was thirty-three home runs closer to Babe Ruth. I had also closed the distance between myself and Hank Aaron. I trailed him now by seventy-eight home runs. I had an outside chance of catching Ruth the following season, and sometime after that going beyond Aaron.

I worked as hard that winter as I ever had. I was not as concerned about Ruth and Aaron as I was about myself. I had one goal for myself from the moment I lost the home-run title—and that was to get it back. I checked what I did against every memorandum I had ever made on batting. I made sure that my condition the following spring would be excellent. When camp came, my motto was that I would be in better shape than even the hungriest rookie. For the Giants and myself, 1976 would be different.

The Giants, to be sure, did not stand still over the winter. In one of the biggest trades in years, we acquired a top hitter from the Pacific League, Isao Harimoto. Mr. Harimoto, like me, was a left-handed batter. He was more of a line-drive hitter than I was, but he could hit home runs, too. The Giants' hope, soon to be borne out, was that the "O-N Cannon" would now be replaced by an "H-O Cannon."

We won the pennant in 1976, edging out the Tigers by just two games. Even though we lost the Japan Series, which followed, we clearly exhibited good fighting spirit. We lost the first three games of the series to a strong Hankyu Braves team. But then we won two games at Nishinomiya and returned to Tokyo. We took a ten-inning victory in the sixth game, tying the series, but then lost the seventh and final game at home, 4–2.

Isao Harimoto finished second in hitting in the Central League. He hit twenty-two home runs, batting ahead of me, driving in ninety-three runs. He was a strong and helpful teammate. He was also a person with more character than people gave him credit for. He came to the Giants with something of a bad-boy reputation. He was not the most admired of players, though clearly the fact that he held the all-time season record for hitting (.383) gained him respect. It turned out, though, that he and I had a good deal in common.

Like myself, Mr. Harimoto, though born in Japan, held a foreign passport. He had never tried to change his Korean identity. He was the same age as I was, entering professional baseball in 1959, the same year I joined the Giants. He lost a sister in childhood, too. He lived in Hiroshima, and his sister was killed in the atom bombing of 1945. He and his mother happened to be walking on a hill just outside the city when the surprise attack occurred, and she shielded him against herself in the shade of a tree. His brother was a survivor, too, and became something of a surrogate parent, working to allow Mr. Harimoto to pursue a career in professional baseball.

But he impressed me most by who he was and not just by what he had been. When he joined the Giants, his position was particularly difficult, because, like Davey Johnson, he had a specific role to fulfill. Unlike Davey Johnson, he was a star within the Japanese baseball system to begin with. Thus he had the dual problem of accepting both more responsibility and somewhat less status. He told me very early on that he had always regarded me as a rival even though we had played in different leagues. As I had set a standard for myself with Nagashima-san, so he had set one with me. But, he said, he had long since given up trying to chase me. Doubling his own effort was the only reasonable way he had of striving as a professional. He wound up asking me to take him to Arakawa-san's to be taught— which I did. It turned out he had a most humble attitude toward this work, the attitude of a beginner though he was a real star. He was a seven-time batting champion, a master at using all ninety degrees of a baseball field (where I could use only forty-five), but he was genuinely humble, and he became my friend. We could equally share the middle of the Giants' batting order and a good round of sake.

The year 1976 marked my return to form, too. I hit forty-nine home runs, drove in 127 runs, and hit .325, and I won two of the three batting titles. But now, no matter what I did, there was this pursuit not only of Japanese records but of world marks as well. With each passing week of the season, particularly as my home-run production ran far ahead of the previous year's pace, the likelihood grew that this would be the year I reached the 700 mark. There was even the chance, growing stronger through the summer, that I would surpass Babe Ruth.

On July 2 I hit my thirtieth home run of the season. The following day, I hit two more, leaving me one shy of 700 career home runs. Till then I had not felt the pressure of having to produce a "special" home run—for myself or for anyone else. All of a sudden, 700 seemed like a real barrier. I found myself trying, and in trying, trying to stop myself from trying. It was an exasperating and peculiar sensation. Of course I knew I would soon get 700, but one week stretched into three before it finally happened. On July 23, in a game against the Taiyo Whales in Kawasaki, in the same park where I took my first swings as a flamingo hitter, I became the only player in Japanese baseball to reach 700 home runs.

By coincidence, Arakawa-san, who had taken a job as a television commentator, was there covering the game that night. I also think Fortune permits you to play-act a little. In line with his official duties, he formally interviewed me after I hit the home run. We met on the field and very seriously shook hands before the cameras.

"Congratulations, Mr. Oh," Arakawa-san said, most soberly standing straight, with one hand behind his back.

"Thank you very much, Arakawa-san."

"Tell me, Mr. Oh, what kind of pitch did you hit?"

"Well, Arakawa-san, I believe it was . . . "

And so on and so on. Afterward, when the crowds were gone, the last interviews and autographs given, we headed off for a little out-of-the-way restaurant where we had *sushi* and sake. I don't know how long we stayed or how much we drank, but our years together made this private celebration the very best imaginable. I did not have a good game the day following.

Because it had taken longer than expected to reach 700, I was not certain that I would surpass Ruth's record that year. I wanted to. I wanted to get past it and reach Aaron's mark as quickly as possible so that I could get back to playing my own game. I believe that records can help a player set standards for his own individual efforts. But they are individual. When they become a planned part of the season, when managers, for example, are pressured to go out of their way to help them along, then the spirit of professional baseball is violated. A record is between a player and himself and cannot be pursued at the expense of his team.

I found myself too caught up in the records ahead. The pressure this brought upon me and my team—not to mention my family—was most unwelcome. And I did not handle it as well as I might have. Yet I could not blame the fans. Their excitement was natural, and their hopes for my success even became a help when I found that my own efforts, so affected by tension, needed something extra.

I did not do especially well after 700. I hit two more home runs in July and then only three in August and none in the first half of September. Fortunately, we were locked in a close pennant race, thus making it easier for me to concentrate. As we fought off the Tigers down the stretch, I began hitting home runs again. From the fourteenth of the month to the end of September, I hit six home runs in twelve games. With season's end sixteen days away, I stood three homers away from passing Babe Ruth.

On October 10, in our 125th game of the year, I hit home runs 713 and 714. I was one away with five games to play.

Nagashima-san and I in the clubhouse. We were side by side for so many years and yet we never spent a single social evening together.

Shigeo Nagashima at an ancestral tomb.

229

王756号！最高峰に立つ

ついに世界を征服 前人未到の大金字塔よ永遠に輝け

ニッカウ井スキー

756号を放った王。「今日はものすごく手応えがあった。打った瞬間に入ると思った」両手をあげ世界新の喜びをかみしめるようにゆっくりとダイヤモンドを一周

I have just surpassed Hank Aaron's record. I can go back to playing baseball again.

230

At the ceremony following the record home run, I decided to honor my parents. I gave them the floral award that had been presented to me. But I could never honor them adequately for what they had experienced and suffered.

Hank Aaron and I prior to our home-run hitting contest in 1974. It was my loss, too, when he retired.

With another American friend.

I took my duties as an assistant manager as seriously as I did as a player. Here I am lobbing baseballs for "toss batting" practice. You had better believe I am into it.

As we were playing at home and as our opponents were the Hanshin Tigers, the expectation became tremendous. We had a full house the following day, and each time I came to the plate I could feel the excitement and the urging of the fans with me. We took an early lead in the game and held it going into the last of the eighth, 4–1. I came up with two men on base, two out, and worked the count full. I connected solidly on the next pitch. The ball rose on a trajectory toward right field. Straight down the line, however. While I knew instantly that I had enough distance on the ball, I didn't know for sure that the ball would stay fair. I watched it for a second or two. It seemed more like a full minute. The ball seemed to be moving in slow motion as it passed just to the inside of the foul pole.

What I did then—what I had never done as a professional before and have never done after—was to joyously leap into the air with both arms extended wide over my head. There was no planning this. It happened almost in spite of myself, as though, perhaps, my "other" had taken over. Oh, yes, how happy I was! I was surely happy for the record. And yet, in thinking about it, I was also happy that the ball was fair and that this home run decisively turned a crucial game in our favor. All of it. But I was surprised at myself nonetheless. Reporters had many times asked me why I didn't show more emotion when I hit home runs, and I always answered as frankly as I could that there was never any point in further punishing an opponent. Photographers, who, after all, had a job to do, always wanted something more than a poker-faced trot about the bases, so I had worked out with them that I would make a happy gesture of some sort, briefly lifting my arms out, for example, so they could get better pictures. This time, my own feelings simply had their way.

The person most affected by this home run—really, I think, by my reaction to it—was my brother. He was, as were other members of my family and the Arakawa-sans, very pleased for me. But, in private, my brother was also very much moved by this reaction of mine. For him it was not a small gesture of triumph but something very different.

"Sada," he told me, "I've been waiting twenty years to say this to you. You remember in high school when I chastised you for being so open about your feelings in the Kanto tournament?"

As if I were likely to forget!

"Well, I've thought about this a great deal, and I must tell you that I was very wrong when I did that."

I, too, was moved when I saw how deeply this affected him and how long he had obviously been living with it.

"I apologize for having done that, Sada! I am deeply sorry. Please, forgive me!"

There was nothing to forgive him for. My brother in recent years had gone from being a kind of elder statesman, with whom only limited confidences could be shared, to being a friend with whom I could share everything. While I surely understood the source of his guilt in this, I wanted to assure him that there really was no need to apologize. If I had had a life not of my own choosing and had so limited my own natural expression, it would have been one thing. But I had spent my life doing what I loved. I certainly envied those who could freely and openly express happy feelings, but I did not really lose because I could not. I gained a peculiar form of self-confidence in the way I limited myself, and I also gained in effectively dealing with opponents. Things are never one-sided, and what is lost in one place is found in another.

Babe Ruth's record, it turned out, was no longer the record by the time I passed it. Ahead was Hank Aaron's. And the end of the 1976 season marked yet an additional milestone along the way. Hank Aaron retired. For the first time, his home-run record was now fixed at a certain number—755. It was immediately apparent to baseball fans, and many, many others in my country, that sometime in the very near future—the following season or, at the very latest, the season after that—I would pass that mark.

I happened to meet Hank that winter in Hawaii. We talked for a while in a hotel room. I was sorry he had retired, because knowing what he did in America kept me sharper in Japan. We talked a lot about hitting styles. It was odd, though. Hank told me that my swing was artistic and beautiful to watch. I, who certainly had been impressed by his batting form for many years, was struck by the look of gentleness and clarity in his eyes. "I'd like to be there when you break my record," he told me. "I remember Stan Musial greeting me at first base when I got my three hundredth hit."

I finished the 1976 season with 716 career home runs. I needed forty home runs to reach a new record. It was far enough away in needed playing time to afford me an interval of ordinary days before the pressure would again build. But in measuring this, perhaps I was also engaging in some wishful thinking. There was to be no letup now in the fever that swept the country. Every day there were requests for interviews and pictures. What was I doing to prepare for 756? Was I in the best condition? Did I have a target date in my own mind for the world record? Even the press beyond Japan began to take an interest now. With Hank Aaron's retirement and my being in such an obvious position to pass his mark, American journalists reported on my doings. The press in Asia, having regularly reported on Japanese baseball, seemed as eager to pursue the story as media people in Japan.

With the coming of the 1977 season, this "Oh fever" actually became a kind of industry. Everywhere, I am told, baseballs with reproductions of my signature were sold as fast as they could reach the stores; companies began producing medals, towels, T-shirts in advance of the commemorative moment; another company manufactured a plate with my portrait as its principal design; restaurants announced incredible bargains on steak dinners to be offered the day following 756 (the cost of a steak dinner is well beyond the reach of most people in Japan); the media even turned up a story about a Mah-Jongg parlor in Yaesu that happened to have the name Oh and that, as a consequence, announced a 40 percent reduction in prices for the day following the big home run. Whether I wished it to be otherwise or not, there was to be no letup in the pressure surrounding me.

In many ways I was lucky to have had the experience of pursuing an earlier "big" record. It was a kind of rehearsal. I learned from it. I had not handled the pressure as well as I might have. I had also found myself resenting the increased public attention. In a way, that was exactly the problem. All the "atmospherics" surrounding my pursuit of the home-run record had interfered with the way I played the game.

As I had on so many other occasions, I returned to Arakawa-san. In June, while the record was still distant, I worked with him every day for a week. We worked from eleven at night until around two in the morning, just as we had in the past. I approached our training sessions as I always had—bowing to my teacher and formally requesting his instruction. We performed the exercises that by now were familiar but that could not be successfully done unless there was absolute concentration.

I approached the problem of excessive public attention in the only way I knew—by disciplined work as a batsman. The way of the flamingo hitter was something I had grown to love. It had yielded its rewards only with persistent effort. Its promise to me had been a kind of proof that effort does effect change. And the change I was looking for was the one I had always been pursuing—oneness with my skill.

What I found in this "interval" between records was something that I was not quite looking for but that was the very thing I needed most. I came to have a changed attitude toward all the attention I was receiving.

I had become quite conscious that the demands placed upon me by the public—for time, autographs, appearances, interviews, and the like—were interfering not only with my play but my life as well. Because crowds had regularly begun to gather outside my house, for example, it was no longer possible for my daughters to go out and play as ordinary children would. My wife could not go to the market, nor could we, if we wanted, go off to a restaurant or have an evening to ourselves. We had to send out for many of our meals, and our children had to accustom themselves to indoor activities, as though imprisoned in their own house.

During my career I had always made it a point to be accessible to fans. This was never something I did reluctantly. I normally enjoyed the relationship I had with them. I have several fan clubs, for instance, and by participating in their events over the years, I have come to meet many interesting people I might otherwise never have known. Mr. Shimei Cho is the best speaker of Japanese among my many Chinese friends. He organized a club after my fifty-five home-run season consisting of Chinese and Japanese members. They hold various events, as does another club organized in Toyama Prefecture by friends of my mother. I attend the annual parties the clubs hold, and they in turn have been very protective and caring toward me. Members send me gifts and cards, which I always respond to in my own hand, and they perform helpful services for which I have been deeply grateful. One member of a fan club regularly visits my twin sister's grave and offers prayers and flowers for me during the regular season when I am not able to attend to this myself.

By midsummer in 1977 two things had become clear. One was that the Giants were not nearly as hard pressed in the pennant race as in the season before. We were well on the way to taking the Central League championship, so the pressure to keep pace, though keen, was not really so draining. The other factor was that I had maintained a steady enough home-run pace to bring Aaron's record within reach by the end of the season. I had twenty-six homers by August 1 and needed fourteen for the record.

On August 4 I got my twenty-seventh home run. I homered again on the sixth, twice more on the ninth, then once again on the tenth, eleventh, and twelfth. With rainouts and breaks in the schedule, we managed to play only three games between the thirteenth and twenty-third. I hit my thirty-fourth home run of the season on the twenty-third, another the following day, two more the day after that. On August 31 I hit career home run number 755. I was one away from the record.

All the while the uproar around my life grew daily. Each day crowds of people gathered at my house, awaiting my comings and goings. The crowds became so regular that police were assigned to the area to keep order. I had no private life of any kind now. From the moment I got up to the moment I went to bed I was accompanied every step of the way by people who awaited this record with me. When I left my house in the morning, I hoped it would give my family some quiet time. It never did. People simply remained or were joined by others awaiting my return. In traffic, cars, camera crews, motorcycles accompanied me, and at stop signals people waved to me and called out greetings. There were times when I could not move from one place to another without benefit of a police escort. Any time I was on a street anywhere, I was sure, in a matter of seconds, to be engulfed by people.

And yet I did not feel as I had earlier. The people who waited for me at my house—children, families—all wished me well and wanted my home run to come soon. When I came down the steps toward my carport, children would hand me bouquets of flowers, some of them quite carefully and beautifully arranged. They had gifts and mementoes, prayers and little capsule messages of good fortune from local shrines. There is a room in my parents' house where all these keepsakes have been preserved. There was a statue of a dragon, my special protection, rising from a baseball; the Overseas Chinese Club presented me with a figure of Hotei, one of the Seven Gods from Chinese mythology, the one who gives long life and luck; a well-known sculptor did a carving of a fish leaping from the water, this the representation of that in all of us which reaches higher amid the limitations of this world. There were drawings, woodblock prints, dolls, brushwork decorations of every kind. In all of this, instead of resisting a loss of privacy, I took into myself the added strength of these good wishes. I became conscious of how much I was supported in my own efforts.

I had always made it a point to sign autographs. I was never troubled by this, because the time it took cost me so very little. But I had a problem at this time, because the crowds around my house had grown enormously. Over the years I had learned how to sign many autographs in a short while. I could carry on a conversation and sign a baseball or board at the same time. Because it got to the point where I was often faced with many people simultaneously asking for my autograph, I made a study of just how many I could give within a certain period of time. In the past I had not always been able to sign for everyone. It bothered me when this happened, and I did not want it to happen in this special situation at my house.

The best way I could deal with this was to add on an extra fifteen or twenty minutes before I had to leave. I calculated exactly. The greatest number of autographs I could sign in a minute was ten. Before I left the house, I counted the crowd. If there were 150 to 200, I knew that I could sign for everyone within fifteen or twenty minutes. If there were more than 200, then I would sign for no one that day. The point was to sign for all or none. When I got outside, sometimes I would borrow a bullhorn from a policeman and request that people form a line so I could more easily handle their requests for autographs.

There were days when it was impossible to accommodate people. But there were many other days when I could. I was pleased to do this, and in the end I believe it even helped on my way to 756.

On September 1 we finished a series at home against the Taiyo Whales. The next day we began a three-game set against the Yakult Swallows. I was not able to hit the record home run in the final game against the Whales nor in the first game of the following series. If the home run did not come in the next two days, the chances were it would occur on the road, where we would be playing till the middle of the month.

It was strange waiting for this moment. Really, it was as inevitable as something could be, given the finite and unpredictable character of events. Yet it was like living in the midst of a storm. The storm, of course, would pass. But for me the task was to try to find its center so that I could concentrate on what I had to do. One to go. It was almost as though the only place left in the world where I had room to move my arms freely was the playing field during game time. Reporters, photographers, cameramen were with me now even as I took practice, sometimes getting in the way as I tried to run or throw. I realized how fatigued I had become over these many months. Except for sleeping, I could not remember the last time I had really been alone.

The evening of September 3 was filled with the same expectation as the previous evening. Traffic was brought to a halt as I made my way from my home to the ball park. Swarms of people surrounded me right up to game time. I remember sitting on a metal chair in front of my locker after the press had finally cleared the clubhouse. My teammates were milling around, shortly to take the field. I felt drained of all energy, as though I had not slept for days. Suddenly a door opened. I thought for a moment I was imagining things. It was my mother. No one was allowed in the clubhouse at this point, and she was entering an area that was normally closed to the press. I will forever remember the look on her face, sweet and beckoning. She was dressed very plainly, as though the occasion was an ordinary visit with her son. I rose to greet her. Her eyes spoke so much to me—certainty that I would make it that very night and also that it was even more important that I take care of myself.

My mother is a very small woman. As I leaned over to catch her words, I remember wondering, absurdly, when it was that I first became conscious that my mother only reached the middle of my chest.

She reached out and handed me two parcels, one rather large, the other small.

"I brought some apples for you and your teammates," she said. "Please distribute them. The smaller package is for your daughters."

I began to thank her, but she went right on.

"I brought some *suzumushi* for them. Such crickets are hard to find in the cities these days, aren't they? Take good care of them, and take good care of yourself." She then turned and left, heading back for the grandstand.

I brought the packages back to my locker. What a strange gift at such a time! I held the small package to my ear to see if I could hear the crickets inside. Yes! They were quite alive. Their wings whirred and whirred. I became so caught up in listening to them that the noise of the locker room and the heavy sea tide of the crowd in the stadium completely disappeared. There was only the music of these summertime crickets and the immense silence that their voices invoked.

When I left my locker and headed for the field, I had no feeling of tiredness. I could feel in my bones that this indeed was the night. I came upon the lights and noise of Korakuen almost as if they didn't exist. The quietness my mother had brought me surrounded me like a spell. It was not going to be broken. I hit in the first inning and then in the third. The third inning. One out, no one on base. The pitcher's name, in this twenty-third game of the year against the Swallows, was Kojiro Suzuki. The goal, Arakawa-san had always said, was oneness of mind, body, and skill. You and the opponent together create the moment. The *ma* is the one you create but in which you are not at all separate from your opponent. The pitcher and I, the ball—and the silence my mother gave me—these were all one. In the midst of whatever was going on, there was only this emptiness in which I could do what I wanted to do. The count went full. Mr. Kojiro Suzuki threw a sinker on the outside part of the plate. I followed the ball perfectly. I could almost feel myself waiting for its precise break before I let myself come forward. When I made contact, I felt like I was scooping the ball upward and outward. The ball rose slowly and steadily in the night sky, lit by Korakuen's bright lights. I could follow it all the way, as it lazily reached its height and seemed to linger there in the haze, and then slowly began its descent into the right-field stands.

The crowd erupted, almost as a single voice. A huge banner was suddenly unfurled that read, "Congratulations, World Record!" Everywhere—but on the diamond—people were running and lights were flashing. For me, it was the moment of purest joy I had ever known as a baseball player.

No one can stop a home run. No one can understand what it really is unless you have felt it in your own hands and body. It is different from seeing it or trying to describe it. There is nothing I know quite like meeting a ball in exactly the right spot. As the ball makes its high, long arc beyond the playing field, the diamond and the stands suddenly belong to one man. In that brief, brief time, you are free of all demands and complications. There is no one behind you, no obstruction ahead, as you follow this clear path around all the bases. This is the batsman's center stage, the one time that he may allow himself to freely accept the limelight, to enjoy the sensation of every eye in the stadium fixed on him, waiting for the moment when his foot will touch home plate. In this moment he is free.

Obviously, 756 was special. How could it be otherwise? I know it was not a "world" record (there is no world competition). I don't believe I would have reached 756 if I had played in America. But it was my record and it was baseball's record nevertheless! It was the devotion of a professional's career.

When I reached home plate, all of the noise and excitement I had left behind were there in full force, happy and surging with energy. I don't know where in the midst of all the congratulations that followed it occurred, but someone said to me:

"Your parents, your parents, let your parents come to the field!"

My parents are very shy people, and I was not sure how they would feel in front of so many people. I was uncertain what to do. Also, I did not really want to monopolize things. My home run belonged to many people other than myself. My teammates and my opponents shared in this moment, though no lights found them. I needed no more for myself than my foot touching home plate. But, yes, I did want to share this moment with my parents. If I had planned it exactly, I could not have calculated the depth of thanksgiving and pride I suddenly felt now. By all means, I wanted to stand with them.

Just then a congratulatory message from Hank Aaron flashed on the electronic scoreboard, and, most eerily, his voice boomed out over a loudspeaker as the crowd became hushed. He must have been speaking by telephone hookup.

"Congratulations," his voiced resounded. "I had hoped to see you break my record there in Japan, but I haven't been able to make it. . . . Continue slugging for your fans. And again, congratulations."

By now ceremonies were under way. Both teams were lined up in front of their dugouts; a microphone was placed in the center of the diamond. My parents were on the field. They looked so happy and so startled by all the commotion. My mother later told me, contrary to what I saw in her eyes, that she and my father had not really dressed for the occasion because they hadn't expected the home run that night. Just then, my parents impulsively walked over to the players on our team. They bowed to each of them and shook each one's hand, thanking them individually for helping me. It was hard to keep from crying. I was so moved and proud of my parents. I have always believed that success in this life owes to a strong will, and there were no people I knew who were stronger in this way than my mother, who was also tenderhearted, and my father, who had endured so many indignities and who so stubbornly persisted in his dreams anyway. The press made much of how generous I had been to others. In my circumstances, it was easy. My father extended himself when it wasn't so easy. He believed in repaying hatred with virtue not when he was surrounded by an admiring public but when the prejudice of officials and the hands of torturers cut his body and tried his soul. In over seventy years of life he has never once gone back on his deepest belief that the goal of any man's life is to be useful to others.

I was presented with a very large floral award, the official recognition of my achievement. Many cameras were whirring; this was the moment the whole nation had been waiting to celebrate. I could think of nothing more fitting to do then than to bring this award to my parents and offer it to them. I did this. I handed them the award, and I bowed deeply to them—and they to me.

I stood, finally, on the mound with all the lights of the stadium turned off save for a single spot on me. I took my cap off, bowed in four directions, and spoke a few words. I told people that my dream had finally come true, thanks to all those who had given me support. To receive such warm applause and feelings made me a happy man, and I promised to keep playing as long as my body would permit.

Later, I told the press that I was sorry for the pitcher, Suzuki, but that I was relieved to have finally answered the expectations of so many fans. Above all, what I wanted now was to get back to my own style of play. This, however, was still a wish.

There were official parties and functions to attend that

night and no end of pursuit by the press. When I got home at two o'clock in the morning, there were over 600 people in front of my house! They greeted me happily and noisily—so much so that my most immediate thought was for the peace and quiet of my neighbors. I had no wish to ruin my fans' happiness either, so rather than have the police ask them to disperse, I signed autographs for them all and to each one said good night.

There was a party in full swing in my house. My parents, my wife, my three daughters, my brother and his family were all there, and so we toasted each other over and over again before we all called it a night.

There was one last matter to attend to. I placed a call to Arakawa-san. He was not with me in the house nor in the entourage that surrounded me before and after the game. I would have liked him to be there, of course, but it was not possible. We might have raised a cup of sake in the midst of all the bedlam, but that would not really have mattered. He knew and I knew—independent of this extraordinary tumult—what we had done together. This night was his, too, and its outcome had been fashioned a long time before.

"Arakawa-san?"

"Yes, it's me."

I said to him what I always said whenever I left one of our training sessions—when I bowed, acknowledging his mastery.

"Domo arigato Gozaimasu."

I thanked him with all my heart, because without him there would have been no record.

Chapter Thirteen

I played for three more years before I retired in 1980. In 1978, less than a year from the time I broke Hank Aaron's record, I hit my 800th home run. Once again there was celebrating and good wishes from many, many people. But it was not really the same—800 was a number, not a rival's record. Each home run I hit was a new record, but I was my own rival now and the challenge, though real enough, was different. I knew, even in 1978 when I felt strong and spirited, that my playing days would not last forever. I tried not to think too much about it.

"My goal now is to hit nine hundred," I said when I hit 800. And had I reached 900 in good playing condition, I probably would have made a similar speech setting 1,000 as my goal. But I did not reach 900, with all my best efforts to do so. In fact, the numbers game would never have been enough to sustain me. When Hank Aaron retired, I was genuinely sorry, because he was a kind of invisible helping spirit, forcing me to play harder each day that he, too, was playing the game.

I would have been quite content to go on forever, to reach one plateau after another. In my countrymen's eyes, I was the world's Oh. Prime Minister Fukuda presented me with the first and only People's National Award after I broke Aaron's record; I personally was congratulated and received by President Carter and by Ambassador Mike Mansfield. I had the support of ministers, diplomats, and millions of fans to help me toward any new record I went for. If the support of others had alone been enough to sustain me, I never would have retired. But an athlete, more than most people, is limited by time. The years of a baseball player's active life, though different for each individual, cannot be extended too far into middle age. At the halfway point of most people's lives, when they are just approaching their most productive years, an athlete's life is over.

I was, of course, very aware of age. Arakawa-san had always said that I would play till I was forty. And though I had once thought of that as a kind of bench mark—like Ruth's record—to enhance my sense of concentration, I began to see it as something else as I actually approached that age. In the back of my mind it became a waiting and unwelcome guest that I knew I could put off for only so long.

I knew I was not the player I had been earlier in my career. My home-run production fell to thirty-nine in 1978, not enough to win a title, but I still was a hitter. I had to make adjustments in order to keep up, but I was able to. I never once had the idea that because I had made this or that record I could just lie back and play the star. If anything, I worked harder than ever. I used everything I knew, everything Arakawa-san had ever taught me, everything I had ever picked up on my own, all the attention and good wishes showered upon me by fans, whose loss, I understood in a positive sense, would have shamed me: all this I used to keep my eye—and my bat—on the ball.

I sometimes had difficulty seeing as well as I had. My reflexes, while still good, were not quite what they had been. I found by strict attention and study that if I moved my contact point slightly forward, I could compensate for this natural loss of quickness. In my best days I could "stay back" till the very last split second, meeting the ball as it crossed the plate rather than out in front of it. This gave me a tremendous advantage, because I had that much longer to "read" a pitch. As it was growing harder for me to do this, and hence as it was easier for pitches to come at me hard inside, I made this slight change that allowed me to continue hitting with full power to the right side. It was a kind of intelligent cheating that only a sharp-eyed first baseman would have been able to pick up. Formerly, when I would swing, you could not see my face if you were standing at first base. After I made this adjustment, it was possible to see my face.

I mention this only because with such detailed work, I made myself believe that I could extend my playing career for many years. Age, after all, was a process, like growing up. You did not get to it overnight. With intelligence, hard work, and spirit, you could keep the dark guest pacified and willing to wait longer and then perhaps beyond that. But in this, more certainly than anything else I can think of, I was completely deceived. As though I were staring into the face of a sudden wave in a calm sea, I saw the end of my career rise up in a single game. The date—August 14, 1980—is as memorable to me as any other in my twenty-two years as a player.

There was certainly nothing else unusual about the day or the game. We were playing a night game at home against the last-place Chunichi Dragons. For some time now—since 1977—our team had ceased to be a power in the Central League. The days of V-9 were surely behind us, and on this warm August evening there was no expectation of a Giants "miracle" in the air. We were on the way to a third-place finish, far behind the Hiroshima Carp.

It was the bottom of the first inning. Darkness had not yet fallen, and the lights of the stadium had not fully taken effect. The Dragons' pitcher that night was Yoshinori Toda, an eighteen-year veteran who, like myself, had seen his best days. I remembered him from the Pacific League champion

Hankyu Braves, because I had hit a huge home run off him in a Japan Series game at Nishinomiya Stadium. The ball went so far, it carried over a high black screen in dead center field. I was looking forward to standing in against him now.

The first two batters on our team failed to hit. As they came back to the bench, I asked, in the customary fashion, what the pitcher was throwing.

"Not much," was the answer. "No velocity. Movement's easy to pick up. We'll get him."

Regardless of what my teammates thought, I discovered when I stepped in against Mr. Toda that his fastball seemed extra fast. It was by me before I could time it. I remember saying something to that effect on the bench later, and my teammates assumed I was joking. The second time I batted it was no better. Mr. Toda threw one pitch that I thought was a foot inside. It was called a strike. I simply could not handle what he was throwing. He might have been the young Masaichi Kaneda or Bob Gibson or Tom Seaver in their prime as far as I was concerned. I sat on the bench trying to hide the sense of shock and disbelief that assaulted me. My "strategic" decline, it turned out, lasted only to this finite point—one summer evening in Tokyo. And between the time the evening began and ended the idea of "retirement" emerged from the shadows to take me by the hand.

I was, of course, not prepared to act so quickly. My first hope was that this was just a passing thing and that in another day or so I would shake this off. I had, after all, been in slumps before.

But this was not a slump in any sense I understood. As it had been with Mr. Toda, so it was with other pitchers I normally liked hitting against in our league. Again and again I found myself overmatched. I was knocked to the ground in situations where formerly I might have pulled the ball deep or stepped easily away. One day I faced my toughest rival from many years before, Yutaka Enatsu. He was the pitcher who, in 1971, when I was struggling to find my own way without Arakawa-san, had offered the decisive challenge that enabled me to regain confidence. He had had in those days an overpowering fastball. But it had long since deserted him. He had been in recent years a wily but not a powerful opponent. I had been able to read his pitching all too well. But now, once again, he was the old Enatsu— only he was not. He leaned upon me as in the old days; his steamless fastballs thundered past me like hot cannon-balls.

In our game, ever so team oriented, there is a high moment of drama reserved for that contest that takes place between one strong batter and a strong opposing pitcher. We give the name *shobu* to this moment, and it is as if the struggle of one team with the other is narrowed and intensified in this desperate and decisive surrogate combat. It is the highest kind of individual struggle, but it bears with it the potential for victory or defeat for an entire team. Yes, I loved the *shobu*. The more intense the challenge, the more intense I was. I was just not up to this now. Whether I wanted it that way or not—and I certainly did— my performance on the field had direct bearing on my team. I had a certain pride as a professional player, which meant more to me than any record. And my pride, more than anything, revealed what it was I was facing. For the fact of the matter was that in this "slump"—as opposed to any other—I had lost all desire for combat. In my earlier days, when I had done badly, I had come back to the bench in a fury. I was already afire with desire for my next chance. Not now.

I struggled against this, of course. I did not want to admit that my spirit, which had served me for so long, had seemingly faded. Perhaps with renewed spirit, I thought, I would find enough in my body to return to some semblance of form. I began to sign my autographs with the word "spirit"—rather than, as earlier, with the words "patience" and "effort." I also went to my Sensei and, as I had done when

252

I first began working with him, bowed before him, palms to the floor, and with all the yearning of my heart begged him to once more teach me.

Arakawa-san and I worked without letup for three days—just as we had in the past. Standing in my shorts, I swung bat and sword until my body was pouring sweat; I listened carefully for the low whistling sound of my sword; I measured carefully the kind of cuts I made through the swinging cards; in everything, in every motion I made, I concentrated *ki* in my one point and projected it downward into the ground and out through my forearms into the secret lengths of bat and sword.

"What shall I tell you?" Arakawa-san said at the end of our time. "You still can hit."

"But what has happened to me?" I asked.

Arakawa-san shook his head. "You still can hit," he repeated softly.

He knew what I was thinking without my having to spell out anything for him. There was no discussion of retirement or of my fears.

"I have no anger anymore," I said finally. He shrugged.

"Mastery in Aikido means loss of desire for combat. You have been a master for many years."

And so we left it there. I went back to this torture rack of decline that season's end brought with it. Nothing changed. There were no flurries of recovery, no sudden changes of spirit. The fire was gone.

Retiring eventually became a kind of logistical combat over when to make an announcement. As many people would be affected by this, it was not simply a question of following my own inclination, which was just to call a press conference, make a brief statement, then withdraw. The Giants, of course, did not want me to leave, and they tried to persuade me to stay as a player and then, when it was clear that I would not, to accept a place on the team as assistant manager. I wanted only to make my statement and go. But on the night before I was to do it, the Giants called me and informed me that Nagashima-san himself was announcing his resignation as manager the following day. I was thunderstruck. Obviously I was forestalled from even being able to hint at my own plans at the same time. The resignation of Nagashima-san became the biggest sports story of the year. Sometime afterward, after many days of consultations and exhortations—especially in light of my team's recent misfortunes—I was able to retire. But I also accepted a position on the team as an assistant manager. With Nagashima-san gone and my old friend Mr. Fujita now entrusted with the team's leadership, it was not possible to simply walk away. Responsibilities neither begin nor end with exclusive personal wishes. Though I would never have sought out such a position on my own, I could not in good conscience have walked away from the demands it placed upon me.

It is hard to explain what the position of assistant manager really is about. There is no equivalent position in American baseball. The part that suggests manager is perhaps misleading. As I understood it—or rather, as I preferred it, my role was to be with the players. To me, then and now, the game is for the players. And hence, the very day after my retirement, the day I became an assistant manager, my role changed. If others saw me as the same figure in the same uniform, I knew the work I now was to do was not the same.

The morning after my announcement, I left my house to go to the Tamagawa Grounds to address my teammates. My youngest daughter, who had been very struck by all the commotion surrounding my retirement, stopped me at the door.

"Daddy," she wanted to know, "have you become an important person?"

I laughed, but I could not really explain to her what was very clear to me even then: that the players are the important ones. For me, who had known so many years as a top player, the difference was obvious. My task now, as surely as it had once been to become a top player, was to give as much in this new position as I could. Even more, to accept this change of role not as a loss but as one of life's inevitable changes—something every bit as much to be "understood" as standing on one leg.

My life as an assistant manager began that very next morning. When I got to the Tamagawa Grounds, even though it was early, there was already a large crowd waiting at the fences.

"Oh-san! Oh-san!" people called out to me.

"Please do not give up. Please go on playing!"

"I would like to see your one-legged batting again!"

I could barely speak. To all these cries, I could only mumble, voicelessly, "Thank you, thank you."

The players were waiting for me in a circle in the center of the field. I strode up to them, my teammates only twenty-four hours before. I had thought all night about what I might say to them. Nothing was clear except that now I was an assistant manager and that for me the best I could give meant somehow being an assistant player. I faced my colleagues. The words, the ones I most wanted to say, seemed to erupt from my body. I was conscious of how loud my voice was:

"As you know, I retired yesterday. Thank you for being with me for so many seasons. I have one thing to say. It is said that life is short. But baseball life is even shorter. It passes in a moment. So please learn to make every moment count. Life should be lived as fully as possible and a baseball life even more. Thank you. That is all I have to say."

There is no plan or program for an assistant manager. As I had through my playing days, I turned for advice to Arakawa-san. But this was new ground for him, too. Still, he was not about to turn away from facing a challenge just because it was unfamiliar.

"Well," he said, "first you must stop playing Mah-Jongg. This is essential. Then you must keep a lot of books with you and stay in your room reading."

We had a little laugh together, but, as always, my instructor was instructing me. By prohibiting Mah-Jongg, Arakawa-san was reminding me that young players might feel inhibited in coming to me if they saw I was in the midst of a game. By staying in my room reading, I did not have to excuse myself from others to invite someone to me. All I had to do was to lower my book—a choice purely my own to make.

I was ready to give what I could to younger players. I had certainly been blessed by having a master teacher, and if I could ever give to just one young player a fraction of what was given to me, my role would be fulfilled. I did not ask for nor did I expect to receive special considerations based on the stature I had acquired as a player. During practice, I made it a point to pull and push batting cages around, to pick up balls, and to do other ordinary grounds-keeping chores. I ate and lived among the players. I chauffeured them to and from the hotel and ball park. All I wanted was to be able to pass on something of what I had learned over twenty-two years as a professional: mainly, to practice and play as hard as they could for as long as they could. I searched out every opportunity to pass this on as clearly as I was able. It was not hard labor per se I advocated but an attitude toward what might be accomplished with it. In fungo drills I did not stand aside and give advice. I took the bat in my hand and worked as hard swinging the bat as the players did fielding. We had a drill with catchers, for example, where two or three of them would take ground balls at fairly close distances from the coach. Though catchers do not often field ground balls in game situations, the purpose of this drill was to sharpen reflexes, so that catchers might better handle wild pitches and sudden throws to the plate. I always began this drill hitting balls easily, picking up the pace gradually until, by the end, I was smashing the ball at the fielders, who barely had time to move this way or that. The goal was to keep them moving—up to the very end—so that even with the hardest hit balls, their reflexes would be much sharper.

It was important to make this more than a drill, more than a punishing exercise—which it surely was. As I hit, especially as I hit harder, increasing the likelihood both of misplays and of the players guessing in advance where the ball might be going, I talked and laughed with the players, trying to buoy their spirits, keeping attention always on *their* performance. I worked myself into a sweat with them—but they made the plays.

"That's it, that's it!" I would call out. Or, when they missed a ball, "Cheer up, boys! Here's another one coming!"

I drove them this way and that, faster and faster.

"Don't guess from the way I'm fungoing!"

. . . Harder and harder.

"Not with the glove, the whole body!"

. . . Till they could barely handle them.

"Ha! Ha! Ha! Right through your legs! Do it again."

. . . Till they were ready to drop from exhaustion, till all of us, soaked through our uniforms, knew that together we had used our time well.

During spring training the following season, we traveled to the United States to spend several weeks with the Dodgers at Vero Beach. One of the Dodger coaches, Manny Mota, suggested that I take part in an exhibition game so that some of the other players might get to see my one-legged style. At first I consented, but then when I realized the game would be televised back to Japan, I decided against it. But I was not upset by this. It reaffirmed quite clearly my original decision.

America, though, was "a land of opportunity" as far as my new work was concerned. I had played against American teams on several occasions during the spring and post-season periods and was very impressed by what I saw. As

I myself had learned, so I could now more easily share what I knew with our younger players. The great skills of the Americans were more than matched by the spirit and professionalism they brought to the game.

One evening a group of us were walking through Dodgertown. The day's activities were long since ended. As we crossed the deserted field, we saw a solitary figure in a warm-up suit running up and down the stadium steps. He ran from field level to the top of the stadium, going up one aisle, then down another to the field again. When we got close enough, we saw that it was Steve Garvey. As I was always very impressed with Pete Rose for his obvious fighting spirit, so I was impressed with Steve Garvey for the kind of quiet, persistent dedication he reflected. I pointed out to the young players with me that even a great star like Garvey understood the meaning of extra effort. He did not have to do what he was doing, I noted, but wasn't this what being a professional was all about? I used any opportunity I could to illustrate that professionalism and persistent mind went hand in hand.

As I had been a strong batsman for so many years, I especially looked forward to what I might be able to teach hitters. The younger players certainly respected me and always listened attentively when I spoke to them. But there is only so much you can show.

When I retired, I was in the process of building a new house. The design was modern, but one room—a training room—was built in the old style, with tatami mats and *shoji*. I had originally intended to use the room for myself, but when it was finished I thought I would use it for teaching. As Arakawa-san had once trained and transformed a young player named Sadaharu Oh, so I dreamed a little that one day a young player might come to my house searching for the same skills. I would be ready if ever there was a student who, with bare feet on the tatami and a willingness to trust to something a little different, sought a power in himself beyond strength.

But no one ever came.

One day my old friend Mr. Shibata, "Red Glove" Shibata, dropped by to visit. I showed him the room and told him my feelings. He nodded his head and laughed.

"I wouldn't come either," he said.

"Why?" I asked, surprised and perplexed.

"You need real courage to practice here. It is an awesome place. And you are an awesome person. If it is so for me, how much more would it be for a young player?"

I know what I accomplished as a player and also what skills I naturally possessed. They cannot be copied simply with hard work or good intentions. But I also know my "first mind" as I know myself. No matter how others see me, I know that I am a person like any other, no greater, no smaller. My tastes and my heart are much as my father's, simple but stubborn. I am not fooled by decorations, nor do I think anyone else should be.

But no one has come to my tatami room.

It has never been used.

Each morning I wake up, the smell of new tatami is in my nostrils, as though the room had been built only the night before. Perhaps I was not meant to be a teacher. I am not really sure. I am not even sure how long I will stay in baseball.

During my first spring training after retirement, I was standing at the batting cage watching the young players take hitting practice. I was very intent on watching them, and even so, I suddenly became aware that someone was standing alongside me. It was Arakawa-san. It flashed through my mind that twenty years earlier I had had this same strange sense of his approaching me almost as if I were having a premonition of some sort. It was indeed Arakawa-san. We stood side by side for some time without speaking. Finally, he said:

"There isn't a single player to carry on the flamingo batting, is there? It lasted but one generation."

I kept watching the players.

Arakawa-san continued, "You are the first and last batter on one foot. To try this is to risk everything. A pro, first and last, wants to remain a pro. There'll never be another like you."

I did not have an answer, but I realized Arakawa-san was not looking for one. He was telling me something.

"I don't think there can be another relationship like ours either," he continued. "I don't think it can happen again. You took my advice well. You were blessed with a strong body, but you also happened to have a pure heart.

"We got along so well. We were both young then, weren't we? I'm a little too old now. I don't feel excited by baseball anymore. Perhaps you're occupied enough now. If so, that's good. But I think things are for a generation only. It's hard to keep it going."

And with that, just as he had twenty years before, he turned and walked away. But unlike the earlier time, I did not wait for his return. We each had different things to do. Arakawa-san will always be my teacher. He is a sensei as others are statesmen or poets or . . . baseball players. Not too long ago, Arakawa-san came across a twelve-year-old boy in Hiroshima who is five foot ten and weighs 165 pounds, is tremendously gifted, and is hungry for baseball. As he has told me since, "Whenever there is the real talent, passion to teach returns."

My Way was the Way of a baseball player—and as is customary with this Way, it came to an end when I was in the middle of my life. I have half my life to live. But unlike Arakawa-san, the old passion can never return for me— just as my youth will never return. It will have to be a new passion. And what that might be, I simply do not know. I am like any other athlete in that sense. Mine is a perfectly ordinary dilemma shared by most athletes. I may stay in baseball, then again I may not. . . .

I have spent more than half my adult life in the public world of professional baseball. For over half my years, the ordinary, private moments of life have been special moments for me. On those occasions when I did have a "vacation" with my family, I found in some way that I was almost not prepared for such leisure. Reporters often asked me what I talked about or what I did. With baseball always on my mind, the answer was "not much." I explained that I was not trying to hide anything. The truth was that outside the world of baseball, I was a fairly boring fellow.

What would I do if I were "free"? I have always, literally, wanted to see the world. I intend to. Someday my wife and I will get on a boat, and we will take a whole year, maybe two, sailing to every part of this planet, seeing and meeting people we never would otherwise have crossed paths with in this life. We will visit places where no one will recognize me or ask for my autograph or even know that among the world's peoples, some of them play a game called baseball.

If this seems like a dream, I must point out that I am not much of a dreamer. A Westerner I know, someone interested in psychology, I think, once asked me to describe some of my sleeping dreams. I had an extraordinarily hard time, because I forget my dreams to the point of being able to remember only ones like: "I have just joined the Giants. I come to bat with the bases loaded. The pitcher throws. I hit a grand-slam home run." He had a hard time with that, so he persisted in trying to get me to remember others. But I couldn't. I honestly couldn't. Instead, I offered to make up a dream just to put an end to the discussion. To my surprise, he seemed quite willing to listen.

"It will be a lie," I said.

"No it won't," he replied. "It will be coming from you."

This is what I told him:

I am dancing with Audrey Hepburn. Her hair is short, much in the manner of *Roman Holiday*. I am her lover. She can never get older. I hold her, and we continue dancing. We are very happy.

"Ah," my Western friend said, as though he had picked up the significance of it, "you're in Rome?"

"No, of course not. *Tokyo*," I replied.

The point is that I am a modern, urban Japanese man at middle age. My father came from a village so remote that even today only the most detailed map will mark its existence. If I had lived in the world my father came from or the one he hoped I would live in, the way ahead would be very clear for me. But my life has been very different, a radical break from centuries of deeply established ways of living. I am like many others in that regard. My Way has led me to accomplishment and through it to mystery. I don't know what the second half of my life will bring or even if it will in any way match the first part. I learned from Arakawa-san, my greatest teacher, that the way is long and mastery of any sort is not easy to achieve. Above all, what I learned from my Sensei was how to wait. I believe I learned the "meaning" of waiting on one foot. If I understand anything in this life, it is how to wait. It is not an answer. But for me it is everything.

Nin

On November 8, 1983, Sadaharu Oh was named manager of the Tokyo Yomiuri Giants.

GLOSSARY

Aikido Literally, the Way of Spirit Harmony, a form of martial arts developed by Ueshiba Morihei in the 20th century from earlier, traditional forms.

amae Tender feeling. The word really does not translate well. It implies all that invites indulgence but which also demands resistance. It is best understood in the context of obligation. It is an opposing force but one which, for that, is necessary.

begoma A traditional childhood game.

Budo The Way of the Warrior, the name for the many martial arts as a whole.

do The Way. As the Way leads to mastery, this is also a specific stage of accomplishment in any of the spiritual disciplines. Leading to mastery, a student proceeds through three earlier distinct stages: *gi,* the stage of acquiring technique; jutsu, skill; and *gei,* the stage of art.

enka Popular Japanese songs. They fall somewhere between pop and folk but represent a unique Japanese form.

furoshiki Wrapping for an old-style bundle of baggage.

geta Traditional wooden sandals.

hachimaki A cloth headband worn under a mask (*men*) in Japanese fencing.

hakama The traditional divided skirt or trousers used in many martial arts.

Iai Nuki The study of withdrawing and replacing the Japanese long sword.

irimi An "entering" or thrusting technique in Aikido. *Tenkan,* by contrast, is a movement that involves pivoting.

Kendo The art of Japanese swordsmanship. Literally, Way of the Sword.

ken no michi "The path of the sword." Some aficionados consider this a more "spiritual" study of swordsmanship than Kendo, others see it as simply another name for the same thing (Kendo, by the way, means the way [as opposed to the path] of the sword).

ki Spirit, but the word is untranslatable as several of its different applications in the book indicate. Ki, however, is as specific in Japanese as "soul" is abstract in our language.

kiai Another combination of "spirit" and "harmony" here representing a technique of shouting in the martial arts, whose purpose may be inferred from the literal meanings of the word.

kirikaeshi Repetition of sword strokes in Kendo practice.

Kokutai The National Amateur Athletic competition. It is, by law, for Japanese nationals only. The strict definition of nationality in Japan—birthright is determined by the identity of the male parent—was the basis for Mr. Oh's exclusion from this tournament.

Koshien The national high school baseball tournament, held once in the spring and once in the summer at Koshien Stadium in Osaka.

kotatsu Heavily draped table whose center is a heater or foot warmer. Used extensively in unheated Japanese homes, this traditional piece of furniture was designed with the idea of many people—the members of the family—sitting together.

ma The interval or space between. It is a concept important in music, dance, and the martial arts. Time as well as space are defined by this interval.

menko A traditional childhood game. Both menko and begoma are played almost exclusively by boys.

metsuke Point of focus or observation.

nabe Pot. In Japanese cooking, this is a special term that indicates the particular combination of foods within the vessel as well as the skill of the preparer.

nage "Thrower" or defender in Aikido (*uke* is the attacker).

nin Another almost untranslatable term. Mr. Oh frequently added this word to autographs he signed. The Zen master Shunryu Suzuki described the word as follows: "The usual translation of the Japanese word *nin* is 'patience,' but perhaps 'constancy' is a better word. . . . *Nin* is the way we cultivate our own spirit. *Nin* is our way of continuous practice. We should always live in the dark empty sky. The sky is always the sky. Even though clouds and lightning come, the sky is not disturbed. Even if the flashing of enlightenment comes, our practice forgets all about it. Then it is ready for another enlightenment. It is necessary for us to have enlightenments one after another, if possible, moment after moment."

Onegai shimasu Traditional greeting of student to master, "please help me."

Ryou yu narabi tatazu "Two heroes cannot coexist."

seiza A sitting pose in many martial arts.

shobu A baseball term indicating an almost game-stopping duel between two opposing stars. Gossage vs. Brett in the 1980 American League playoffs is a good Western model. The individual players in shobu carry the fate of their teams with them. It is never done for the sake of the individuals alone.

shoji Paper sliding doors.

suburi Any of several basic movements in Kendo and other martial arts that employ the use of swords or staves.

suzumushi Cicadas.

tatami Straw matting.

tenkan A pivoting movement in Aikido.

tenranjiai A baseball term used to describe a game that is unusually close and tension-filled.

tokuda Another baseball term used to describe special or particular batting practice. *Tokushu* is a particular fielding practice used to test specific skills at a given position.

tsuka The handle, usually made out of leather, of a wooden practice sword.

yakitori Literally, grilled chicken. *Yakitori* shops abound in Japan. The decor of the places—scrubbed white wood—is usually as attractive as the fare. A Japanese *yakitori* shop of merit is probably the closest one will come to finding a four-star fast-food restaurant on the planet.

Yamabiko no michi "The path of an echo." An Aikido technique in which your movement forces an "echo" movement from your opponent.

yukata Summer-weight kimono.

zanshin A martial arts term meaning follow-through. As with other technical terms, it is to be understood that this cannot be performed without maximum extension of spirit. In baseball it is something more than "putting everything" into a swing, because *zanshin* can only be performed correctly if the technique leading to it is also sound.

Appendix I

In the course of his twenty-two-year career, Sadaharu Oh and the Yomiuri Giants crossed paths with American baseball several times. In spring training, post-season exhibitions, all-star tours of Japan, Oh-san came to have limited—but often very cordial—relations with our players. In my discussions with him, it was clear that he had studied them well. It was also clear, in subsequent discussions I had with American players, that they had watched him pretty closely. The point that should be made, I suppose, is that this cross-ocean contact was nevertheless limited. Among professional ballplayers this meant diminished opportunity to compete together—a handful of "meaningless" games rather than the full beauty of a championship season. For fans in America, the consequences were somewhat different. Those of us who love baseball and who have followed it in one degree or another over the last two decades have been deprived of even seeing this great Japanese star perform. There is no plaque honoring him in Cooperstown, no photographs or film clips—or even mention of his accomplishments. It is as though, according to *the* Baseball Hall of Fame, he never played the game. The random impressions American ballplayers have had of Oh-san, though admittedly limited and confined almost exclusively to his playing abilities, are, in no particular order, presented for those who may be curious:

Tom Seaver:

You know, he *looks* like a power hitter. You'll be surprised when you see him. He's not a small man at all. He has a very powerful lower body—the kind of heavy thighs and rump you see on most home-run hitters. Physically, he's right in the mold.

He sure hit me. He was a superb hitter. He hit consistently, and he hit with power. If he played in the United States, he would have hit twenty–twenty-five home runs a year and, what's more, he'd hit .300. He'd be a lifetime .300 hitter. He had tremendous discipline at the plate. He knew the strike zone extremely well, almost never went for a bad pitch, and was always willing to wait. In that stance he had a sense of timing that was perfectly suited to the kind of hitter he was. It enabled him to stay back to the last possible second. A lot of hitters, a lot of power hitters, will open up too soon. Oh-san didn't. He could pull your hard stuff, and you couldn't fool him off-speed. He was very, very impressive.

Oh-san took a group of us out to a Chinese restaurant one night—in Osaka, I think, I'm not sure. Well, it was a very elegant place, and Oh-san was obviously the most honored guest this restaurant could have. Everyone—management, waiters, busboys, patrons—was just magnetized by him. Nancy [Seaver's wife] was the only woman in our party. And Japanese culture being as male-oriented as it is, she wound up feeling pretty much out of it. By the time the food came, it was as though she had become invisible. Though he clearly was the center of attention, Oh-san never lost sight of what was going on. The food was brought out and placed on this very lovely revolving lazy susan—right in front of Oh-san. It's the custom there for the head of the table to serve himself first. Well, when the food was set down, Oh-san suddenly turned the lazy susan around, so all the dishes were in front of Nancy, so she could serve herself before anyone else. He didn't make a big deal of it. It was done so smoothly and graciously you almost didn't even know it had happened. But he turned the atmosphere in that room around, too. Nancy and I were both very moved by that. He didn't have to do that—but he did.

Sparky Anderson:
Oh was . . . just different. He understands what it means to be a star. The biggest problem in our country is a lot of 'em don't know how to be a star. . . . He knows how to be the king. He knows he's the king an' he understands what is expected of a king—that's probably the greatest tribute I can pay him.

Hal Macrae:
Oh had tremendous patience as a hitter. He kept his head right down on the ball, his body was rooted, he got his bat head out front, his follow-through was natural—hits something like Al Oliver with that one leg. But he had good power. I don't know how many he would have hit here. Let's say you start with twenty, start with that at least. He was a great all-star. He'd have been a Hall-of-Famer.

Al Oliver:
I was with Texas, and their team came through Pompano Beach. An' you know I wear the number "0"—an' his name was Oh—so some people thought it would be a good PR stunt to get us together. So I shook hands with him and congratulated him on the career he had had—I did get an opportunity, though, a few years before when I was with Pittsburgh to see him swing the bat—in batting practice— you know, I mean you can tell then whether or not the guy has a good stroke—an' he sure did.

Amos Otis:
We were in Fort Myers, waiting around for his team to come through. All of us were just hanging around, waiting for Oh, waiting for Oh. We didn't watch his team. All we did was watch him.

Reggie Smith:
In style, he didn't remind me of anyone. He had his own style. In terms of the results he achieved, you would have to compare him with Ted Williams.

Pete Rose:
There's no question in my mind that he wouldn't have hit eight hundred home runs if he'd played here, but if he played in a park tailored to his swing, he'd have hit his thirty-five a year. He'd do his thing. But he'd hit .300, I'll tell ya' that.

... Another town we went to—(on our tour of Japan) these people are Sadaharu Oh fans. All they do is wait for him to come there. So Sparky got real good and friendly with Nagashima—and we're playin' this team and these people hadn't seen Sadaharu play for many years because they're up in the hills somewhere—a real small town—all of a sudden, it's the first inning, first guy makes out, second guy makes out, third guy hits a double—and Harimoto wasn't playing that day, there was a right-handed hitter batting after Oh. So Oh walks up to the plate, and Sparky goes like this—walk 'im. We put him on and these fuckin' people go crazy. They want to see Oh hit. I'll be goddamned if next time up it wasn't the same situation. They just don't do that over there. See, he [Sparky] was trying to show Nagashima the value of the intentional walk—to take the bat out of the star's hands. And the second time up he did the same thing, and after the second time then they had to tell the cops to watch our bus so they could just get us outta there alive.

Charley Lau:
He hit well for the same reason Mel Ott did ... he hit mechanically well. The leg lift enabled him to get himself back, and when he got back he went forward and had a good weight shift. . . . He had to be good with those numbers. He had to have great body control, was never panicky or tried to muscle a ball. . . . To hit through the kind of shift they employed on him, you've got to be awful good. The average hitter would wind up hittin' .200.

Walt Hriniak:
I saw films of Oh once or twice, saw that stance. People laughed at it like they laughed at Mel Ott's front-leg kick— but it was mechanically sound, mechanically very sound because anything you do in sports—whether you're swinging a golf club, a tennis racket, a baseball bat—in order to

get the maximum out of the swing, you have to go back to go forward. That's what Sadaharu Oh did, that's what Mel Ott did—they're goin' back to go forward. Just like a pitcher who winds up. Same principle.

George Bamberger:
He was very, very impressive. Everyone who saw him felt the same way. Saw him in spring training in Miami when I was with Baltimore. He could hit, really hit. If you stand on your head and can hit, so be it. He'd be right up there with the Frank Robinsons. He'd be a Hall-of-Fame player, no doubt about it.

Tommy LaSorda:
He was one of three guys I saw in Japan who could play here—Nagashima, Kaneda, and Oh. He'd be a good hitter in the big leagues. He had good power . . . had a good, good idea of the strike zone. That stance was similar to Mel Ott's. Oh, yeah, he'd 'a' been good.

Frank Howard:
A lot of Americans say he wouldn't do that well over here. Well, maybe he wouldn't hit forty-five or fifty, but you can kiss my ass if he wouldn't have hit thirty or thirty-five home runs a year and hit anywhere from .280 to .320 and drive in up to 120 runs a year. The point being, he rates with the all-time stars of the game. In other words, he would play in any league, any time, including our own major leagues, and he would star in any league. Make no mistake about it. He's a champion.

Don Baylor:
Oh could have played anywhere at any time. If he played in Yankee Stadium, being the kind of left-hand pull hitter he is, I have no doubt he'd hit forty home runs a year. Consistency is his hallmark. His stats tell you that. He didn't hit thirty-five one year and five the next—but he did the same year in and year out.

Steve Kemp:
I only met him once.
Q: What did you do?
A: Asked for his autograph.

Bob Gibson:
He was a good player, I guess. Just look at his record. I only faced him once, didn't get anything off me. I can't compare him with anyone. I imagine anyone who can hit can hit anywhere. I would imagine he still would have been a home-run hitter because he had that stroke. . . . I didn't see him enough.

Tim McCarver:
Shit. Hoot's got the worst memory. He hit one off Gibson. Beat Gibson that first game (of our tour). My dominant recollection of Oh is his picking up that foot. He was always ready for a fastball, he was an outstanding hitter. He had big thighs and a big ass, and he used his power. He could hit. He would have hit over here, and he would have got his home runs.

Mike Torrez:
We all heard of the legend of Sadaharu Oh. . . . I got to pitch against him, he got a hit off me, not a home run, he hit the homers off Steve Carlton and Ron Wilkes. He could have played for any major league team. . . . When I pitched him, I thought, don't give him anything inside, sink the ball away from him. He was a good fastball hitter, but I think he just waited for a pitcher. . . . Anyone who hits that many home runs, I don't care if it isn't .330 all around, you still have to hit the ball. He was very disciplined. He waited good. If the pitcher got behind in the count and had to come in with a fastball, he was ready. He hit 'em a long way.

Joe Torre:
He was pretty good size. He coulda competed over here.

Jon Matlack:
We heard a lot about the man before we went over there. His stats spoke very loudly about what he had done, all the home runs he had hit, the unique style he used. That piqued everybody's curiosity. We wondered how in the world a guy could hit that way. But he obviously could. At first he really didn't do that well against us. First time I faced him, no problem. Threw a little bit of everything. Show him the

ball inside, change speeds away. Same as I'd do with any left-handed power hitter in the States. But then he caught on. He adjusted pretty quickly. He got just about everybody over there. It was like he started to get a feel of what we were doing and then had a much better idea of what he was doing at the plate. It made it that much more difficult to pitch to him. He could hit all pitches. The thing that impressed me most about him was his ability even with that unique stance to keep his hands back and wait on the off-speed pitches.

Jerry Koosman:
The first thing that impressed me was the balance and timing he had because of the way he hit by lifting up that front leg . . . so I figured with him doing that I should be able to get him out with my good fastball. But the guy's just got awesome timing by the way he uses that leg. And he did hit a home run off me there in Tokyo. . . . No, he's a good hitter.

Don Drysdale:
He would have hit for average and power here. In a park tailored to his swing, there's no telling how many he would have hit. The Dodgers toured over there, and we saw him in spring training in the sixties. Believe me, he was something. You try to keep him off guard an' see how long he could balance on that left leg of his. . . . He was pretty damn successful at it. He could do it about as long as he wanted to. See, when we first went over there, they did not have change-ups, and the first change-up they got a really good taste of was Erskine's [Brooklyn Dodger pitcher Carl Erskine]. He might have had one of the greatest ones ever. That was '56. Anyway, we'd try that with him to get him out. You might throw him a few change-ups, make him supply his own power, see if you could get him off balance, make him think about it at least, so, boom, now you can come in with the fastball. Oh never had the problems with it that the others had. He was always ready for anything we threw him. We were all impressed.

Jeff Torborg:
We tried everything on him . . . change of speeds, busted him hard inside . . . he hit four consecutive home runs off

us, I remember . . . he was out on one of 'em because he passed a runner at first base. . . . He hit one that went pretty far out and then he really cranked one that almost went out of the top of the stadium. For sure, he would have been a bona fide power hitter, and playing in Yankee Stadium, oh my! Being a catcher, I tried to think how to get him out. I actually saw him enough. We'd throw slow curve balls and think we'd have him fooled, and he'd hit the ball down the left-field line. He was just a fine player. He was tough even against left-handed good breaking ballers like Perranoski. We never got him out consistently. . . . Having caught behind other hitters, I know he was an outstanding hitter.

Greg Luzinski:

He had an odd batting stance, but there's no question in my mind that he'd have been a great ballplayer in the United States, that he was a super-talent. We played some exhibition games in spring training when I was with the Phillies and then we played the American League—National League series over there. He hit the ball really well whenever I saw him play—he was a really impressive ballplayer.

(Remembering the Aikido demonstration with Arakawa-san):

A: (Long pause) I don't know . . . I don't remember. . . . Oh! Wait a minute! You mean that little guy! Oh, yeah, he was showing me about body balance and not focusing your eyes properly. We were just talking—and he just asked me to pull. He was demonstrating body balance, that was it—I was a big guy and he wanted to demonstrate with me. He *did* have good balance. He wasn't goin' forward or backward.

Q: What happened when you pulled?

A: (Short pause) Nothing.

Roy White:

One of the highlights of my playing baseball in Japan with the Tokyo Giants was the opportunity of playing with Mr. Oh. I didn't get the chance to see him as a young player, but I did not have to to know that this man was a special, great player. . . . I will also always value his friendship, as he was of particular help to me as a player in Japan.

Jim Palmer:

He hit a long home run off me [Orioles tour, 1971]. From a pitcher's standpoint he's a very impressive hitter because he hit so many home runs. When you were winding up and he lifted that leg it was very disconcerting . . . made you lose concentration. You'd be turning and he'd be doing that, you'd notice those things. . . . He was a lot like Yaz . . . got mileage out of his career. He wasn't big in stature, but he had tremendous bat speed and could hit any pitch you threw him for a home run. Which is obviously the sign of a home-run hitter. Yaz had great years, but he had a much bigger swing than Oh. Oh had, like, a perfect swing. Very relaxed. The whole key is to have good bat speed. Be relaxed and get the bat head out, and that's what he did . . . it was beautiful to watch. Not if you're a pitcher, obviously. But he did what you're supposed to do. The rest took care of itself.

Brooks Robinson:

Oh had a slow start (on the tour), but the last half of the games we played, he wore us out pretty well. He was the best player I saw in Japan. He could have played right here in the big leagues with the best players in the world. He would have hit here. Not as many home runs, but he would have hit his share and hit for average. He was just an outstanding hitter.

Frank Robinson:

He was a little larger than I thought he would be. Very good hitter. Not only for power but also knew the strike zone, hit for average, drove in runs. . . . He had a very odd stance as most people know it, but he would stand and pause on one leg, and you thought you could throw a fastball by him or throw a change-up, but he would slow down and just hesitate and just stand there on that one leg and react to the ball. . . . I know he would have very respectable numbers up here in the big leagues. . . . I'm not saying he'd hit forty to fifty home runs, but I'm sure he would have hit in the thirties and probably the low forties. Because he could hit the ball, he was a good hitter. . . . It's correct that thirty home runs a year add up to over six hundred home runs, and he'd do that if he played the same number of years here that he played there.

Jim Frey

(Remembering a home-run contest during the Orioles' tour):

. . . And when Oh got in a groove he was like a guy hitting off a golf tee at a driving range. He just kept hitting every ball, looked like he was hitting five-irons up in the seats. . . . Shit, he musta hit fifteen out of twenty at one stretch. It was incredible. I don't think I've ever seen anybody consistently hit the ball hard up in the air like he did in that contest.

Duke Snider:

He had a kind of Musial stance that way, but you could tell right away he was an outstanding hitter. He was strong, strong enough to pop the ball—the ball just jumped off his bat. When you're scouting, scouting for a hitter, why, you always look for the ball to jump off his bat—and with him, it sure did.

Clete Boyer (who, with the Taiyo Whales, played against Oh for five years):

A lot of people over here don't know Japanese baseball, and they think it can't be nearly as good as baseball over here is. But I've played in the big leagues—fourteen years— and I've played there five years, and when you're around the athletes . . . you know, athletes are athletes . . . and I've played with Mantle, Maris, Berra, Howard, all those guys; I went to Atlanta, played with Hank Aaron for five years, Cepeda . . . I played with guys that as far as I'm concerned were way above my head. I mean, I guess I was a decent big-league ballplayer, but when you see talent, you know who was better than you, and you get the feeling of how much better. I've always compared Oh to Hank Aaron. Very durable, very intelligent, knows not to get hurt on the field, doesn't do anything silly on the field, you know, like running into walls, stuff like that. I saw a guy break his leg on a fence one night. Score was ll–2 or something in the ninth inning an' he's tryin' to save a home run. Well, to me, you know, that was stupid, it ruined his career. So to me, Oh is in the class of Hank Aaron. I admired the guy so much. I loved to play against him because there was electricity.

He had electricity like a Mantle or a Mays. I saw him in the Triple Crown years—twice in a row—he had fifty-one one year and forty-nine the next. And they only play 130 games! One of those years, I'm not exactly sure, he had something like 170 or more bases on balls—well, that's forty games of nothing! Okay, so ninety games he hit fifty-one home runs. I saw him hit balls clear out of the ball parks over there, all right . . . an' they talk about the short fences! I don't care if you're in high school. You've got to hit it okay. An' he could hit left-handers, right-handers, it didn't make any difference. But to me, he was just one of those great athletes that you go to the ball park early just to watch take batting practice.

Bowie Kuhn:
I met him [Oh-san] on a number of occasions and found him to be a warm and engaging man. . . . He was outstanding both at bat and in the field. . . . He would have been a star in American baseball.

Q: Should baseball stars from other countries, like Mr. Oh, be included in the Hall of Fame?

A: It would be doubtful it could be achieved as a practical matter.

Appendix II

OH'S FINAL STATS‡

*League leader

	YR	G	AB	R	H	2B	3B	HR	TB	RBI	SB	BB	INT.BB	SO	AVE.
1	'59	94	193	18	31	7	1	7	61	25	3	27	(1)	72	.161
2	'60	130*	426	49	115	19	3	17	191	71	5	72*	(5)	101	.270
3	'61	127	396	50	100	25	6	13	176	53	10	67	(3)	72	.253
4	'62	134*	497	79*	135	28	2	38*	281*	85*	6	84*	(9)*	99	.272
5	'63	140*	478	111*	146	30*	5	40*	306	106	9	129*	(12)	64	.305
6	'64	140*	472	110*	151	24	0	55*	340*	119*	6	122*	(20)*	81	.320
7	'65	135	428	104*	138	19	1	42*	285*	104*	2	144*	(29)*	58	.322
8	'66	129	396	111*	123	14	1	48*	283*	116*	9	149*	(41)*	51	.311
9	'67	133	426	94*	139	22	3	47*	308*	108*	3	137*	(30)*	65	.326
10	'68	131	442	107*	144	28	0	49*	319*	119	5	131*	(18)*	72	.326*
11	'69	130*	452	112*	156*	24	0	44*	312*	103	5	116*	(12)*	61	.345*
12	'70	129	425	97*	138*	24	0	47*	303*	93	1	125*	(24)*	48	.325*
13	'71	130*	434	92*	120	18	2	39*	259	101*	8	126*	(17)*	65	.276
14	'72	130*	456	104*	135	19	0	48*	298*	120*	2	114*	(18)*	43	.296
15	'73	130*	428	111*	152*	18	0	51*	323*	114*	2	128*	(38)*	41	.355*
16	'74	130*	385	105*	128	18	0	49*	293*	107*	1	166*	(45)*	44	.332*
17	'75	128	393	77	112	14	0	33	225	96*	1	124*	(27)*	62	.285
18	'76	122	400	99*	130	11	1	49*	290	123*	3	127*	(27)	45	.325
19	'77	130*	432	114*	140	15	0	50*	305*	124*	1	132*	(16)*	37	.324
20	'78	130*	440	91	132	20	0	39	269	118*	1	115*	(17)*	43	.300
21	'79	120	407	73	116	15	0	33	230	81	1	94*	(10)*	48	.285
22	'80	129	444	59	105	10	0	30	205	84	0	75	(8)	47	.236
		2831	9250	1967	2786	422	25	868	5862	2170	84	2504	(427)	1319	.301

	YRS	G	AB	R	H	2B	3B	HR	TB	RBI	SB	BB	INT.BB	SO
OH	22	2831	9250	1967	2786	422	25	868	5862	2170	84	2504	(427)	1319
AARON	23	3298	12364	2174	3771	624	98	755	6856	2297	240	1402	(293)	1383
RUTH	22	2503	8399	2174	2873	506	136	714	5793	2209	123	2056		1330

	AVE.	HR/AB	F.A.	TRIPLE CROWN	BATTING TITLE	HR TITLE	RBI TITLE	MVP	ALL STAR	GOLD GLOVE
OH	.301	10.7	.994	2	5	15	13	9	18	9
AARON	.305	16.4	.982	0	2	4	4	1	9	3
RUTH	.342	11.8	.968	0	1	12	6	—	—	—

‡Courtesy Japanese Baseball Newsletter

3PM

TransAtlantic Video

6 rue de deux Ponts

Ile St. Louis

Metro

Pont Marie

3,635
NY-P